DEADLY HERO

Also by Jason Lucky Morrow

The DC Dead Girls Club:
A Vintage True Crime Story of Four Unsolved Murders in Washington D.C.

Famous Crimes the World Forgot:
Ten Vintage True Crime Stories Rescued from Obscurity.
Volume One
Silver Medal Winner, 2015 eLit Book Awards, True Crime Category.

DEADLY HERO

The High Society Murder that Created Hysteria in the Heartland

JASON LUCKY MORROW

Historical Crime Detective Books
Tulsa, 2015

Published by: Historical Crime Detective Books, Tulsa, OK
Printed by: CreateSpace Inc.
Editor: Gloria F Boyer, gfboyer.com
Cover Design: Jason Morrow

ISBN-13: 978-1511991711
ISBN-10: 1511991712
ASIN: B00XLSKNI2
First Edition, 2015
10 9 8 7 6 5 4 3 2

For Mom.

Additional photos related to this story can be found at:
HistoricalCrimeDetective.com/deadly-hero-photo-gallery/

Contents

A Special Note on Historical Accuracy

Because I am former newspaper reporter, my style of writing is to craft an entertaining story, but also to stick with the facts. I go where the research leads me and in the end, the story is the story. All of the dialogue, quotes, and events in this book are as they appeared in the original source materials. I have not recreated any dialogue or manufactured events to make the story more dramatic. In some cases, especially during the trial portion, I had to trim excess verbiage to make the content flow more efficiently.

To help bring the characters to life, I relied on an enormous amount of newspaper coverage to guide me in portraying body language, facial expressions, mannerisms, gestures, and tone of voice. These character traits are used to enhance the scene and set the mood, without altering the facts. About half of such character traits were specifically described in the research material. The other half of the character traits portrayed in this book are based on clues found in the research material and should be considered semi-fictional.

This book was written by referring to approximately 640 newspaper articles, magazines, books, maps, census reports, interviews, and other resources. Although I have done my best to verify the information I have included, in any work of nonfiction, it is inevitable that some facts or interpretations will be incorrect.

Footnotes: I have used footnotes throughout this book to provide clarity, perspective, or additional information. If you are reading this book on an e-reader, I encourage you to click the footnote links for information that will enhance your understanding of the events and your experience of the story.

Part One: The Murder

His teeth chattering so that he could hardly speak, Oliver refused details until he had pushed those who met him into the safety of the baggage room at the Claremore station.

"He is going to kill me," Oliver squeaked. "My God, why did I say that I would name the man who killed Gorrell?"

— *Tulsa Daily World*
December 2, 1934

Chapter One

Friday, 12:05 a.m., November 30, 1934

WESLEY CUNNINGHAM JUST WANTED TO get home. After his family's Thanksgiving[1] meal, the seventeen-year-old met up with friends for an evening out in downtown Tulsa that included a 9:30 showing of *College Rhythm*, followed by sandwiches and Nehi pop at the Orpheum Theater's lunch counter. Around midnight, Wesley said his good-byes and sat in his family's Ford DeLuxe while the engine warmed up. The weather had turned ugly, and the mixture of rain and sleet would impair his visibility for the drive home. It was time to get going.

Driving south, Wesley was just a minute or two from reaching his stepfather's driveway, when he saw something unusual in the road. In front of him, on a triangular median wedged between Victor Avenue and Forest Boulevard in the heart of Tulsa's exclusive Forest Hills residential area, the front end of a Ford sedan had gone partway over the median, with the back half blocking the street. Although his headlights could barely pierce the elements to illuminate the car, he thought he could make out a figure slumped behind the steering wheel. Since it was a holiday weekend and college students were back in town reconnecting with old pals, he first thought it was a rich kid living nearby who'd had too much to drink.

He lived two blocks away and knew the area well. The square mile of land that radiated out from the troubled car was one of

---

[1] Thanksgiving was celebrated on the last Thursday in November until it was changed in 1941 to the fourth Thursday of the month.

the wealthiest in the state. Several hundred yards to the west, the seventy-two-room Philbrook Mansion sprawled out over twenty-three acres crafted into a garden that would rival the estates of Italy on which it was modeled. Its owner, Waite Phillips, was the younger brother of the founders of Phillips Petroleum. With the rest of the country mired deep in the Depression, oil-rich Tulsa was surviving marginally better than other major cities. And within that square mile lived most of the oil barons and elite of Tulsa society.

The area was unusually dark, and Cunningham noted that several streetlights in the vicinity were out. His car was equipped with a spotlight, and as he pulled abreast of the Ford, he guided the beam toward the cab.

"I saw a man, very pale, with blood running down his face," he would later tell police. But as he studied the situation more carefully, he slowly began to understand that it was no drunk driver. *That fella looked dead.*

Accelerating to get out of there, Cunningham sped to his home nearby and told his stepfather, who called police. When the patrolmen arrived on the scene five minutes later, they checked on the driver and saw what looked to be a bullet hole in his right temple. Blood streaks had gravitated down in jagged lines that took several different directions. Their first assessment of the situation led them to believe the young man had shot himself while the car was still in motion, which might explain why it had gone over the curb. They did find a gun in the car, but it wasn't where they thought it would be. Instead, it was tucked neatly in a leather shoulder holster that lay on the seat next to him.

That was odd.

From the description given by Wesley's stepfather, the police dispatcher assumed the Ford's occupant was dead, and at 12:20 a.m. he notified Sergeant Henry B. Maddux, who was on duty. Maddux was the police department's criminologist and second-in-command of the detective bureau. He'd been hired in

January by a progressive new fire and police commissioner, and his boyish face misled others into thinking he was much younger than his thirty-five years.

There was virtually no traffic on the wet streets as Sgt. Maddux, accompanied by Detective George Reif, drove to the scene. When they arrived at the triangular median, the investigators found the whole area unusually dark. Looking around, they noticed several streetlamps were out. They would need more light. Maddux ordered a patrolman and Detective Reif to reposition their patrol vehicles so that the victim's car was in the middle, lit by four headlight beams.

Peering through the open passenger door, Maddux immediately noticed the death car was still in gear, and the ignition switch had not been cut off. When the Ford jumped the curb, it had apparently shut the motor off. Turning his attention to the dead man, Maddux found that aside from the streaks of blood and a small bruise over his right eye, the young driver appeared peaceful. His clothing was in perfect order, and his dark, wavy hair was still carefully in place. His feet were still on the clutch and gas pedals, and his right fingers were touching a leather holster that held a revolver.

That didn't sit right with him. How does a man with a bullet in his head put a revolver back in the holster? He didn't know where this case was going to lead, but his training told him photographs of the dead driver would be needed. As Detective Reif pointed a flashlight toward the cab, Maddux adjusted the Kalart flash, peered through the Kodak's viewfinder, and snapped a picture.

After handing the camera off to Reif, Maddux carefully reached into the dead man's coat and, from an inside pocket, retrieved a wrinkled envelope addressed to John Gorrell Jr., at 1205 Linwood Boulevard, Kansas City, Missouri. The return address was 2116 East 15th Street, Tulsa, Oklahoma, and the letter was apparently from the boy's mother.

John Gorrell Jr.?

Maddux didn't know the name but Reif did; John Gorrell Sr. was a prominent local physician, and if this was his son, it was a bit of a surprise to both of them. There had been a lot of suicides lately, but most of those were by men who had lost fortunes or were beaten down by the Depression. But as he tilted the boy's head and aimed Reif's flashlight toward the grisly wound, he made a discovery that would eventually turn the entire city of Tulsa inside out.

There were two bullet holes in the side of Junior's head.

Maddux called Reif to take a look and told the young detective to keep the fact that this was now a murder investigation a secret. Maddux made an instant decision to throw off the killer by letting him think the police believed it was a suicide. He wanted the shooter to relax and let his guard down.

The sergeant then turned his attention to the revolver jammed tightly into a leather shoulder holster on the seat next to him. With his handkerchief, Maddux lifted the holster from the edge and gingerly placed it in a paper sack. If it was the murder weapon, then fingerprints might link it to the killer. The barrel protruded through the bottom of the holster, and judging by its smell, it had recently been fired. But a more detailed examination would have to wait until later that morning, after Maddux notified the boy's parents.

In spite of the late hour, the commotion attracted a small crowd of onlookers. Across the street, the grounds of the Cornelius Titus mansion were well lit, but not enough to reach across the street. Parked in a car nearby were two security guards who worked for Mr. Titus. Sergeant Maddux, a man who lived with his wife in a modest apartment, looked around the area and understood that this was the part of town where the rich people lived. It was not going to be a routine murder investigation.

As he warned the patrolmen to guard the scene until the coroner arrived, one of them directed the senior lawman's attention to Wesley Cunningham, who had returned to the area.

"As I turned off Forest Boulevard, I noticed the car," Cunningham explained to Maddux. "It looked as if there had been some sort of accident. I stopped when I was abreast of the car and turned on my spotlight."

He then told of how he had seen the lines of blood on the right side of the man's pale face and had sped home to tell his stepfather, who then called police at 12:15 a.m. He estimated five to ten minutes had passed from the time he discovered the car to when the phone call was made.

That would put the time of death sometime before midnight, Maddux would later report.

When the police sergeant reached the Gorrell home, a reporter for the *Tulsa Daily World* had already broken the news to the family. With a lack of sensitivity, the writer asked Dr. Gorrell if he thought his son could have committed suicide, a theory being advanced by police.

"Ridiculous," Dr. Gorrell said, while standing in the doorway, dressed in his pajamas. "John was in the best of spirits yesterday. He had been attending dental school in Kansas City and only got home yesterday morning for the holidays. I know that he would not kill himself. He was not the type."

Both parents were emphatic in their opinion that John had had no reason to commit suicide. He was a normal, vibrant, young man who was intensely interested in joining the dental profession and was engaged to an attractive young woman living in Pittsburg, Kansas.

With a scornful look to the reporter, Sgt. Maddux introduced himself and was let into the Gorrell home. At the same dining-room table used by the family just hours before, Maddux proceeded slowly with his questions to the grieving parents. He needed a timeline of their son's activities that day, where he was, and who he was with.

John had returned early that morning from Western Dental College in Kansas City, where the twenty-one-year-old shared a room with two other Tulsa boys, Richard Oliver and Jess Harris, the parents told him. Oliver had stayed in Kansas City, but Harris and Gorrell drove back to Tulsa in the Ford. Around noon, John reconnected with his pal Charles Bard, who was home from Oklahoma A&M.[2] The two of them then attended a University of Tulsa football game before having Thanksgiving dinner at the Gorrell home. It was a normal day, but what they told Sgt. Maddux next caught his interest.

Thirty minutes into the family dinner, they were interrupted by a telephone call. Mrs. Gorrell pushed her chair back from the table to answer the phone, but John was already out of his. There were eight people at the dinner table that night: John and his younger siblings, Edith Ann and Ben; Charles Bard; Dr. and Mrs. Gorrell; and two adult guests.

"No, I'll go, Mother," John had said as he walked to an adjoining hallway where the family telephone was located. His mother couldn't make out what he was talking to the caller about, but when he returned to the dining room, she could tell something was wrong. The sparkle had left his eyes, and his face was blanched and tight.

"He looked to be in a state of suppressed nervous excitement," Mrs. Gorrell said. "When I asked what was wrong, he said 'nothing.'"

But just a few minutes later, John announced he and Charles had dates that night, and they excused themselves from the table. They ran upstairs to John's room to get ready and came back down around 7:20 p.m. When they came back down, his mother could hear the clicking of the telephone dial as her son made a call and then John speaking in a low mumble. After he was done, John and Charlie walked by the crowded dining table

---

[2] Now Oklahoma State University.

toward the front door. She asked her son where he was going and received a terse reply.

"Don't ask me, Mother."

That was the last time she saw her son alive.

BACK AT THE CRIME SCENE, reporters for the *Tulsa World* and *Tulsa Tribune* were moving through the growing crowd, looking for neighbors to interview. Frank Moss, one of the night watchmen for the Titus estate, had heard five shots earlier that night. At nine o'clock, he had heard three shots, then the sound of a car speeding away, and then later, two more shots. His partner, Carl Rust, had also heard shooting.

"I heard three shots and then the sound of racing cars," Rust told a *World* reporter. "They came around the curve from over the hill, and then there were two more shots. The cars separated. One of them drove toward town, and the other turned down in such a way that it could have been just where this one was found."

Rust assumed it was young people still celebrating the holiday. He judged the incident as unimportant until he noticed all the activity where Gorrell's car was found. Somehow, the two night watchmen had not noticed the Ford until the police had shown up.

Sergeant Maddux's strategy of publicizing a suicide theory, with the intention of getting the killer to let his guard down, lasted only a few hours. As reflected in the morning paper, reporters had learned Gorrell had been shot in the head, twice, and the probable murder weapon was his own revolver, which was returned to the shoulder holster that rested on the seat. That information came from police Captain J. D. Bills, who apparently wasn't in on the secret.

After the body was removed by the coroner, Maddux and Reif directed their attention back to the streetlights. Two of them were out, including one with a shattered bowl that was near the Gorrell car. They weren't sure what to make of this detail, or if it was even connected to the murder. For now, they needed to find Charlie Bard, and they needed to find the two young ladies the boys had been with the night before. To solve this case, Maddux and his detectives would have to reconstruct every minute of the nearly five hours between 7:30 p.m. and 12:10 a.m.

Chapter Two

LATER THAT FRIDAY MORNING, NEWSPAPERS throughout Oklahoma showed little interest in the Gorrell murder. The dailies of adjacent states—Texas, Arkansas, Kansas, and Missouri—only had a three-column-inch stub from United Press, or two inches from Associated Press, each with conflicting information. Nobody had bothered to wake the Tulsa stringer for Oklahoma City's *Daily Oklahoman*, and even the *Tulsa Daily World's* front-page story seemed inadequate and stoked the mystery with more questions than answers. The *World's* staff had worked all night and crammed into the report everything they knew while the printing press was warming up. The story revealed they had followed Maddux and his detectives back to headquarters and the coroner's office, where the preliminary findings indicated Gorrell had most likely been killed with his own gun. Two fired shell casings and one bullet were removed from the cylinder, and powder burns on the victim's head indicated the barrel was approximately twelve inches away when it was fired.

Maddux and Reif roused Charlie Bard out of bed at six in the morning and noted that the eighteen-year-old seemed genuinely distraught and deeply affected upon learning of his friend's death. He was anxious to tell all he knew, and, step-by-step, Bard went over everything that had happened the day before.

The detectives had already learned from the boy's mother that her son had arrived in Tulsa around three o'clock in the morning in a used car he and Richard Oliver had recently purchased. When he got home, John went to bed, slept until midmorning, and ate lunch. He then picked up Charlie, and the two had gone to a football match to watch the University of

Tulsa Hurricanes play the University of Arkansas Razorbacks. John was in high spirits as he followed the tight game, which ended 7-7, Bard said.

As Maddux already knew, the boys then ate Thanksgiving dinner at the Gorrell home, where John received the mysterious telephone call, but he never told his friend anything about it. After they were excused from the table, they went upstairs so that John could change clothes for his date that night. He was still wearing the knee-high leather boots and riding-crop pants of a dashing pilot, an outfit he had chosen to wear to the game. Charlie had to help him pull off the boots.

The phone call he had made before leaving turned out to be no mystery at all. It was to his date that night, Eunice "Alabama" Word, a student nurse who lived, worked, and trained at St. John's Hospital. He would pick her up at 7:30 p.m., he told her. Then, Gorrell did something strange, Bard said. Instead of taking him along to go pick up Eunice, John went alone to the hospital, at 21st Street and Utica. John insisted that Bard stay behind, saying he had to do something first. Bard didn't know what that was, but he waited by the front door for his friend to return. Twenty to thirty minutes later, John arrived with Eunice, and the young trio then drove to Charlie's house, where he placed a call to his date, Hazel Williams. And it was here, while he was getting ready for his date, that Charlie said he saw something that might be helpful to detectives.

"John showed me a revolver," he said with a dramatic pause. He could see the detectives' eyebrows go up. "It was a .22-caliber. He asked me if I had any cartridges to fit it. I told him that I had none. He put the pistol back in a holster at his right side, after showing me that there were three cartridges in the cylinder."

He was right about the three cartridges; Maddux had only found two empty shells and one unfired round in the cylinder.

After fifteen minutes, by Charlie's estimation, the boys then went to Hazel's house. There, John showed off his revolver again and laughingly remarked that he was prepared for bandits, Bard said. The group then drove back to Charlie's house. They were only there ten minutes when John suddenly announced he had to leave.

"I've got to see a friend," he had told Charlie. "If I don't see him tonight, I will miss the contact. I'll be back soon."

And then he left with Eunice Word. Charlie never saw him after that, and he had no idea whom John was supposed to meet.

The trail was clear to Maddux and Reif; they needed to follow up with the two girls and learn what they could about the man he was supposed to meet. However, the job of tracking down alibi witnesses and double-checking stories was going to grow exponentially as the case moved forward. From here on out, Maddux would need his seasoned team of investigators to help manage this case. He needed reinforcements, and detectives Leslie Kern, Isaac Fisher, and Louis Boyd were called into a meeting back at the detective bureau that Friday morning.

"I don't have to tell you how important this case is," Maddux reportedly told his detectives. "We're going to work twenty-four hours a day until it is cracked."

In the office of the nursing supervisor at St. John's, Eunice told the detectives that from Charlie's house, the two went to a motel on the outskirts of town called Cook's Camp. After spending a few hours in one of the tiny bungalows frequented by travelers, Gorrell took her to a roadside food stand, where John bought pork sandwiches for both of them. While there, he recognized another young man and waved to him, but he never told her who it was.

Yes, John did say he had an appointment to meet someone, but he never made that meeting while she was with him, she told detectives.

"We returned to the hospital before 11:00 p.m.," Eunice declared. "I think it was 10:50. John walked up the steps to the front entrance with me. We stopped only a few seconds while we said good-night. I went inside. That was the last I saw him."

When Maddux asked the young woman if she had seen the revolver Gorrell was carrying, she gave the detective an important clue.

"I saw John put a pistol in the door pocket [driver's side] as we came back to the hospital," she told him. "John parked his car in front of the hospital and left the car door open and the motor running."

If Gorrell was indeed killed with his own pistol, Maddux realized, then that little mistake may have cost him his life. Based on his examination of Gorrell at the scene, the young man was likely murdered thirty to forty-five minutes before he was found, and shortly after he left Eunice, the last known person to see him alive. He was supposed to meet someone that night—but the killer may have found him first.

The young woman told her story in a frank, direct manner. There was no reason to doubt anything she said, but Maddux needed to be certain about the time frame for everything. Sister Gratiana, who was in charge of the front desk that night, checked her log book and confirmed she had signed Eunice back in at 10:50 p.m.

Back at headquarters, Det. Reif was going through Gorrell's pockets and found he only had one dollar and thirty cents on him when he was killed. John had left home with about two dollars that his father had given him on his way out. They knew Charlie had loaned his friend fifty cents after he had asked for spare bullets. Two dollars and fifty cents wasn't much of a motive, but maybe the killer didn't know that before he shot Gorrell.

By noon, the autopsy report from the coroner was ready. The two bullets had traveled in a horizontal line and shattered the skull plate, where the coroner found them just below the scalp on the left side.

"One bullet entered the right temple and was fired at a distance of ten or twelve inches," Maddux would later tell reporters, who were always swarming around police headquarters. "The head had fallen and the blood ran down toward the upper part of the jaw.

"The second shot entered above the right ear and was fired with the muzzle pressed close, as indicated by the scorched hair. The head was then thrown forward in some way, for the stream of blood ran down toward the front of the face, crossing the first stream of blood."

The reporters lapped up everything Maddux had to say, and he was making sure he told them just about everything he could. An impression needed to be made to everyone in Tulsa that his department was doing all it could to solve this case.

"Gorrell must have been killed while the car was in motion by someone who sat in the front seat beside him while Gorrell was driving," he continued. "This person must have been someone he knew and trusted."

The gun, he added, had been wiped clean.

He then turned his attention to performing a ballistics test. After firing test bullets into cotton, Maddux placed a clean round next to one of the death bullets in a Gravelle comparison microscope. Despite heavy damage to one of the bullets retrieved from the young man's skull, the lands and grooves of the other bullet confirmed it; Gorrell was killed by his own gun.

While Maddux was working in his lab, the city's grapevine was on fire. News that a young man from a prominent family was found murdered in his car in the rich part of town ignited the imaginations of 150,000 Tulsans, and switchboard operators struggled to keep up with all the calls. Radio Station KVOO blasted out the story with their morning news broadcast and ran updates throughout the day.

"Rumors and tips began to seep into Headquarters even before the early editions of the newspapers were on the streets," a high-ranking police official would later write. "Some of that information, at first cast aside as unbelievable, as utterly preposterous, was later to be found of value. In Tulsa's homes and on the street corners, the death of young Gorrell was the one subject of conversation.

"The feeling that something terrible and sinister was about to be disclosed swept over the entire city before nightfall. But I know none realized the wake of horror and revulsion that was to be left as the case progressed. While at the time there was nothing tangible, a feeling of apprehension prevailed in official circles."

When Sgt. Maddux broke the news of the ballistics test to his colleagues, Police Chief Charles Carr called a meeting of all detectives in his office. It was a private meeting, behind a closed door and a stern secretary. But before it was over, they would have the name of the man who killed John Gorrell.

Sort of.

Chapter Three

Friday afternoon, November 30, 1934

EDWARD LAWSON WAS A HARD-CHARGING Tulsa oil executive who hated stagnation. He thrived on movement and action, because that meant accomplishment, which meant money in the bank. He had contempt for the bureaucrats of the world who could wrap more red tape around a drilling rig than there was wood to hold it up.

As a close friend to the Gorrell family, he knew John and his wife were devastated. He didn't like that. He had to do something about that. And so he did the one smart thing nobody had thought of yet; he called John's roommate in Kansas City, Richard Oliver. Oliver was from Tulsa. Maybe he knew something about what was going on. And when Lawson spoke to John's roommate, he struck oil.

After telling the young man that John may have committed suicide or been murdered, Oliver blurted out, "Impossible! I know John did not kill himself—and I know who killed him."

The story, as he told it to Lawson, was that nearly two weeks before, a fella from Tulsa had come up to see John.

"He was introduced to me as 'Bob Wilson.' But before I met Bob Wilson, John told me something. He said: 'If I am ever killed or wounded, you will know that Wilson did it.'"

Lawson told him not to move, and to stay close to the phone. His next call was to Chief Carr, who answered his phone while still meeting with his detectives. Carr took immediate action by issuing two orders to his detectives: find out who Bob

Wilson was, and contact Oliver and make arrangements to get him here by train as fast as possible. Railroad timetables were consulted and arrangements were made. Oliver's train from Kansas City would arrive in Tulsa early the next morning on the Frisco line. Lawson and two detectives would meet him at Union Station and escort him to police headquarters.

A search of arrest records did not uncover anyone with the name Bob Wilson. The city directory showed there were half a dozen Robert Wilsons, but after those who were too young or too old were ruled out, the remainder went by Rob or Robert. Not one police officer from top to bottom had ever heard of Bob Wilson. Blank stares greeted detectives when they made inquiries with the Gorrell family and John's friends.

Bob Wilson? Who in tarnation was the Bob Wilson that met with Gorrell?

The Tulsa grapevine that had been burning up with news of the murder began to work in the detectives' favor. Their telephones rang constantly with new tips from the public, many of which seemed preposterous and farfetched.

One confidential source told detectives that Gorrell was linked to an extortion-and-kidnapping plot against one of the richest families in Tulsa. Another lead revealed a scheme Gorrell had allegedly concocted during his time in flying school. It involved "frequent trips to Mexico" that would "make a lot of money."

Mexico? Frequent trips? A lot of money? It wasn't hard for detectives to figure out what that was all about—if it were true. In a department that already had its own narcotics detective, they knew some of the young people were messing around with marijuana. Unheard-of ten years ago, it had first appeared on Tulsa streets in the past four years. It was known to be an import from Mexico and was often referred to as "that Mexican weed."

Detectives also learned that Gorrell had had a passenger when he drove home. Lon Lyle was another Tulsa native and a dental student in Kansas City. But when detectives found him, he could shed no light on John's murder, and he had never met the Bob Wilson who had come to Kansas City two weeks ago.

After Chief Carr's meeting Friday morning, twenty-two-year-old George Kearney walked into police headquarters on Fourth Street and asked to speak to detectives. He may have seen the killer last night, he told them. Just like Gorrell, Kearney had had a date with one of the student nurses and had escorted her back to the main entrance a few minutes before Gorrell and Eunice arrived.

"We, my companion and I, were standing near the hospital entrance when John and Miss Word drove up. It was just a few minutes before eleven. I was ready to go home.

"As John and Miss Word walked up the steps, I turned and walked to my car which was parked north of the hospital on Utica Avenue. I noticed a man standing beside Gorrell's machine. When I started to drive away the fellow jumped into his own car and followed me.

"I paid very little attention to him until I slowed down to turn into my home driveway. The man pulled up alongside me and stopped [and] rolled down his window. I thought that he wanted to say something to me. He cut his lights off, but a split second later, turned them on again. Then he jerked back and drove off. I watched as he wheeled his car around at the next intersection. He returned down Utica Avenue, traveling back to the hospital."

Kearney knew John, and although his story was interesting, it wouldn't bring Maddux any closer to the killer. The young man didn't really get a good look at the driver and couldn't describe him. He couldn't even say what the make of the automobile was. Nevertheless, the information filtered out to all patrol officers. Employees of both the Crawford Drug Store, across from the hospital, and the hospital itself were questioned about the strange man and the car he was driving.

But nobody else had seen him.

Later that evening, Maddux had another impromptu meeting with his detectives. They had learned a lot over the first twenty hours. They had two possible witnesses to the killer—Kearney and Oliver. And that's when Maddux started to get nervous. What if the killer had learned of Oliver's return to Tulsa? There were a lot of print and radio newsmen swarming around, and he couldn't contain all the information. If the killer knew Oliver was on that train, he might try to silence him when it reached Tulsa.

Maddux couldn't risk it. So far, Oliver was the best lead he had. He sent a telegram to the train station in Vinita, Oklahoma, for Oliver, informing him that detectives would meet him in Claremore, thirty miles northeast of Tulsa. Detectives Reif, Kern, and Fisher would escort Oliver off the train and bring him to Tulsa by car.

Before the *Tulsa World* went to print the next morning, Maddux enlisted their cooperation. Mixed in with the story tomorrow would be a bold proclamation that two local witnesses knew more than they actually did, and that an arrest was imminent. If the killer kept up with the news, he might lose hope and surrender.

"If their story is correct, and if they are able to identify the man they saw, this case will be solved," Sgt. Maddux was quoted by the *Tulsa World*. "We believe the trail is growing warmer."

As a reward for their assistance, Maddux told those same writers that his men would be in Claremore to pick up Oliver and bring him back to Tulsa. Following the detectives the next morning would be a car with reporters and a photographer. When Oliver's picture hit the newspapers the following day with a story that he was talking to police, Bob Wilson might come out of the shadows.

In spite of all the precautions Maddux took, and the safeguard of sending his best men to protect his star witness, he could not have predicted the astonishing coincidence that was about to take place aboard that train.

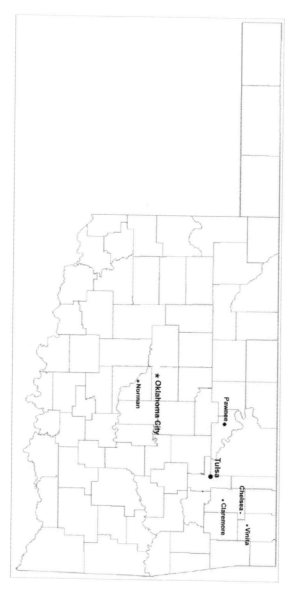

Map of Oklahoma showing Tulsa, Claremore, Chelsea, and Vinita.

Chapter Four

AT 5:46 THE FOLLOWING MORNING, the daily south bound Frisco train ground to a halt in front of the Claremore railroad station. Three detectives from Tulsa, followed at some distance by reporters and a photographer, approached the conductor.

"We are looking for a young fellow, Richard Oliver," Detective Reif said with a flash of his badge. "He's on the train and—"

"I know he's on my train," the uniformed conductor interrupted. "That boy is scared to death. He is locked up tight in my compartment."

With amazement and near-disbelief, the detectives listened as the conductor tried to explain in a few hasty sentences what had transpired in the past hour. Anxious to get the boy off the train, the conductor excused himself for a moment and returned with a young man who clearly didn't want to be there.

When Detective Reif got a look at Richard Oliver, everything about his demeanor conveyed the dental student's belief that he would be horribly murdered at any moment. From his wild, expressive eyes to his quick, sharp glances in every direction, to his pulled-up coat collar that he tried to hide behind, their witness looked as if he would break into pieces if anyone screamed, "Boo!"

"Are you the officers from Tulsa? Thank God you are here," Oliver said as he turned and pointed back at one of the cars down the track. "The man who killed Gorrell is on that train!"

The newsmen were there to catch Oliver's frightened state. "His teeth chattering so that he could hardly speak," a *Tulsa World* reporter wrote, "Oliver refused details until he had pushed those who met him into the safety of the baggage room at the Claremore station."

"He is going to kill me," Oliver squeaked. "My God, why did I say that I would name the man who killed Gorrell?"

Detective Reif didn't know what to think. Maybe the boy was one of those easily excitable types prone to delusions. Or a nervous type. Could the killer they've been hunting now for thirty hours actually be on that train? Coming back to Tulsa? It didn't seem right, but the boy did look as if he had seen the devil himself.

By the time Oliver finally calmed down, the train had left the station. He was thrust into a sedan and taken back to Tulsa with a carload of newsmen following close behind.

Back at police headquarters, Oliver told his story.

"He got on the train at Chelsea. He was wearing a tan suede jacket and gray trousers. Almost at once I recognized him as Bob Wilson. He was the man John feared.

"Wilson recognized me. I could feel his eyes boring through me. I got up and moved toward the rear of the train. Wilson followed a few minutes later, taking a seat behind me.

"In desperation, I went to the conductor. I had received a telegram at Vinita[1] from the Tulsa Police Department advising me that they would send detectives to meet me at Claremore as a precautionary measure, and I showed it to the conductor and he protected me." The conductor had locked Oliver in his private cabin and then locked the door to the coach.

---

[1] See map end of Chapter Three.

In Chief Carr's office with detectives and a stenographer, over donuts and coffee, Oliver told how he'd first met Bob Wilson.

"John was a happy-go-lucky fellow," Oliver began. "He seemed to always invite risks and danger, but he made friends wherever he went.

"The night of November 15, he got a telephone call from Tulsa. I was there at the time; also Jess Harris, who shared the apartment with John and me. He appeared to be worried and said, 'There's a fellow coming up from Tulsa. He is in a jam down there over some slot machines we own and I am afraid that he is coming up here to get me.'

"The next day, John told Jess and myself that when this fellow got up here he would introduce him to us as Bob Wilson and explained that while that was not his real name, it would suffice. He asked that we take a good look at Wilson for if anything ever happened to him, Wilson would be the one responsible.

"'If I am ever murdered or wounded,' John said, 'you will know that Wilson did it. Remember, Wilson will be the man.'

"About eleven o'clock, the night of November 20, he received another call. This call had come within Kansas City and was from Wilson. John talked to him for about five minutes. The conversation ended with John agreeing to meet Wilson in the apartment lobby at midnight.

"A few minutes before midnight, our apartment bell rang. Gorrell went down to the lobby, remaining there six or seven minutes. Then, John and Wilson came into our apartment. After a brief introduction, they went into the bedroom where they remained about an hour. I noticed that Wilson carried a long parcel.

"Both left the building, neither returning that night. Later, when I went into the bedroom, I found the package. It had been opened and I saw that it was a box which had contained surgical gloves. The brand was *Aid* and as John had a girl in trouble, I figured that Wilson was probably a medical student he knew who was going to operate on the girl.

"The next day, Gorrell said nothing about Wilson's visit, although the man called twice for him. Wilson said he was staying at the Phillips Hotel. Once, when he called, I answered the telephone. He said his name was Hake, but I recognized his voice.

"A couple of days later, I asked John what had happened to Wilson. He answered shortly, saying that nothing had happened to him. A few minutes later he made this remark: 'I guess he went back on a Braniff [Airways] plane. That's the way he came here. He had a round trip ticket.'"

The lineage of the revolver was of interest to detectives, and Oliver was able to clear that up. The weapon was borrowed from roommate Jess Harris. Gorrell's parents knew he carried the revolver on long trips but were unaware that he had been murdered with his own weapon.

"He said he wanted it for self-protection," Oliver explained. "We thought his self-protection talk was nothing more than make-believe."

When asked to give a description of Bob Wilson, Oliver said he was of medium height and stocky, with thick dark hair and dark eyes. He appeared to be well developed muscularly, but above all, his friendly personality had been his outstanding characteristic.

As Oliver waited outside the chief's office, Carr and his detectives discussed the young man's statement. It hadn't provided the smoking gun, but it gave them a lot of leads to work. A wire was sent to Kansas City Police to check the registration records at the Phillips Hotel and the passenger list at Braniff Airways. Detective Fisher would check the airline's records in Tulsa.

Around the same time Oliver was telling his story, a chubby, bald-headed, middle-aged man walked into the Kansas City Police Department Headquarters and asked for a private meeting with Chief of Detectives Thomas Higgins. While Tulsa detectives were still trying to track down Bob Wilson, this new witness had an amazing story to tell of the twenty-four hours he had spent with John Gorrell's killer.

And he knew Bob Wilson's real name.

Chapter Five

Saturday mid-morning, December 1, 1934
Kansas City, Missouri

THOMAS J. HIGGINS DIDN'T LOOK like a detective. At least not in the way those Hollywood flickers portrayed hard-nosed, gum-shoe detectives. He was short, wore wire-frame glasses, and had a comb-over that failed to mask his bald dome. But where others were brash and forceful, Higgins was methodical, patient, thoughtful—qualities that led to his posting as chief over all detectives in Kansas City, Missouri.

And when airplane parts dealer and unlicensed pilot Floyd Huff sat across from his desk that Saturday morning of December 1, Higgins detected the nonverbal clues of a nervous man anxious to tell a story that he felt was important. If this fella believed his story was significant, Higgins was patient enough to hear him out. In an article that appeared the following year in a crime magazine he coauthored, Higgins recounted the statement Huff gave.

He began by handing Higgins a newspaper clipping about the murder in Tulsa of John Gorrell Jr., a student at Kansas City Western Dental College. Attached to the Associated Press article was a clipping from a local newspaper that had pursued the Kansas City angle, with a short but unproductive interview of Dick Oliver. Higgins read each item twice before asking Huff the significance of the clippings.

"Chief, that boy was murdered and I know who did it!" Huff exclaimed. "The murderer told me in so many words that he was going to kill Gorrell. He told me how he was going to do it. It fits to the letter with this story.

"That fella will come back here and kill me. He gave me his name, address, and telephone number. I'm not going to leave here until that man is arrested."

"Let's get this straight, Huff. Start right at the beginning," Higgins told him. "I'll listen. And if your story is worth anything, you'll get the action you want."

"I had known Gorrell for some time," Huff began. "I knew that he was a licensed pilot. He was a frequent visitor at the airport.

"The afternoon of November 21, he and another young chap came to my hangar at Fairfax Airport. They wanted to rent my plane for a flight. Flying conditions were bad, almost what we call zero-zero. I refused to let my ship go out.

"Evidently, what I said confirmed Gorrell's opinion on the weather, as he was a good pilot. His friend, however, seemed to be disappointed. We talked for a little while. The boys said they had no way to get home. I offered to take them to Gorrell's apartment.

"Gorrell's friend wanted to go to the Kansas City Airport, so I drove across the intercity viaduct into Missouri. The fellow sent a telegram at the postal branch and then went to the airport ticket office. He left the unused part of a round-trip airline ticket with the agent. He said he didn't want to lose it.

"From there, we drove to 2015 Linwood Boulevard,[1] where Everett Gartner lived. Both boys seemed to be well acquainted with Gartner.

"We had been there some time when Gorrell's friend brought up the subject of his return to Tulsa. He wanted to return that night, but all the flights from Kansas City had been canceled.

---

[1] Not to be confused with Gorrell's address of 1205 Linwood Boulevard.

"Gartner offered to buy the unused airplane ticket. The deal went through. I then said that I planned to drive to Oklahoma, and that I would go as far as Bartlesville. That is about fifty miles from Tulsa.

"'If you will take me on into Tulsa, I will buy the gas and oil for the trip,' this young fellow said to me. That was satisfactory.

"About 4:30 that afternoon we started for Tulsa. We stopped at a store and bought a bottle of Scotch whiskey. We opened the bottle shortly after we left the city, headed south. We had a drink or two. The weather and roads were all we talked about for some time. For a long while neither of us said anything. Suddenly, the boy said:

"'Do you know why I came to Kansas City?'

"I told him 'no.'

"'I came up to kill John Gorrell.'

"I looked at him and laughed. He said:

"'You don't believe me, do you?'

"This boy opened his bag and pulled out a long dagger. He said he had some rubber gloves he had intended to use when he stabbed his friend.

"I thought that was all boy talk and that the chap was trying to impress me. Then he told me why he had been so disappointed about the airplane that afternoon. He said he had planned to crack Gorrell over the head with a wrench and then bail out. That would make it look like an accident. His little plan would have cost me just about $8,000 for a new plane, too.

"The boy showed me a bump on his head which he said he suffered in an automobile crash, and I still thought that perhaps he was just drunk and maybe a little irrational from that crack on the head," Huff told Higgins.

"He kept talking about how he was going to kill Gorrell. Listen, Chief, he said this: 'Gorrell is coming to Tulsa next week. I'll get him then. I'll drive him out on some lonely road, [and] pretend I have a flat tire. Then he'll get it!'"

Higgins would later write that he wasn't sure if he should believe Huff, who seemed as if he were trying just a bit too hard to sell the detective on his wild tale. But there was one item in his story that matched with what the AP reported: "was found in a motor car in a lonely south side park area." And Huff had just quoted the killer to have said, "I'll drive him out on some lonely road..."

"I had become impressed," Higgins wrote in his magazine article. "This was a case 300 miles out of my jurisdiction, across two state lines, but that made no difference. I questioned Huff. 'What was this fellow's name?'"

Huff reached into a shirt pocket, retrieved a scrap of paper, and extended it to Higgins.

Phil Kennamer. Philtower Building. 4-0219.

"That's the name he gave me," Huff said. "When I left him in Tulsa the following morning he gave me that scrap of paper, first writing his name on it."

"Why did he want to kill Gorrell?" Higgins wanted to know.

"Why, he had some rigamarole about a girl he wanted to protect. He showed me a letter he said was an extortion note; that it demanded $20,000 from a man named Wilcox. He explained that the [extortion] letter threatened the life of Virginia Wilcox, the girl he loved.

"I didn't read the letter, [because] it was sealed. Kennamer simply showed me the envelope, which was addressed to Wilcox. Wilcox is a very wealthy oil man, according to what the boy said.

"I asked him what he was going to do with the letter, where he obtained it.

"'Gorrell gave it to me to mail in Tulsa,' he said.

"'Are you going to mail it?' I asked him.

"He said he was undecided just what he would do with it. He was very positive in saying he did not intend to turn it over to police."

Huff ended his story by reporting that he and Kennamer had spent the night in a hotel in Pittsburg, Kansas, and had arrived in Tulsa midmorning on November 22, where he dropped Kennamer off at the Philtower Building.[2]

Higgins found the story to be credible. Astonishing, but credible. There were too many rich details a fabricator wanting a little notoriety couldn't have plucked out of thin air. While he waited for a long-distance connection with Chief Carr to advise him to arrest Phil Kennamer, he had no idea of the storm he was about to unleash.

"This story, with the lightning-swift developments that followed in its wake, was to rock Tulsa to its very foundation that Saturday afternoon," Higgins wrote. "It would be difficult to find adjectives describing the bombshell it created in Tulsa Police Headquarters. The name, which had meant little to me, was a potent one in Tulsa. There was prestige, both social and professional, behind it."

Phil Kennamer, aka Bob Wilson, was the son of Federal Judge Franklin Kennamer.

Tulsa was about to be hit by a tornado.

---

[2] A twenty-four-story, art-deco-style high-rise built by Waite Phillips and completed in 1928.

Chapter Six

FRANKLIN ELMORE KENNAMER WAS BORN in Alabama in 1879. After graduating high school, he attended a private college and studied the law under several apprenticeships. He moved to Oklahoma in 1901 where he taught school and continued his legal studies. In 1905 he was admitted to the bar and joined a law practice in Madill. In 1908, he associated with attorney Charles Coakley in a long-running partnership that oversaw a large amount of Indian land litigation and important criminal cases, in addition to representing the local interests of several railroads.

He was a city attorney for Madill from 1915 to 1916 and mayor from 1919 to 1920. In 1919, he was a delegate to the Republican National Committee and supported Warren Harding for president. A Republican resurgence in November 1920 propelled him to the Oklahoma State Supreme Court. In 1924, while other prominent men were considered to be front-runners, President Coolidge chose Franklin Kennamer to serve as Federal Judge for the Eastern District of Oklahoma. Exactly one year after that appointment, Judge Kennamer was moved to the newly created Northern District of Oklahoma, with a federal courthouse in Tulsa. He quickly became well known throughout the state as a stern judge with zero tolerance for bootleggers.[1]

When his brother, Charles, was moved up from federal prosecutor in Alabama to the bench in 1931, the two Kennamers were the only brothers in US history to serve as federal judges at the same time. Other Kennamer brothers occupied important government positions from Washington DC to Alabama.

When Philip was born in 1915, he was the youngest of four siblings. Although extremely intelligent with an IQ of 120,[2] it became clear from an early age that Phil was also a troubled child with psychological problems—a fact that would become public knowledge in the months ahead.

As a morning paper, Saturday's edition of *Tulsa World's* coverage was mostly a recap of everything that happened the day before. Across the Midwest, the early papers in adjacent states showed no interest in what was then viewed as a local story for Tulsa. By later that afternoon, that would all change.

Reporters in Kansas City had gotten wind of Huff's statement and "literally were burning the wires in efforts to substantiate it." The sudden flurry of phone calls coming down from the north sparked wild rumors that made their way into the offices of the *World* and *Tribune*, and then out to the gaggle of reporters waddling around the courthouse, looking for the next big angle.

But when they looked around for chatty Sgt. Maddux, they were told he was in a meeting in County Attorney Holly Anderson's office with Chief Carr. In fact, all the city detectives

---

[1] Oklahoma didn't need the 18th Amendment to outlaw alcohol. Prohibition was accepted as part of the state constitution in September 1907, two months before it became the 46th state in the union. Oklahoma never did get around to ratifying the 21st Amendment, and the sale of distilled liquor was illegal statewide until 1959.

[2] At the time, an IQ of 120 placed him in the 91st percentile.

on the case were in that meeting, along with the coroner, and Assistant Prosecutor Tom Wallace.

Higgins had telephoned Chief Carr at 10:55 a.m., and the meeting he called together had started just after 12:30. One o'clock came and went, then two. Whatever was going on in there, it had to be big. Where the *World* reporters had time, the *Tribune* staff had run out of it by 2:30. If there was a big scoop coming, Tulsa would read it about it first in the *World's* Sunday edition.

A scoop was coming—a lot of them, in fact. And they were all jaw-droppers.

Around 2:40 that afternoon, two distinguished-looking men dressed in fitted, dark suits walked up the short flight of steps at the west entrance to the courthouse. As they entered the lobby, the elder of the two was greeted with deference by those who knew him. His name was A. Flint Moss, and he was the most highly regarded criminal defense attorney in Tulsa. He had moved to Oklahoma in 1900 following his graduation from Cumberland University in Tennessee. He was active in Democratic Party politics and was a former county attorney for Kay County in north-central Oklahoma. He then migrated to Oklahoma City, where he practiced law for six years before settling down in Tulsa in 1913, just when the city was booming. As the defense attorney for many high-profile murder cases, he quickly gained the respect of his peers, and it was said about him that he "could laugh a murder case to acquittal."

Half a step behind him and to his right was a young man in a blue serge suit who looked as if he didn't have a care in the world.

Inside the sheriff's office, Moss leaned against a waist-high counter and called out to Deputy Nathan Martin.

"This is Phil Kennamer. He wants to surrender. He killed John Gorrell," Moss declared.

Martin chuckled. He looked at Moss and waited for the punch line that never came. But this was no joke. The older man in glasses was serious. Kennamer stood there quietly with a smug look on his face that would become his trademark. Martin then looked to his left at Chief Deputy John Evans, twenty feet away, who caught the confused look on his face. When Evans reached the counter, Moss repeated his statement.

"This is Phil Kennamer. He wants to surrender. He killed Gorrell."

A wave of silence rolled through the wide room as deputies, secretaries, and clerks stopped what they were doing and stared quietly at the two men. It was as if Bruno Hauptmann himself had walked into the room.

"Have you been in trouble?" Nathan Martin asked the young man.

"Yes, I shot Gorrell. I had to do it. It was self-defense," Kennamer replied.

Inside the county attorney's office, an excited secretary broke into the meeting with the surprise announcement. Those old men, with their paunch bellies, backaches, arthritis, and other ailments, sprang up like they were young boys again and hustled down the corridor to where Moss and Kennamer were standing.

It was going to be a long day.

Deputy Evans escorted Kennamer and Moss to the sheriff's office with a dozen officers, detectives, and newsmen crowding close behind.

"Phil told me this morning the facts and circumstances surrounding the killing and he wanted to surrender," Moss began with a raised voice to quiet the chatter. "I said I wanted to talk to his father about it. I knew his father would concur with me and Phil that the rightful thing for him to do was to surrender.

"Phil's thought was that some person would be arrested and charged with this offense who had not been [involved] with the killing. His confidence in the righteousness of his defense satisfied him the outcome of this prosecution would be in accordance with the truth and his complete vindication.

"Kennamer knew Gorrell for several months but was not an intimate acquaintance of his. Phil admits he shot Gorrell but did it in self-defense. After the shooting, Phil went home. He did not say anything to his father, and I was the first person he discussed the matter with this morning. Judge Kennamer approved completely Phil's determination to voluntarily surrender."

For all the confidence Moss had in his client at that moment, it would soon melt away when he would learn from new witnesses that half the proclamations he had just made were not true. If he didn't know it then, he would soon learn: Phil Kennamer had a big mouth.

Moss then told his audience of lawmen and journalists that Kennamer killed Gorrell in self-defense with Gorrell's own gun. When a reporter asked for further explanation, Moss pushed his glasses back and stared directly at the young man who asked the question.

"Suppose I was having a difficulty with someone and he tried to kill me with his gun and we both fought over it and in the end, he was killed with his own gun. There would be nothing extraordinary about that."

Kennamer did have that part going for him. It wasn't his gun, it was Gorrell's. But like everything else that would come up during the case, there were many layers to the truth.

"The family environment of Phil Kennamer," Moss continued with an air of self-righteousness on his client's behalf, "makes it of necessity true that there some powerful underlying reason for the trouble that finally came up between the two young men."

Sergeant Maddux and his senior detectives stood back quietly and watched the spectacle unfold. The client was with his lawyer, and his lawyer was grandstanding in front of reporters who were asking all the questions. But when they probed and prodded for concrete answers to specific queries, Moss would fire back, "you can't ask these questions! It was self-defense and that's all we have to say now."

Soon after the lawyer left his client in the custody of deputies, Sgt. Maddux and his detectives took a crack at him. But as much as he liked to talk, and talk about himself, Kennamer was sticking to his lawyer's guns; it was self-defense. All the salient details of his story would just have to wait.

Afterward, the newsmen scrutinized Kennamer once again and were impressed with what they saw. His dark-brown, wavy hair was parted on the left side. He had strong wrists and hands, and a determined jaw that hung low and full. His heavy eyelids punctuated the cocky expression he always had, and his 185 pounds on a six-foot frame could intimidate a lot of people.

He was, they said, a nineteen-year-old who carried himself with the poise of someone twice his age, and they noted that he looked much older. Some of them knew him personally from the short time he was a cub reporter for an Oklahoma City paper. They also recognized him from the circle of chiselers and crumbs and schleppers and spoiled young swells that clung to the illegal gambling and drinking dens of Tulsa's quasi-underworld.

"He speaks fluently, unhesitatingly, and interestingly. He has a habit of mixing metaphors and embellishing his statements with aphorisms. He is quick on repartee and has a sense of humor," a *World* reporter observed.

Although his appearance and diction were impressive, Kennamer's calm composure and confidence puzzled them. In their experience of covering crime, young offenders booked into jail were often nervous, unsure of what would happen next. But not Phil. He was one cool customer, and it seemed to come from within, not from who his daddy was.

"Did you kill John Gorrell?" asked *World* reporter Pat Burgess, who was well acquainted with Kennamer.

"I did."

"Why did you kill him?"

"It was self-defense."

"Why was it self-defense?"

"I sincerely regret that it was necessary for me to kill John Gorrell, but under the circumstances, it was necessary and I did it."

"Why did you do it?"

"I had to save my own life."

"Were you involved in the purported plot to extort money from Homer Wilcox in a kidnapping scheme?"

"Certainly, I was not."

"Did you know the Wilcox family?"

"Yes."

"Were you implicated or involved in any other extortion plot?"

"Such a thing never entered my head."

"What caused the fatal fight?"

"I'll tell that to the court at the proper time as my lawyer has directed me."

"How do you feel about this killing now?"

"I regret it. It was necessary to do and I am sorry for John Gorrell, for his family and for my own."

The query, *what caused the fatal fight*, turned out to be a question Tulsa would debate for years.

The interview was cut short by deputies, who formally arrested Kennamer and lodged him in the jail matron's living quarters. This was the first of many actions Sheriff Charlie Price would take that were controversial. Price, it would soon come out, had a lot of axes to grind, and Kennamer's cell was a very comfortable room. It was modestly furnished with a cast-iron bed, an ivory-toned dresser, a green rocking chair, and a battered and scarred radio cabinet. When Kennamer walked into the room, he observed a private lavatory to his right, and to his left, a door, which was supposed to be locked, that led to the matron's office with a desk and typewriter.

For some untold reason, a low-hanging portrait of Governor Martin Trapp was left behind to adorn the pastel colored walls. Trapp had left office nearly eight years before. It might have been left in place out of respect, since he was the one who had established the State Bureau of Criminal Investigation. He had also curbed the power of the Ku Klux Klan by passing an anti-mask law.[3]

To everyone involved, it looked like special treatment, which Sheriff Price admitted it was, but not because he liked Judge Kennamer—he hated Judge Kennamer.

"I wanted to show Judge Kennamer how kind I can be to his son, in contrast to what he once did to me," Sheriff Price later explained.

"When Price was undersheriff several years ago," the *Tulsa Tribune* reminded its readers, "Judge Kennamer sentenced him to three months in jail and ordered him fined $500 when he would not tell a grand jury about reported drinking among officers at the jail. Price said he knew nothing about it. He served a month in the Vinita jail and was freed when his fellow officers paid the fine for him."

Sheriff Price failed to win reelection, and in four more weeks, he and twenty-six deputies were out the door. Feeling as if he answered to no one, he was going to do whatever he damn well wanted to do.

Once they had the motive of self-defense, reporters began chipping away at the alleged extortion plot involving the Wilcox family. Second only to Kennamer's surrender, this was the next big angle. Homer Wilcox was a sickly man when he came to Tulsa in 1909 and got into the grain and elevator business. He soon regained his health and, with investors, began drilling for oil, which had recently been discovered in the area. But after he came up empty-handed time and time again, they started calling

---

[3] Anti-mask laws penalized individuals who covered their faces for political or religious purposes.

him "dry-hole Wilcox." Wilcox persevered and, with a new strategy, began drilling deeper than anyone else. This approach paid off, and he applied it repeatedly. By 1922, the *Tulsa World* estimated he was worth $20 million.[4]

By late afternoon that Saturday, Tulsa reporters knew about Floyd Huff's statement made in Kansas City just a few hours before. According to Detective Higgins, Huff said Kennamer told him he was going to kill Gorrell, because John was the mastermind of a $20,000 extortion scheme which threatened to harm Virginia Wilcox, the woman Phil Kennamer was in love with, if the money wasn't paid.

However, the whole bizarre story was more complicated than that. Those same reporters would soon learn, from Phil, that Gorrell's original plan was to kidnap Virginia, and that Phil had acted as double agent and had gone to Kansas City to convince Gorrell to change his plan from kidnapping to extortion. Then, with the extortion note in his possession, Phil could put a stop to it.

The day before, credible rumors had filtered into the newsroom that a shakedown against a wealthy Tulsa family had already taken place. But when they interviewed Wilcox, he denied ever receiving a note, and no other families came forward to claim they were the victims of an extortion plot. If the Wilcox letter described by Huff was never sent, it was unclear to everyone where it was or who had it.

At 3:30 p.m., Chief Deputy John Evans arrested big Wade Thomas, owner of the Idle Hour, a food and beer joint that operated illegal slot machines and craps tables in the back. No charges were filed, and Thomas was held in solitary confinement—away from the newspaper reporters, who were never given a straight answer on why he was arrested. The Tulsa papers made a big deal of his arrest and insinuated there was a possible connection to the murder, extortion plot, or both.

---

[4] The 2014 equivalent of $277 million, when adjusted for inflation.

For all the jaw-droppers and hard news that investigators and reporters were trying to make sense of that Saturday, there was the soft news of a broken family coming to terms with the loss of their son. More than five hundred people attended the funeral services for John Gorrell Jr., held at the First Presbyterian Church. The entire student body of the Spartan School of Aeronautics attended en masse. After the graveside service, a *Tribune* reporter followed the Gorrells home, where the family tried to reconstruct what they knew about their son's ties with Phil Kennamer.

"The first time I heard of Phil Kennamer," Mrs. Gorrell said as she leaned back in her chair, "was last summer when, for about a week, he would come by the house for John accompanied by another boy. The friendship was short-lived. It just spurted up and then as suddenly died down. I never heard much of Phil again until Thanksgiving Day.

"Before John came home that day, Phil Kennamer called for him. I forgot to mention it to John until that night at the dinner table. Doctor Gorrell had just served John with a second helping, and I told John that Phil had called twice for him. He looked very funny and didn't take another bite of dinner. He went out at about 7:20[5] and shortly after that, Phil called for John again.

"Now, I am sure Phil was just keeping in touch to see that John was in town and couldn't get away from him by his calls [on] Thanksgiving. And to think he shot John with John's own gun."

The *Tribune* reporter was the first to break the news to the family that Kennamer might have killed John over an extortion plot against the Wilcox family, allegedly masterminded by their son.

---

[5] She was in a different room in the house and wasn't aware that John had left Charlie behind and then returned to pick his friend up.

"John couldn't have been mixed up in anything like that," Mrs. Gorrell fired back in disbelief. "Why, when the Lindbergh kidnapping and the others were in the limelight, John was the first to express his horror and disgust. That was one thing about John. He was never cruel. He could never have been that way to anyone.

"And as for ever wanting $20,000, John wasn't like that. He never wanted big amounts of money. He only wanted small amounts to do little things."

"If John had only come to us with all that was worrying him instead of keeping it to himself, but he wouldn't do that," his father chimed in. "Evidently, he had been threatened in Kansas City by Phil Kennamer, and that was why he was so upset. But he figured that he could get out of it without disturbing or worrying us."

The *Tribune* writer did not press them about rumors that John had gambling debts owed to Wade Thomas, or that there was a rumor he'd dreamed up some scheme involving frequent trips to Mexico.

Before ending the interview, the Gorrells expressed their belief that Phil Kennamer had an accomplice—someone who drove him away from the murder. That conviction was also shared by Sgt. Maddux and his detectives, even though Kennamer was telling anyone who would listen that it was a solo job.

At six o'clock that Saturday night, the judge himself walked into the courthouse and held a thirty-minute private meeting with his son in Sheriff Price's office. Reporters caught up with him as he was leaving.

"I never dreamed such a thing could happen. I had always instructed my boy to never touch the hair of a human unless it was a life-and-death struggle," Judge Kennamer said with tears in his eyes. "Life, it seems, is full of tragedy."

Feeling the need to explain himself, the judge said his son had accompanied him on a quail hunt at his farm, near Chelsea in Rogers County, on Friday. Later that night, Phil asked his father for a ride to the local train station early the next morning, explaining that he had to return to Tulsa on business. Phil then met with Flint Moss in Tulsa, who agreed to take on his case, but demanded that they travel back to his father's farm in Moss's car to speak with Judge Kennamer first. They returned to Tulsa that afternoon and surrendered at 2:40 p.m.

As it turns out, Oliver was right. "Bob Wilson" had gotten on the train at Chelsea, a mere nineteen miles northeast of Claremore.

The Sunday editions of both Tulsa newspapers were going to shock everyone. They had it all: Richard Oliver stalked by the killer on the Frisco train, Floyd Huff's statement, an alleged kidnapping or extortion plot involving the Wilcox family, Phil Kennamer's surrender, the funeral, the mysterious arrest of Wade Thomas, the Gorrell family reaction, and Judge Kennamer's response to his son's arrest. It should have been enough, but this was no ordinary day. Later that Saturday night, a tall, young man about Gorrell's age pushed his way through the crowded courthouse lobby and marched down the corridor to the sheriff's department on the first floor. Standing behind the same bannister from which Kennamer and his attorney had announced their surrender just hours before, he asked to speak with Sheriff Price.

"I want to tell him something about Phil Kennamer and John Gorrell," he said. "They were planning some hold-ups and other things a lot worse."

That got him a first-class ticket to the sheriff's private office. His name was Ted Bath, and he was a Tulsa boy who worked at a refinery in Longview, Texas. He was a close personal friend of John's, he said, and had been a pallbearer at his funeral that day. Chief Deputy Evans, who led the investigation for county authorities, took his statement with a stenographer.

"Last September I was home on a short vacation," Bath began. "One day, in the Brown Derby Café on South Main, I met John and a boy he introduced as Phil Kennamer. We sat at a table, talking about a number of things.

"Kennamer remarked that he needed some money. John and I laughed. Both of us said we always needed money. A little later Kennamer said the fact that my car had Texas license plates might be useful. He said there was a place on East 11th Street [the Idle Hour] that we might hold up and get $300 or $400.

"He had something else in mind because he went on to say this money could be used to further other plots.

"I didn't like the idea and said so. I said if he did, it could mean bloodshed and maybe someone would get killed. Phil made a gesture as if to say 'what does it matter?'

"At first I thought he was joking, and when I learned he was serious about the matter I quickly told them I was not interested because I had a good job and was doing pretty well for myself.

"The conversation switched, and in a few minutes I left. I returned to the place a short time later. Phil and John still were there. Kennamer spoke to me.

"'Do you know Barbara Boyle?'

"I started to say no, when John interrupted.

"'You leave her name out of this,' John said. 'She is a close friend of the family.'

"Kennamer then asked me if I knew Virginia Wilcox. I told him that I did not. He wanted to know then if I could take a couple of weeks off from work. I said not unless it was for something important.

"Kennamer suggested that I ingratiate myself with Miss Wilcox and try to get her into a compromising position. He wanted to obtain some pictures of her. He said he would defray all my expenses. I said I would not be interested. Shortly after that we left the place."

As tired as he was after a long day, Deputy Evans was ecstatic. Bath's statement confirmed some of the rumors they had been hearing. It also refuted Kennamer's assertion that the extortion plot was all Gorrell's idea. Kennamer was in on it from the get-go, and it could break apart his claim that it was all self-defense.

When the news of Kennamer's surrender first rolled through the city that Saturday night, more young Tulsans came forward with incredible stories of their own that allowed detectives to piece together everything that had happened that fateful night.

Chapter Seven

KENNAMER'S SURRENDER ON SATURDAY, DECEMBER 1, came at an inconvenient time for the *Tribune* and afternoon papers nationwide. A few dozen evening editions across the country were able to squeeze in a short piece about Kennamer's surrender, his self-defense claims, and Huff's statement.

By the next morning, the story had exploded across the country with front-page coverage in all forty-eight states. In nearly every AP and UP report, it was never about the young victim; it was a story about the son of a federal judge committing murder. Phil's identity was enmeshed with his father's, and nearly every headline drove home the fact that it was the son of a federal judge who was now charged with first-degree murder. He was often referred to as "young Kennamer" and "the judge's son." In the few cases in which a photo was published, it was his father's image that appeared.

The story was hot enough that the wire services and major newspapers in Kansas City, Chicago, St. Louis, and New York City sent in their best word-slingers to cover it. They were called newshawks and were veterans at covering major crimes. When they blew into town, it raised the stakes for everyone. The most celebrated of them all was Lowell Limpus of the *New York Daily News*. He was an Oklahoma native who had covered many important criminal cases of the last decade. His claim to fame was his personal investigation into the infamous 1922 Hall-Mills double murder that had led to police reopening the case.

Before the shock of a federal judge's son confessing to murder could evaporate, reporters started digging into Judge Kennamer's past. After his appointment to the state supreme court, he had moved his wife and children to Chelsea in Northeast Oklahoma, where he bought a farm he would own the rest of his life. When appointed to the federal bench in February 1924, the family, with two girls and two boys,[1] moved to Sand Springs, a town eight miles west of Tulsa. There, Phil thrived in school and was twice elected class president.

"Phil was endowed with natural leadership ability, and was one who would take a project and literally just put it over," his elementary school principal later recalled. "Although he did not stand first in his class, he was a superior student, ranking in the top ten percent. He was quite well liked by his teachers and he was an able debater."

In 1928, the family moved to Tulsa, where Phil began his freshman year. At home, there had always been signs of trouble, but in Tulsa, the boy fell apart. He would often confide to his sister Opal that he wished he were dead because he felt he was misunderstood and out of tune with the world. He first ran away from home when he was six, and he ran away again soon after the family moved to Tulsa.

In 1930, his father sent his troubled son off to military school in New Mexico, where he ran away before the school year finished. He earned just six and one-half credits the semester he was there and failed to complete his French, biology, and art courses. His highest grade was an 84 in modern history. He was next sent to a boarding school in Durant, Oklahoma, but when his mother's illness with cystic fibrosis worsened, he accompanied her to San Antonio,

---

[1] Oldest to youngest, they were Opal, Juanita, Franklin Jr., and Phil.

Texas, where the warmer climate would ease her condition. Instead of aiding her, young Kennamer abandoned her. Authorities found the sixteen-year-old in Galveston on a fishing boat, where he said he was preparing to fight in a South American revolution but was unsure of which side to join. He later ran away to New Orleans and then on to Miami, where he was stopped by a federal lawman. When asked to explain why he was so far from home, Kennamer said he was going to enlist in the French Foreign Legion. Sent home, he continued to talk about joining foreign armies and expressed his belief that he could rule a South American country and be a popular dictator.[2]

In the 1930s, boys from poor families who ran away from home were arrested and brought to court, where they were frequently branded "delinquents." This label would often earn them a sentence in a state reform school, where abuse by guards and other boys was common. But every time Phil Kennamer ran away, his father rescued him. In 1931, Kennamer attended Tulsa's Central High School where an intelligence test revealed his high IQ. But his teachers took note of his inability to apply himself, and he left after just three months, receiving no credit. In 1933, his father made a last-ditch effort to provide his son with a secondary education by enrolling him in Tulsa's prestigious Catholic school, Cascia Hall.

Just like at Central High, three months was enough before he quit.

Judge Kennamer then used his influence to get his son job after job, none of which lasted more than a few months. His most notable profession, and one that led to his current trouble, was as a reporter for the *Daily Oklahoman*. While working for the Fourth Estate, he got to meet *Tulsa World*

---

[2] In 1934, the word *dictator* did not have the same negative connotation it has today.

reporters Preston Cochrane and Pat Burgess, two young men who would figure largely in the Gorrell investigation. He also got acquainted with the fast lifestyle of bootleggers and petty criminals, including Oklahoma City bondsman Henry "Cadillac" Booth, who would play a large role in unraveling Kennamer's intricate plot.

It was not unusual at that time for reporters to rub elbows with criminals, claimed *World* police beat reporter Walter Biscup in a 1979 interview for a Tulsa Junior League oral history project. To get the inside scoop, Biscup and his colleagues would hang out at nightclubs and speakeasies.

"You had a few nightclubs here that were really run by people who had an underworld tie. They weren't part of the underworld, but, on the other hand, they knew what was going on, and you could buy drinks, you could gamble, in fact; while Tulsa wasn't a really wide open town, still it was," Biscup explained. "And that's where most of the action was. It was a different age."

Biscup also frequented the county jail, where he talked directly with prisoners behind bars. "I got real friendly with all of the criminals who were there for a long time and [would] buy them cigars sometimes. Get magazines. First thing you know, they trust you, and tip you off," he said. Biscup, along with Burgess and others, worked on the Kennamer story.

To get Phil to his newspaper job on time, the judge bought him a car, which he wrecked a few weeks later. He bought his son another car but it too was wrecked in less than a month. The third car he bought for his son was wrecked a few weeks after he got it, and only a week or two before he flew to Kansas City to meet Gorrell.

During his short-lived time as a car owner, he was stopped by local police for drunk driving on numerous occasions, but only once was he cited and fined twenty dollars.

Phil had a reputation as a liar and an exaggerator, but he was also known for his complete lack of fear. Stories circulated that he once jumped from the running board of one car to another when both were traveling fifty miles per hour. During a Christmas party the year before at the Mayo Hotel, he crawled out a window on the sixteenth floor and walked along the ledge from one end to the other in order to impress Virginia Wilcox, who was on a date with another boy.

She was not impressed, and the stunt only repelled her further.

If his attorney wanted to build an insanity case, his client surely had the history of outrageous behavior, and County Attorney Holly Anderson forecast that was exactly what Moss would do.

FOR ALL THAT WEEK, city and county investigators labored long into the night, sifting the factual witness statements from the ludicrous assertions phoned in by anonymous tipsters and amateur detectives. The Tulsa grapevine was thriving on rumors that outnumbered facts, rumors that seemed more credible only because they were sensational and satisfied the public's thirst for conspiracy theories and complicated plots. Local officials had their own theories, which evolved daily. Still in the matron's room on the third floor, Kennamer read all the newspaper coverage and followed the investigation with interest.

"It is strange that they apparently overlook the obvious in order to seek the mysterious," he was overhead to say. But they were only doing their job, and unrelenting rumors fogged the investigation.

"There seemed no end to these startling stories," the *Tribune* reported that week. "While officers tend in time to run all of them down, for the present the prosecutors and reporters centered on those that seemed most probably linked with the case."

The *World* also made note of the phenomenon. "Numerous anonymous telephone calls were being received by police in regard to the case. Several informed detectives of interested persons who could shed more light on the mysterious aspects of the slaying. These were all being checked, and from the haze of rumors, whispered information, and suspicions, officers were hopeful of abstracting salient facts."

Wild stories of sexual blackmail, underage drinking, gambling, marijuana smoking, and narcotic smuggling within the young social set of Tulsa's most noted families became the background theme to the entire investigation and seeped into detectives' analyses. Those allegedly involved were associated with the elite Hy-Hat Club, of which Kennamer was once a member. It was a club of rich boys who were selective about who could become a member or attend club dances.

For a gang of young wastrels who all owned automobiles, initiation into the club was rumored to be: "Drink ten glasses of beer, one right after the other, hop into your automobile and drive around a corner at sixty miles per hour." The unsubstantiated activities of the Hy-Hat Club coexisted with the city-wide gossip that swirled around the Gorrell murder until their escapades became exaggerated and distorted, taking on a life of their own.

On Monday morning, Chief Deputy Evans escorted Kennamer to Judge John Woodward's Court of Common Pleas, where his attorney was waiting for him. Moss waived the reading of the charges and pleaded "not guilty" on his client's behalf. Kennamer said nothing during his entire arraignment. He was smartly dressed in a gray suit, gray shirt, and matching gray tie. All eyes in the courtroom were on him, and they saw a young man who was completely at ease—almost as if he enjoyed the attention.

As Moss, Anderson, and Judge Woodward discussed a timetable for the preliminary hearing, Kennamer fingered a button on his suit, glanced down at his freshly polished shoes, and then scanned the audience. Reaching into his pocket, he retrieved a cigarette and match, and lit the match off his thumbnail. He puffed away until Moss whispered something in his ear. He then dropped the cigarette on the courtroom floor and smashed it with his foot.

With five other murder trials in the pipeline, Anderson was able to push the preliminary hearing to December 17. Judge Woodward ordered Kennamer held without bail. As he was escorted from the courtroom, he smiled at acquaintances. His father was notably absent.

Kennamer's immaturity was not lost on those present, and a *Tribune* writer took note of his attitude.

"When the boy went to jail, he did so, apparently, without a word of advice from his father about his conduct in jail, or about other matters of court and jail procedures of which a federal judge could be presumed to know a great deal. He told the boy he was in the hands of his own attorney. He didn't tell him not to talk or not to pose for photographers, or to drop his light-hearted air."

Moss did tell his client not to talk, but Kennamer couldn't stop himself if he wanted to. In the weeks leading up to the murder, he spoke often of the necessity to kill John Gorrell to stop him from carrying out his kidnapping plans in order to save Virginia. Sometimes, he attempted to be chivalrous by claiming he didn't want to drag her name into it. But he did drag her name into it. When he got back from Kansas City, where he later claimed he talked his adversary into an extortion plot instead, Kennamer showed the three-page letter to ten of his peers and told them of his plans to kill

Gorrell in order to save Virginia. If they happened to see him as a hero, so be it.

There was only one problem he didn't count on: nobody believed him because Phil Kennamer always "talked big." He told Jack Snedden, Virginia's boyfriend, and four of his friends. He told Betty Watson, a friend and sophomore at the University of Oklahoma. He even told Homer Wilcox Jr., who then told his eighteen-year-old sister, Virginia, but neither one of them told their parents because they didn't want them to worry over nothing. In the past, Phil had threatened to kill himself on numerous occasions because Virginia didn't love him, but he never went through with it. Why would they believe his latest rantings?

Kidnappers had been in the news a lot at that time. About fourteen months before, George "Machine Gun" Kelly had gone to trial at the federal courthouse in Oklahoma City for the kidnapping of wealthy oilman Charles Urschel. He and his wife Kathryn were sentenced to life in prison. And then there was the most sensational crime of the twentieth century, the kidnapping and murder of Charles Lindbergh's baby. Bruno Hauptmann had been arrested that September and, by the time Gorrell was murdered, the impending trial dominated nationwide radio and newspaper coverage.

Even with all those headlines in the background to set the mood, nobody believed Phil Kennamer.

When he surrendered that Saturday afternoon, Moss relayed to newsmen that his client chose to surrender because he didn't want an innocent person to be charged with murder. Although noble, there was no chance that was ever going to happen. One hour before the murder, Kennamer told friends he was going to kill Gorrell, and then afterward, he not only told a friend he'd done it, he offered to show him the body.

Jack Snedden, Virginia's boyfriend and the son of a recently deceased oil millionaire, was a primary target of

Phil's boasting. Warping Snedden into his conspiracy was necessary because someone close to Virginia would have to tell her what a hero he was. Like her brother, Snedden told Virginia about the alleged plot. On November 20, Kennamer asked the nineteen-year-old to drive him to the Spartan Airport so he could catch a Braniff Airways flight to Kansas City to confront Gorrell.

"He said he was going up there to see if Gorrell was going through with the extortion plot and, if he was, he was going to kill him," Snedden told police and reporters that first week. "He said Gorrell had a gang up at Kansas City that was planning to kidnap Virginia Wilcox. That he would be back the next day and asked me to be at the airport at three o'clock to bring him in to town."

When Snedden returned to the airport on November 21 to pick up Kennamer, he learned no planes were flying that day because of bad weather. Later that afternoon, he got a telegram from Kennamer which was sent to the Owl Tavern, addressed to him.

"Grounded in Kansas City. Keep your mouth shut."—K

Huff was telling the truth when he said Kennamer sent a telegram from the airport. And why would Jack Snedden have to keep his mouth shut?

When more witnesses came forward that first week of the investigation, all Kennamer's movements and nearly every word he said Thanksgiving night were documented by detectives. When they were done piecing it all together, Kennamer had cooked his own goose. A timeline of how the murder began and ended on Thanksgiving night was constructed by detectives and given to reporters.

At approximately 7:30 that Thanksgiving night, Judge Kennamer gave his son a ride to the Crawford Drug Store, across from St. John's Hospital, where Phil ran inside and bought his father some cigars and a magazine. When he returned to the car, Judge Kennamer claimed he asked his son to come home because the weather was bad. Phil begged off and said he'd be home between 12:30 and 1:00 a.m. After his father left, John arrived,[3] and the two made plans to meet up later at eleven o'clock. Gorrell then walked across the street to pick up his date at the hospital and returned home to pick up Charlie.

Kennamer was next seen at the Owl Tavern a little after 10:00 p.m., where he met up with Snedden, Randall "Beebe" Morton, and George Reynolds. Morton and Reynolds were also the sons of oil millionaires.

"That afternoon, he called me and told me to meet him down there [later that night]," Snedden told police. "He called me in the back and pulled open his coat and showed me a hunting knife. He said he had a date with Gorrell at eleven o'clock. Beebe Morton took the knife off of Phil; it was in a scabbard. I asked him if he was going out there to kill Gorrell and he said 'yes,' then I talked to him about his mother and the Gorrells and the trouble it would cause and he put his hands in his pocket and started whistling.

"I left him talking to Beebe Morton. He turned and went out the front door and yelled back that he would be back in five minutes. I waited there, [but] he never did come back. I imagine it was around 10:30 or quarter to 11 when he left."

Kennamer then walked to the Quaker Drug Store, two doors east of the Owl Tavern, where he ran into his close friend and confidant, Sidney Born Jr. The Owl Tavern, Quaker Drug Store, and Sunset Café were clustered together on 18th Street and were the main hangouts for the children of Tulsa's elite. They referred to it as the "Jelly Bean Center," and it was where they often congregated before and after dances or movies. Born was the president of the Hy-Hat

---

[3] It is unclear when John and Phil agreed to meet at the Crawford Drug Store, but it most likely occurred during Thanksgiving evening when John got up from the table to answer the telephone in the hallway.

Club and was the nineteen-year-old son of a University of Tulsa research professor and petroleum engineer. Earlier that night, Sidney had been ice-skating on a group date with his girlfriend. Afterward, he had taken her home and then made his way to the drugstore, where he was hanging out with other friends when Kennamer walked in.

"I want you to take me someplace," Kennamer was quoted as saying, in a statement Born gave to police. But Born was busy and tried to hand off his car keys to him, to which Kennamer replied, "No, you come on and take me."

Reluctantly, but willing to do Kennamer a favor on a bad night, Born told Maddux and his men that he drove the one mile to St. John's Hospital at approximately 10:45 p.m. Kennamer asked him to drive one block past the hospital, and when Sidney stopped at an intersection, suddenly and without warning, Phil jerked open the door, sprang out of the car, and yelled back that he would see him later. Born could not see which direction he went because of the bad weather.

Police then theorized that Kennamer recognized Gorrell's car parked in front of the hospital. Miss Word stated that Gorrell had placed his revolver in a pocket in the driver's side door and had left the door open while he escorted her to the hospital's front entrance—a distance of about one hundred yards. Sister Gratiana had signed her in at 10:50 p.m.

It was a sad twist of fate that Gorrell had left his revolver behind and his car door open.

As it turns out, Kennamer didn't need his hunting knife after all. After Morton had taken the knife away, he gave it to Snedden, who later turned it over to police when he gave his statement.

There was never any struggle or fight, police claimed. The photograph Sgt. Maddux took showed that, they said. Kennamer shot Gorrell in cold blood near the triangular median, and a minute later, after the car had stopped, placed the barrel against his head and fired again. Then he wiped off the fingerprints, returned the revolver to the holster, and walked away.

When he surrendered, Kennamer told detectives he had walked home after killing Gorrell. But witnesses came forward who proved that was not true. From the murder scene, Kennamer walked two miles northwest back to the Quaker Drug Store. To get there, he probably walked right past his own house, which lay halfway in between. Instead of going home, he needed to tell someone of how he had just saved Virginia by killing Gorrell in order to put a stop to his devious plot to extort the Wilcox family.

By the time a wet-haired Kennamer got there, Born had left. Kennamer then went next door to the Sunset Café. Inside, he greeted several friends before he took pal Robert Thomas[4] aside for a private conversation that took place around midnight.

"Phil asked me how I was. I said okay. He said he had something to tell me," Thomas told Anderson.

"'What is it?' I asked.

"'I've just killed John Gorrell,' Phil said. Of course, I didn't think he was serious. I thought it was a joke so I wasn't serious.

"'Did you do a good job of it?' I asked.

"'Yes, I did,' Kennamer answered. He then said he killed Gorrell because of an extortion note.

"'What extortion note?'

"'This one,' he said. 'Read it.' I didn't want to read it. He insisted and handed me an envelope. It was soiled but had never been mailed. There were three sheets of writing paper in the envelope, I think. The letter was written in black ink; it wasn't typewritten.

---

[4] No relation to Wade Thomas.

"I didn't pay much attention to the note but I remember it said if Mr. Wilcox didn't pay a $20,000 ransom, they were going to kidnap his daughter, Virginia Wilcox. I remember it said that if he was to get in touch with them, he was to identify himself over the telephone as H. F. W. As I remember it, the letter was signed Mr. X. I'm not sure of that though.

"Phil said Gorrell was a dirty rat [and] asked me if I wanted to see the body. I told him I wasn't interested. I still thought he was joking. Phil wanted to tell me more about it. He put the letter back in his pocket.

"Phil said he killed John Gorrell because of this extortion note written by John. He said it was the work of a gang in Kansas City. I didn't pay much attention to any of the conversation because I didn't believe it. It was the first time I heard Phil mention Gorrell's name. I didn't know Gorrell.

"Phil didn't seem excited. He looked kind of wet. Something like he was perspiring.

"I also remember now that Phil, when he put the note back in his pocket, said that he would never show anyone that or use it because he didn't want Virginia's name brought into it."

Robert Thomas was then asked how the conversation ended and what Kennamer did next.

"Phil asked me to take him home but I already had a car full and told him so. Phil said he would take a cab. I told him that wasn't necessary because Tommy Taylor was there and he would take him home. I asked Taylor and he said he would. I then left Phil."

Thomas didn't learn of the murder until Saturday night, and he heard that Phil had surrendered earlier that day. He told his parents about Kennamer's confession, and they took him to Anderson's office Monday night.

When questioned by police, Tommy Taylor told them, "Phil asked me if I minded taking him home. I said I did not.

I finished eating my sandwich and we took off together." Taylor was a seventeen-year-old polo player at the Oklahoma Military Academy in Claremore and was, like most others in Kennamer's social group, the son of a wealthy oilman. His account also made it into newspapers that week.

"Phil turned on the radio in my car," Taylor continued. "An orchestra was playing. After I had stopped the car in front of his home, Phil asked me to wait until the end of a piece of music.

"We talked for a minute or so. I don't remember the things we discussed, but they were not important. I told Phil that I had promised my mother I would be home by 12:30, and that I would have to leave. He got out and walked toward the house."

Taylor also said that it appeared as if something were bothering Kennamer, but since the two were only slightly acquainted, he didn't probe further. He estimated the time he dropped Kennamer off to be 12:15 a.m.—about the same time the Cunninghams were calling police.

The story by Thomas and Taylor should have cleared up a couple of things for investigators. Kennamer didn't have an accomplice, and the rumors that Wilcox Junior drove him home after the crime were not true. Even so, Junior wasn't off the hook yet. As it turned out, Kennamer wasn't the only one shooting a revolver that night.

When witnesses started coming forward to build an honest account of what had occurred before and after Gorrell was killed, Moss could see the story was shifting away from a simple case of self-defense. Three days after Kennamer surrendered, Moss held his first real meeting with his client. In the room with them were three more attorneys, recently added to the defense team. Russell Hayes was a young lawyer married to Kennamer's sister, Juanita. Charles Coakley was the old law-firm partner with Judge Kennamer, and seventy-eight-year-old Charles Stuart was "one of the

Southwest's most prominent attorneys." It was a meeting that began at 9:30 in the morning and lasted well into mid-afternoon. When Moss walked out of the room, he looked exhausted as reporters rushed up to him.

"The whole business is so queer that no normal mind can follow through," he told them.

Anderson had already publicly stated that an insanity plea would be used, and a rumor was flying around that Moss had inquired with a nationally-known psychiatrist. Between the county attorney's speculation and the rumors, reporters asked him if he was leaning toward an insanity defense—one he had used many times in the past.

"When you consider what these kids have done, analyze the conduct of their associates and the acts preceding the actual killing, just how much mental responsibility there is for what has been done is beyond me."

At the heart of it all was the extortion note. Each day that week, newspapers devoted half their coverage to the extortion note and the Wilcox family, and the other half to Phil Kennamer and John Gorrell. Investigators knew of it only because witnesses had spoken of it. There was a congruity in their account of the note, so they knew it must be real, even though they had never actually seen it. Where it was and who had it were mysteries.

"I'm positive that there is an extortion note in existence and I think I know where it is or where it was," Anderson told reporters. "It has been seen by at least ten people."

"Have you seen it?" a reporter asked.

"No, but how I wish I could!" Anderson bellowed.

When Snedden was asked by reporters if he recognized the handwriting in the letter Kennamer had shown him, he said, "I did not recognize the handwriting but I knew that it was not Phil's, as I would recognize his handwriting anywhere."

On Tuesday, December 4, Maddux and Reif traveled to Kansas City, where they searched Gorrell's room and questioned his "gang," which turned out to be a bunch of college boys who drank hard and chased skirts. Before they returned to Tulsa, Maddux told a reporter he had discovered evidence that would lead to an arrest of the son of a prominent Tulsa man.

"The detectives would not divulge the youth's identity or the nature or source of their evidence. Maddux said the youth would be accused as an accessory of the slaying of Gorrell," the *Tulsa World* reported. "The detective said the youth in question heretofore had not figured prominently in the case."

It was a statement that revealed a peculiar characteristic about Sgt. Henry Bailess Maddux; the lead detective had a habit of making major announcements that were vague and mysterious, but he stopped short of clarifying them with concrete facts. This was a major case with a volatile, ever-evolving story line that went far beyond enthralling Tulsa residents, and Maddux seemed to enjoy feeding the fire with purposely ambiguous statements that were soaked in gasoline.

It would eventually get him into trouble.

Chapter Eight

ALMOST FROM THE BEGINNING, Homer Wilcox Jr. was named as a person of interest in the case. Initially, he was sought because he was a close friend of Kennamer. On Sunday, Maddux announced he had no more need to question Junior because other witnesses had come forward to fill in the blanks. Then, new information was received which made an interview with the seventeen-year-old "most important" to the case.

"We cannot help but admit that the investigation, as it now stands, hinges entirely on young Wilcox," thirty-eight-year-old Anderson dramatically declared on Monday, December 3. He was a former mayor of Sand Springs and had recently been reelected to his second term as county attorney. "I cannot impress how vital the presence of Wilcox here is to the future development of the case. Wilcox can be of tremendous aid to us and we need his presence here immediately."

This type of seesawing would become typical for the investigation. But on Sunday, the day after Kennamer surrendered, the entire Wilcox family had left town. Their departure from Tulsa hours before investigators sought them out for questioning was viewed with some suspicion. They had traveled to Toledo to do some Christmas shopping, their servants told authorities. Homer Senior then journeyed to New York City, where investigators were able to reach him by telephone in his room at the Waldorf Astoria. He told them Junior would be home in a few days and would be made available to answer their questions.

The two night watchmen for the Titus estate did hear gunfire that night, but they weren't the muffled shots that killed Gorrell. Junior and three friends of his had some explaining to do as to how the streetlights near the murder scene were blasted out just a few hours before Gorrell was murdered in that same area. The Wilcox name featured prominently in the newspapers for the entire first week while the family was out of town. The extortion note was mentioned nearly every day, but the details of Junior's coincidental involvement with the crime scene were left out. They didn't have to include it. The grapevine was taking care of that for them, and it was feeding into the narrative of a bunch of rich kids who were out of control.

From blackmail photos of daughters from wealthy families caught in compromising positions to cocaine parties alleged by a ne'er-do-well convict looking to reduce his burglary sentence, the Hy-Hat Club and the youth of Tulsa's well-to-do were getting the stink eye from adults. Narcotics detective Sgt. Francis McMillen ran down all the "whispered tips that dope peddlers were involved in the case" but eventually came up empty-handed. Nevertheless, the stories got wilder and wilder.

"There are disclosures of serious trouble among our youth and many signs of modern blight," lectured a December 6 editorial from the *World*.

Governor-elect Ernest Marland's attitude on the matter reflected the times: "What is it that creates a craving for narcotics among our young people? We are an Anglo-Saxon race, and it is not a natural habit."

One Tulsa school board member said in a public meeting that week, "The young people do everything that their parents do and then go on looking for new thrills!"

The statement by Maddux on the impending arrest of another prominent young son of Tulsa seemed only to confirm those beliefs. But by the next morning, the university-trained criminologist retracted it. No new suspects were being sought and no more arrests were planned.

That premature and provocative declaration wasn't the only grenade Maddux lobbed into the investigation's narrative. From day one, rumors had made their way into newspapers that a prominent Tulsa family had *recently* received an extortion note. This turned out not to be true, but what was true was that wealthy oilman Charles Wrightsman had received extortion notes in 1931.

True to his pattern of behavior, Maddux made the announcement to reporters later that week that "an extortion note had been sent through the mails to another Tulsa oil operator." The note he was alluding to was the Wrightsman note. Everybody already knew about the Wrightsman note. It was three damn years old. It had nothing to do with the Kennamer-Gorrell case, but that didn't stop Maddux from using it to add to the mania that was building.

Looking down at the Sergeant's desk, where he saw the letter addressed to Charles Wrightsman, a *Tribune* reporter asked Maddux, "Is that the note?"

Maddux could only smile and avoid the question, but eventually he responded, "You'd give your left arm to see what was in that note."

No, he wouldn't. Phil Kennamer was fifteen going on sixteen in 1931.

More unnecessary excitement was injected into the case that week when copies of the photograph Maddux took of a dead John Gorrell in his car were "leaked" to the *Tribune* and *World*. In a time when photographs of dead people rarely appeared in newspapers, it shocked the entire city, and was grossly insensitive to the boy's parents.

All the press coverage of extortion letters and kidnapping plots caused federal agents to make a cameo appearance in the case. The Kennamer-Gorrell note was locked up by the defense somewhere, and the Wrightsman note was three years old. There wasn't much they could do and, after a day or two, newspapers never mentioned them again.

On December 5, County Attorney Holly Anderson announced to the press that his office and the sheriff's department were closing their investigation. This declaration came after Homer Wilcox Sr. promised that Junior would be made available for questioning upon their return to Tulsa. Newspapers held off revealing Junior's involvement until official announcements were made.

The next day, Anderson, with Dr. John Gorrell, invited Oklahoma Attorney General J. Berry King to assist with the prosecution. King's participation in the case gave the short-lived illusion that the state would be heavily involved in the Kennamer prosecution. But King, like Sheriff Price, would relinquish his office in a little more than a month.

As it turned out, King was close friends with Judge Kennamer, even though he was a Democrat. King had recently lost his bid to be the Democratic candidate for governor in the primary. He'd served as assistant attorney general in the 1920s, and then attorney general for almost six years, with his term ending on January 14, 1935. In those days, his name was just as familiar to Oklahomans as Judge Kennamer's, if not more so.

Like the day Phil surrendered, Wednesday, December 5, was a news-packed day. Around midmorning, a black sedan with a red warning light mounted on top—something new in those days—parked in front of the Tulsa County Courthouse. Five minutes later, Wagoner County Sheriff Clay Flowers and Mr. and Mrs. Basil James were in Sheriff Price's office. The day before Thanksgiving, five robbers had stormed the James home, lined up them and two guests against a wall, and robbed them of eighty-five dollars, several guns, a watch, and forty-five pints of whiskey.

James was the owner of a roadhouse just outside of Wagoner,[1] and when he and his wife saw Kennamer's picture in the newspaper, it looked familiar. Up at the matron's room, they

---

[1] Wagoner is forty miles southeast of Tulsa.

identified Kennamer as the leader of the gang and one of two men who didn't wear a mask and held a .32-caliber revolver with an attached silencer.

"He was the man," James whispered after the group had all peeked in on Kennamer in his room. "He was the man who knocked on my door and the man who first entered the house."

The wife confirmed her husband's identification and for nearly a week, newspapers included this new angle within its coverage. Kennamer and Moss emphatically denied the Jameses' claim, and Tulsa investigators backed off from pursuing it a day or two later. This time, Kennamer was actually telling the truth; witnesses placed him in Tulsa around the time frame of the Wagoner robbery.

On the night before Thanksgiving, the same night the James couple was robbed, Kennamer left home around seven o'clock and walked to Jack Snedden's house. Snedden was taking Virginia Wilcox to a dance at the Mayo Hotel. The trio went to the Quaker Drug Store first, where they stayed until 8:30 p.m. Friends Sidney Born and Jerry Bates showed up around that time, and Phil went with them downtown. At approximately 9:30 p.m., Bates and Born went to the same dance as Snedden and Virginia, but Born loaned his car to Kennamer, who damaged part of it in yet another wreck. Later that night, after the dance, Born met up with Kennamer at the Sunset Café.

From there, Born and Kennamer went back to the Mayo Hotel, where they rented a room for "a wild party." In the morning, one of them, presumably Born, wrote a check for ten dollars, which later bounced, to cover their bill.

Although Basil James persisted, Tulsa authorities were confident Kennamer didn't commit the robbery. If he had access to a .32-caliber revolver equipped with a silencer, he wouldn't have been showing off a hunting knife to friends the night of the murder. Even when his alibi became public knowledge, the robbery accusation fed the public perception that Kennamer had a full-fledged criminal gang that was still on the loose. Several witnesses against Kennamer reported receiving threatening telephone calls and letters to keep their mouths shut. The same day Oliver's name appeared in the paper, detectives were guarding his home after rumors had made their way to headquarters that their witness was in danger. On Sunday night, Dr. Gorrell called to speak with Oliver about his son but was told Oliver was out.

"Do you mean to tell me he had enough crust to go out tonight?" Dr. Gorrell was quoted as saying. "I have heard it from reliable sources that they are either going to implicate him or kill him."

But Oliver was in hiding, and not even the police could find him those first few days.

The roadhouse robbery also supported the rising chorus from parents, pastors, educators, and local authorities that the well-to-do youth of Tulsa were out of control, even though they had nothing to do with the robbery. Looking out over their Christian, conservative city, they imagined sex-mad teens driving dangerously over their streets to get to hole-in-the-wall gambling joints and breast-bouncing dance parties where they would plan big crimes—all while high on marijuana and drunk on 3.2 beer.

Meetings were scheduled. Plans were being made. A crackdown was coming. Phil Kennamer had just gummed up the good times for the fast, young, Tulsa set.

Later on during that first week of the case, after other witnesses had paved the way by coming forward, more young people from Kennamer's small circle of friends gave statements to the police.

Betty Watson, a nineteen-year-old sophomore at the University of Oklahoma, was in Tulsa on Saturday, November 24, and she swung by the Kennamer residence for a dutiful visit.

"I was acquainted with the Kennamer family and had seen none of them lately. I was only going to be in Tulsa for a short-time [she was on her way to Chicago for the Thanksgiving holidays] and went by to pay my respects," she told County Attorney Anderson over the phone on December 5.

"Phil was there and when I left he asked me if I would drive him to the Quaker Drug Store. We drove around for a few minutes and as I drove he talked.

"I thought he was crazy. He had a letter in his hand which he asked me to read. It was addressed to H. F. Wilcox and said that unless $20,000 in $1, $5, and $10 bills was left some place I don't remember, something would happen to Virginia.

"Phil said that Gorrell wrote the note and that he was going to kill him. He said that he had been to Kansas City and got the note from Gorrell there. I let Phil out at the drug store and just put his talk down as something silly and crazy."

When the *Tulsa World* ran Watson's statement the following day, they did not publish her name and only identified her as a sophomore at the University of Oklahoma. Too many names of good Tulsans were already being dragged through the mud, and crackpots were calling up witnesses to make veiled threats. The *Tribune* had just reported that Jack Snedden and three of his friends were warned of death "if they do not keep quiet regarding what information they know."

When Kennamer read Watson's story the next day, he knew exactly who it was, and he didn't like it one bit. Her statement, and those of his other so-called friends, told of a planned murder, a murder in the first degree, a murder charge that could get him the electric chair. With brash arrogance only Phil Kennamer could come up with, he got to a third-floor telephone and called down to Anderson's office while Anderson was in a private meeting with Attorney General King. Kennamer mentioned the news story and inquired if Anderson would pass along a message to Miss Watson.

"If you intend on speaking to her, I would like for you to give her a message for me," Kennamer asked.

Thinking he could learn something new, Anderson agreed.

"Give her my love and a piece of cheese," Kennamer said.

"I understand the love part but what do you mean about the cheese?"

"She'll get it, THE RAT!" Kennamer answered as he slammed the handset down.

The incident, reported in the *World*, revealed two things to Tulsans: Kennamer had just subtly intimidated a potential witness, and he had an incredible amount of freedom from his room on the third floor. But still, Sheriff Price did nothing about it. Kennamer wasn't moving anywhere. And if Kennamer had that kind of telephone access, maybe there was some credence to the stories of witnesses being threatened, although police were dismissing them as crank calls.

Anderson sent his investigator, Jack Bonham, to the University of Oklahoma in Norman to interview Watson who "wept as she gave her statement," the United Press reported. When it was over, "she signed the statement and ran weeping from the living room of the sorority house."

She wasn't the only attractive young coed who had a story to tell police. Barbara Boyle, a Gorrell family friend and Kennamer's first choice for kidnapping, told police Gorrell had warned her of the plot as far back as September.

"Gorrell had warned her to have nothing to do with Kennamer or another boy, a close friend of his,"[2] the *Tulsa Tribune* reported. "She said Gorrell told her that 'they would hesitate at nothing' as far as he was concerned and might go to the extent of giving her doped cigarettes to place her in a compromising position to accomplish their scheme. Gorrell warned her, she said, to say nothing of this to either of the two as he would not answer for what they would do to him for exposing the plot."

---

[2] This could not have been Ted Bath, and the statement is confusing as to whether Gorrell meant a close friend of his, or a close friend of Kennamer.

This statement gave police a new theory that instead of Kennamer going along with the scheme in order to sabotage it, maybe it was Gorrell who was doing exactly that to thwart Kennamer. This idea was corroborated by the dean of the dental school, who told a Kansas City reporter he knew Gorrell "was in a jam" and had called on him before driving to Tulsa to say that if anything happened to him during that trip, Kennamer was responsible.

Dean John Rinehart also said that when he heard Gorrell had been killed, he knew immediately who had done it and that it was because "Gorrell would not mail a letter Kennamer wanted him to mail."

But Rinehart later retracted this statement after he got cold feet over fears the publicity would be bad for the college. He promptly denied he had ever made the report and claimed he knew nothing about the conflict between Gorrell and his accused slayer.

By the end of that first week, the investigation was wrapping up and newspaper coverage was tapering off. Even so, the hysteria that gripped Tulsa was refusing to let go, and the scandalmongers were still churning out gossip.

"Scores of 'self-appointed' and amateur detectives have called at headquarters with innumerable tips and so-called clues in the case," the *World* reported. "Only a few have developed into material facts."

One rumor was put to rest that week when Wade Thomas was eventually released on a writ of habeas corpus. His only involvement in the case was a twenty-five-dollar gambling debt owed to him by Kennamer, and fifty dollars from Gorrell. Together, the three allegedly owned slot machines that were confiscated and piled up at police headquarters for a publicity photo as two officers stood over them with sledgehammers. The Idle Hour was shut down. So was the Sunset Café, temporarily, after it was caught selling 3.2 beer to minors.

December 9, 1934

The December 9 edition of the Sunday morning *World* ran a short cover story with this headline:

"No Development in Gorrell Death"

The top announcement in that little item was a statement from King that, after a conference with Maddux and Dr. Gorrell, the investigation was over.

"Everything that was necessary has been done in this case," King told the media. "The guilty party has been definitely identified and there is no reason for a further statement until the preliminary hearing which will be held in Tulsa, December 17."

As Tulsans read their Sunday morning *World,* Sidney Born was in the front room of his parent's home, writing checks for his father. His father and Czech-born mother left the house at 10:30 a.m. to go for a Sunday drive, and his younger brother, Harold, was away with friends. A few minutes after eleven, Born jumped in his Chevy sedan and drove off.

At approximately 11:30 a.m., he was spotted in a wooded area near 27th Street and Lewis Avenue by four women riding horses in the Woody Crest addition. The undeveloped area was a popular location for those wanting to forget they lived in the city. Seventy-five yards from the street, the horse trail crested over a hump and then dipped down into a draw. Just after topping this rise, the first horse in line shied off and each horse in succession gave a wide birth to a motionless young man by the trail, sitting there smoking a cigarette. Three of the women addressed him as they passed by, but he ignored their salutations and continued his hard stare at the horizon. His face, they later said, was drawn tight and haggard, as if in deep contemplation.

Born returned home around 11:45 a.m., fetched something from the back of a drawer in his father's desk, and then went up to his room. At noon, he announced to the maid he was leaving again.

"Aren't you going to wait for dinner, honey?" maid Josey Henderson asked as he was walking out the door.

"I'll be back in a minute."

Born's first stop was to a tire repair shop to get a tire changed on his Chevrolet. He was reportedly in good spirits as he chatted with mechanics. During the night before Thanksgiving, he had loaned his car to Kennamer when he and Jerry Bates had gone to the dance at the Mayo Hotel. By the time he met up later with Kennamer at the Sunset Café, his friend had wrecked his car, causing fifty dollars[3] in damage to it. Kennamer had promised to pay him back, but that was before he was arrested for murder. The new tire was part of those repairs for which Kennamer owed him money.

At about 1:00 p.m., Born telephoned his girlfriend Betty and was in a cheerful mood as they chatted for a short while. He did not tell her where he was calling her from.

He next drove to the Brookside Drug Store on South Peoria and asked the clerk if he had change for a quarter to use the pay phone. Opening the city directory book to the letter *T*, he found the number to the Tulsa County Jail, dropped a nickel in the slot, and dialed the number.

"I want to talk to Phil Kennamer," he was overheard to say. After a pause of about twenty seconds, Born shouted, "Oh, hell!" and slammed the receiver on the hook.

From the drugstore, Born drove to a quiet area near Detroit Avenue and 29th Street and parked his sedan near a vacant lot one quarter of a mile from his house. The sun was out that day, and by 1:30 p.m. the temperature was comfortable for that time of year. It was a peaceful Sunday afternoon, and as he looked around, he could only see one man off in the distance walking

---

[3] The 2014 equivalent of $870, when adjusted for inflation.

his dog. He stared down at his hands for a moment, studying the lines that crossed his palms.

Born looked around one more time, and when he saw nobody was around he took a deep breath, reached into his coat pocket, pulled out his father's .32-caliber automatic, pressed it firmly against his right temple, and pulled the trigger.

Part Two: The Hysteria

The whole affair has sensational and morbid features which bring undue attention to a large number of young people who have little to nothing to do with the tragic events themselves. While not disposed to be critical of our brother newspaper men, we do object to some of the assiduous efforts to build up a lurid story of "flaming youth" in Tulsa. It is certain some of the stories were far beyond the bounds of propriety, and that they magnified to an unconscionable extent some of the sidelights of the affair.

— Tulsa Daily World Editorial

Chapter Nine

AS THE KENNAMER CASE BEGAN TO settle down by Saturday, one week after he surrendered, the newshawks quietly left town. By Monday morning, December 10, they were all making their way back to Tulsa. Once again, the story was front-page news from coast to coast. In light of the new developments spawned by Born's death, Lowell Limpus of the *New York Daily News* was asked to compare the nationally famous Hall-Mills case of the 1920s with Tulsa's high-society murder.

"That was a third-grade arithmetic problem compared to this!" Lowell exclaimed.

Incredibly, Born didn't immediately die. He was taken to Morningside Hospital, where his grief-stricken parents rushed to his bedside. As Mrs. Born sat by her son, Dr. Born was too distraught to sit still. He drifted back and forth between the room and the hallway, where his son's friends had gathered.

"Word of Born's injury swept over the city," detective Tom Higgins would later write in his crime-magazine article. "It was like a fire roaring in a high gale across the drought-browned prairies."

The circumstances in Gorrell's and Born's deaths were too similar for Tulsans to believe it was suicide, as city police were claiming. After all, that's what they had said at first about Gorrell's death. Both boys were shot in their own cars, with their own guns, and in isolated areas of Tulsa with no witnesses.

When Born passed away at 6:55 Sunday night, one of the four young women waiting in the hallway fainted and fell off her chair. Sidney's father was overheard by a *Tribune* reporter to say that his son's involvement in the case was so minor, he could not believe he would commit suicide. "My boy commit suicide?" he exclaimed. "Impossible. It was murder!"

That Sunday, most of Tulsa agreed with him.

"I do not exaggerate when I say that all Tulsa shuddered that night," Higgins continued. "Here was one of the most popular young men in the city, dead. There was no answer available [in the first few hours] to those who desired to know whether it was suicide or murder. To anxious parents in dozens of the best homes, that question was of very little importance. And, instead they asked: 'Is the name of *our* son to be dragged into this horrible affair?' That fear was to cause many families to leave the city."

Young Born was an immaculate dresser. To his close friends he was known as "Algy," an affectionate nickname. While he always had plenty of money, he was conservative in his spending. He was an A and B student in high school and was doing well in his classes at the University of Tulsa. His name had never been mentioned in any of the minor scandals and salacious rumors that hovered around some of those in Tulsa's young, high-society crowd.

Born was the president of the Hy-Hat Club, whose members congregated at the Jelly Bean Center on 18th Street. Despite what the newspapers were already saying about club members, it mostly formed parties and dances, which were forbidden at Central High School, and couples were paired off by club leaders.

An hour or two after Born shot himself, Robert Thomas appeared at police headquarters to request a permit to carry a pistol. When he was refused, he went to Assistant County Attorney Tom Wallace to make the same request, but he was again denied.

"I told him that we could not issue such a permit and would not under the circumstances," Wallace told a squad of reporters who now occupied the police station.

But Thomas never told authorities exactly whom he was afraid of. Neither did Ted Bath, when he showed up to make the same appeal. He was already carrying a pistol and when he was denied, he dramatically announced he was leaving town.

"Kennamer's gang is still out of jail and they will do everything they can to keep the fellows from testifying," Bath was overheard telling Maddux. "I'm leaving Tulsa for good. The only reason I haven't received threats to keep my mouth shut is because those fellows could not reach me. Plenty of the fellas who told police what they knew about Kennamer and his gang have been warned. So I'm getting out while I'm able. There are too many dark streets and alleys where a shot could seal your lips for good."

Although Kennamer never had a "gang," the rumor mill had created one, and perception was stronger than reality in December 1934.

Richard Oliver reported that he had received a mysterious telephone call several hours after Born was taken to the hospital. When he answered the phone at his room in Kansas City, the voice of an unknown male asked him if he knew Sidney Born. Oliver replied that he did not recall the name. The mysterious voice then told him Born had just been murdered. When Oliver asked who was calling, the caller hung up. Afterward, Oliver still continued attending his dentistry classes but changed his residence, and not even his parents knew where he was living.

On the advice of the family attorney, Jack Snedden went into hiding at a secret location "fifteen minutes outside of Tulsa" after they got the news that Born had been shot in the head.

Charles Bard, who was with Gorrell the night he was murdered, received an anonymous letter that declared he "knew too much about the case." The Oklahoma A&M student was escorted between classes by campus security, and his fraternity brothers kept an all-night vigil for him in case someone tried to murder him in his sleep. When word of Born's death reached him Sunday evening, he "presented himself at the county jail and asked to be locked up for safety." He was turned away. The next day, he withdrew from school.

Owl Tavern proprietor Jack Arnold, who told police that Snedden received a telegram from Kennamer at his tavern, reported he was threatened a week earlier by an anonymous telephone call. Although initially frightened by the threats, he later told police he believed they were crank calls.

Police also reported that Kennamer had written a letter to Betty Watson, allegedly admonishing her for talking to police. Fortunately, her father intercepted the note before she could read it.

"We told Betty it would be best for her not to go out at night and to remain with her friends when it seemed that a murder had been committed," her father told reporters. "When she called home tonight [Tuesday, December 11], I thought it would be all right for her to go wherever she desired."

Although police believed the anonymous threats were from pranksters and wackos looking to stir things up, they took no chances, and several witnesses received twenty-four-hour police protection.

Hours after Maddux and another detective were called to Born's blood-soaked Chevrolet, they were confident in their declaration that it was a suicide. They pointed to several factors, which included powder marks inside the wound and the use of his father's gun. The pistol had fallen into Born's lap and was covered in blood. One nearby resident and a man walking his dog heard the shot, and both reported to police that they saw no one fleeing the scene.

But to many Tulsans, murder seemed more plausible than suicide, given Born's trivial involvement in the case. When asked why Sidney Born would commit suicide, Sgt. Maddux pulled a Sgt. Maddux.

"Fear," he replied.

Fear? Fear of what?

True to his character, Maddux coyly refused to elaborate on his answer and chose the provocativeness of mystery over the enlightenment of clarity.

"Whether he meant that Born feared an attack from the accomplice police continue to intimate aided Kennamer in the slaying," the *Tulsa World* wrote the day after the suicide, "or whether he was of the opinion Born had taken a greater part in the Gorrell case than he had admitted to officers went unexplained by Maddux."

Whatever the reason, Sidney Born's "fear" was certainly real to him, even if it was found later to be blown out of proportion. But when city lawmen learned that shortly before his suicide, Sidney had tried to contact Phil, the sheriff's department received a sharp rebuke from Maddux. He criticized the lax custody of their star prisoner and claimed Born would not have committed suicide if Kennamer was more restricted in his confinement. Ever since it was publicized that he had called down to Anderson's office, folks believed he was freely allowed to use the telephone—including Maddux.

The sheriff's department strongly denied this claim but their only proof was the self-accountability of their guards. They would first claim no calls at the jail were received. This was later changed to the acknowledgment that a call was received at 1:15 p.m., but that the jailer told the caller (Born) that Kennamer was not allowed to use the telephone.

Nearly all the young people whose names appeared in the newspapers came from powerful, wealthy families with patriarchs who gave the veiled impression that they could squash any public official they disfavored. Rumors supporting this notion had trickled back to police headquarters. Maddux, and his detectives, sensed the subtle threat that "their jobs were unsafe," reported Commissioner Oscar Hoop. The issue became such a concern that the retired army colonel and University of Tulsa history professor felt it necessary to push back in the newspapers.

"I told my men yesterday and I'll repeat it now, that their jobs are safe regardless of where this investigation might lead," Col. Hoop said. "There is no one in this town too big or too wealthy for us to include in the investigation if it proves necessary to do so."

Hoop's backing gave Maddux the confidence to criticize the sheriff's department publicly.

"It was our wish that the sheriff's office hold Kennamer in solitary confinement and allow him to talk with no one except his attorney and members of his immediate family," Maddux told the *World*. "We have positive evidence that Kennamer has sent mail to witnesses in this case, and in at least one instance, of a threatening nature. We also understand Kennamer has had the use of the telephone."

County Attorney Holly Anderson was attending a crime conference in Washington DC, when he heard of Born's death. He sent a telegram to the sheriff requesting Kennamer be moved to a jail cell. The reply he received was a sharp rebuke stating that "he had no authority in determining the manner in which a prisoner should be kept."

When Sheriff Price returned to his office on Monday, he gave reporters a logical explanation for Kennamer's unorthodox imprisonment. He pointed out that when the courthouse was built in 1912, the jail on the third floor was designed to accommodate only seventy-five prisoners. By 1934, it was housing two hundred inmates. Cells originally built for four prisoners now held twelve. To place Kennamer in a private cell would force Price to release twelve prisoners because there were threats to Kennamer's safety by inmates who hated his father.

"At least five prisoners have told me," Price claimed to the *Tribune*, "that if Kennamer is put in with other prisoners he will be killed. It's not worth taking the chance of murder to avoid a little criticism."

Born's death came as a complete surprise to Kennamer. The confessed slayer was attending afternoon church services within the jail when he was told by Assistant County Attorney William "Dixie" Gilmer that Born had shot himself. Gilmer later said Kennamer seemed genuinely shocked and affected by the news.

"I'm awfully sorry to hear that," Kennamer said. "He was a dear friend of mine."

It was the first time during his entire incarceration that Kennamer showed emotion, and when he was led back to his room, he wailed about how Born was his "best friend."

Later, when told there was no hope for Born and that he would die soon, Kennamer said, "Isn't that awful?" He then requested a Sunday-night conference with his attorneys. Charles Coakley was the first to reach him and later told reporters his client was "visibly shaken by the news and wept like a child."

The next day, after he had regained his composure, Kennamer told anyone who would listen that he would never believe it was suicide. For him, Born's death had created an opportunity; it was a chance to add unverifiable authenticity to his claims that Gorrell had a criminal gang, which was now responsible for Sidney's death. He would later declare that he knew the three boys who did it and emphasize that Born's testimony would have exonerated him in court.

But Kennamer's appropriation of his friend's suicide wasn't nearly as amazing as other unbelievable rumors that Sunday, which forced investigators and reporters into high gear. Pranksters used his death as an opportunity to crank up the hysteria with outrageous claims.

The first rumor to engulf Tulsa was that Wade Thomas killed himself by swallowing poison, and that his wife would not allow investigators to perform an autopsy. Thomas had been released from jail on Friday, December 7, and he informed those who called his house that reports of his death were "greatly exaggerated."

Another rumor claimed that John Newlin, Hy-Hat member and minor witness in the case, had been kidnapped. His parents declared it was nonsense and reported he was at home, safe and sound. While newsmen were chasing down those lies, another came into the *World* offices saying that the Quaker Drug Store had been bombed and was a smoking ruin. In addition, a bombardment of shots was heard that Sunday afternoon near Born's Chevy, and "mysterious cars" were seen driving away. And poor Richard Oliver, the target of so many incidents beginning with his train ride home, was allegedly slain in Kansas City.

Even though these rumors were easily disproved and dismissed, there was one rumor that would not go away: Sidney Born was murdered.

By Monday morning, the city was equally divided between those who believed it was suicide, and those who knew it was murder. Maddux and city police ruled his death a suicide, based on the physical evidence, and "because of imaginative worries over his connection with the Gorrell slaying and the threatened exposure of his previous escapades with Phil Kennamer."

Born's university professors told police he was a high-strung boy, nervous, and prone to worry over insignificant things. The insignificant thing Born worried over was a threat by Kennamer "to make public the details of [some of their] escapades." The *Tulsa World* quoted an anonymous "police official," who sounded a lot like Sgt. Maddux, saying that he was convinced Kennamer spoke with Born from the matron's quarters sometime between ten in the morning and noon, despite the claims of the county jail employees. Born's effort to contact Kennamer from the drugstore twenty minutes before he shot himself was "one last effort to persuade the imprisoned youth not to reveal their escapade at the Mayo Hotel."

The anonymous police official dodged questions regarding how the telephone communication between the two boys could have occurred. Jailer A. J. Schultz denied any outgoing call had been placed, and the Born's maid, Josey Henderson, told police the phone only rang once that morning and it was for her. Schultz did admit that a young man called around 1:15 p.m. and asked to speak to Kennamer, but the jailer said he told him Kennamer wasn't allowed telephone calls. This was corroborated by the drugstore employees who reported Born only used the phone for approximately twenty seconds before slamming the receiver down.

Even if this "police official" was making provocative statements, the physical evidence lent itself to suicide. An autopsy revealed powder burns and bullet fragments inside the wound, which detectives believed were consistent with suicide.

When Born left the drug store, he bumped into a young female friend who was later interviewed by police. "He left her and told her that he was going to jump into the river," Maddux said later. "That was just a few minutes before he was found shot. Apparently he meant it but changed his mind on the method of suicide."

In spite of all this evidence, the county sheriff's department firmly believed Born was murdered. Explaining his theory that another, unknown man aided Kennamer the night Gorrell was slain, and then later murdered Born, Sheriff Charles Price said, "we have, from the start, worked on the theory that Born's death may have been murder, and [we] are not satisfied with the suicide theory."

The sheriff's department was self-admittedly affected by the rumors flying around Tulsa that it was a murder. They searched for a suspect seen fleeing Born's car after the gunshot echoed across Detroit Avenue, but this turned out to be the man who found Born, and he was running to call for an ambulance.

Sheriff Price then took issue with how Born's body was positioned when found by the ambulance drivers. "The pistol was found in Born's lap," Sheriff Price told reporters. "If the boy had shot himself, I believe the weapon would have dropped straight down to the seat. The boy's hands also were cupped in a manner as to fill with blood. That doesn't seem right to me. The right hand should have been outside the leg."

Also suspicious to the sheriff was the entrance wound in the right temple which was larger than the exit wound on the left. It should have been the other way around, he said. Normally, that would be true, answered city detectives, but when Born pressed the barrel against his temple, the bullet fractured the temporal and parietal plates. When the bullet exited the left side, it punched a small hole in the driver's-side window and kept on going. However, Chief Deputy Evans didn't believe it happened this way. Instead, he put forth the theory that Born's killer was standing outside the car when he shot Born through the window.

But if this was true, where did the bullet go? It wasn't inside his head. It wasn't inside the car, and it didn't open the door and then close it on its way out of Born's Chevrolet. Evans's theory was based on his own assumptions and ignored the plausible answer. Nevertheless, people believed him.

During that entire week, whispered phone calls were made to Sheriff Price, instructing him to look at certain people, or hinting that he should follow this lead or that clue, and it would all bring the mystery man into the light, the *World* told its readers. A young girl, nationally known for her ability to mimic birdcalls, was in the area that Sunday. She reporting hearing a gunshot and then hearing a man running through the bushes. Deputies investigated this report but were never able to substantiate it. Nevertheless, it was more proof that Born was murdered, even though it could never be verified.

When his investigation into Born's death began to stall, Sheriff Price became frustrated and publicly claimed that there were many witnesses with information who were just too afraid to come forward. If they did, he said, they would prove his murder theory.

"I am at a loss to understand this fear," Price said. Hundreds of people knew the boys, and in his mind, one of them held the key to solving both murders, if they would only come forward. "Just because they chanced to know something of the principals in this case does not mean the police will interpret that as meaning they are connected with the case . . . or as anything detrimental to their reputation.

"They should consider it a civic obligation to aid officers in the matter. If these persons will get in touch with us, we will see that they will receive the full protection of this office."

No one ever came forward.

WHILE THE DEBATE OVER BORN'S death continued, one persistent rumor was cleared up when seventeen-year-old Homer Wilcox Jr. walked into police headquarters on Monday, December 10, as promised, to explain his connection to the case. Police and newspapermen had been holding back on reporting that Wilcox, classmate Bill Padon, and their dates that night, had shot out the two streetlights near Gorrell's Ford just hours before he was murdered. The murder, and all the rumors and events that stemmed from it, roused the suspicions of officials and the general public. It was hard for them to believe the streetlights being shot out did *not* have something to do with the murder and was just a coincidence.

Homer Wilcox Jr. and his father arrived at 8:35 in the morning and were both neatly dressed in dark blue overcoats, tailored suits, and fashionable ties. They were unfamiliar with the layout of the police station and appeared confused by the crowd at the door of the municipal courtroom. A helpful reporter directed them to Maddux's office.

While the sergeant and Assistant County Attorney Dixie Gilmer questioned the young man for forty-five minutes, Homer Senior and his attorney waited in the press room of the courthouse and chatted with reporters. Wilcox expressed his belief that Kennamer had "forced his companionship" on some of the younger boys whose names had been mentioned in the case.

"Kennamer often called our house by telephone and asked for Homer, but Mrs. Wilcox consistently discouraged the association, principally because Kennamer was reputed to be a wild driver and had been in several automobile accidents," Senior told reporters. "Mrs. Wilcox didn't want our son to go out with Kennamer and get hurt in an accident. I told the boy to give police any information he might have that would help them. But he doesn't know anything."

The fact that Wilcox and friends shot out the two streetlights nearest to where Gorrell was found dead in his car was mere coincidence, Senior asserted.

Maddux and Dixie Gilmer agreed and seemed satisfied with the boy's explanation that his connection to the crime scene was a fluke, but Junior and Padon had still broken the law. Homer was formally arrested on a charge of malicious mischief and was in the process of emptying his pockets for the desk sergeant when he remarked, "I've certainly gotten myself in a fine mess."

Before he could be jailed, however, his father's attorney made arrangements for the boy's release on a $500 bond. When he appeared in municipal court the next day, the flash of a news photographer's camera brought an admonishment from Judge Andress Hatch.

"This young man is under the protection of the court," Judge Hatch began. "While he's under my jurisdiction, I am not going to subject him to pictures unless he wants them taken."

For such a minor crime and the boy's accidental involvement in the case, the *World* and *Tribune* devoted dozens of column inches and numerous photographs. The story then spread as far east as the *New York Times,* and to California newspapers like the *Oakland Tribune.*

Judge Hatch reprimanded the boy and hinted at the perceived privileges of being the son of a wealthy oilman.

"Doubtless you have been the subject of parental indulgence," he began. "You have had pleasures and conveniences which many your age do not have. You should have had some privations and hardships to make you strong.

Perhaps if things in general had not been so easy, it would be different."

He then fined the boy seventy-five dollars and expressed his desire that it should be deducted from his Christmas allowance. In contrast, the *Tulsa Tribune* noted that the madam of a brothel was fined fourteen dollars plus court costs that same day. Padon was also arrested and fined fifty dollars for his part. The two girls who were with them that night were never charged. Ironically, it was one of them who had shot out the light nearest to Gorrell's Ford after Padon had taken a shot and missed.

Outside the courtroom, Wilcox Senior took offense to the judge's criticism of his parenting and how newspapers and city leaders were shaping the story into a cautionary tale of rich kids gone wrong.

"The amount of money given my children as spending change is so small that I would not name it for fear friends would think it untrue. The children of financially well-off families are wild, in a way, but no wilder than those in less fortunate circumstances. And it is only the prominence of the parents that has brought both stories to the front pages of the nation's press.

"Youths of families living in my neighborhood and who are schoolmates of my son do not have large sums of money to spend, according to their fathers with whom I have talked. I believe my own family is an average one and I know that Junior does not have too much money to spend," Senior said as he adjusted his fedora in preparation to leave. "One does not have to have money to get into trouble. Lack of it is the usual cause for crime. Daily check of the newspaper and courts will show that."

But Wilcox's statement was never given much consideration. For average folks in town, it was easy to cast blame on the shortcomings of all the mothers and fathers of Tulsa's privileged youth. After all, the names of kids from regular families weren't being dragged through the newspaper mud—it was those high-society types. Hours after the news of Born's death had spread throughout Tulsa, Mayor Truman Penney made a rare Sunday evening appearance at the police station.

"The parents are to blame at bottom for this shocking revelation of what our children have been doing," Mayor Penney dramatically declared to a *World* reporter. "While the parents give their time to making money (this left no doubt *which* parents he meant), the children go about ungoverned. I am greatly disturbed and saddened by what happened today and by what has happened in the last two weeks. It has got to the point where I don't know what to do next."

But he did know what he was going to do next. In a meeting of city commissioners led by Oscar Hoop on Tuesday, December 11, city leaders swore to go after the one element which they believed was corrupting Tulsa's youth the most: marble machines—the grandfather of the pinball machine.

"Marble machines and loitering of young people around them have provided much of the background for events that tie into the death investigation," the *Tribune* claimed in a front-page article. However, the precise correlation between marble machines and murder was never actually explained.

"Reverberations of the Gorrell murder case were felt in the city commission meeting Tuesday as Police Commissioner Hoop announced that marble machine distributors would either clean house or the police would do it for them," the *Tribune* continued. Hoop's proposal was to clear the machines from establishments located near the schools, and to establish the city's complete control over them through licensure.

But as Hoop later confessed in that same meeting, he didn't want to just restrict the simple penny-operated games, he wanted to eliminate them.

"I offer this more in hope than in confidence; I believe it will ultimately be necessary to remove the machines," Hoop asserted. And in his mind, their removal from businesses located near schools didn't necessarily mean removal from businesses located near schools. Instead, it meant anywhere young people congregate in their free time for fun and socializing.

"Marble machines, which Hoop and Mayor Penney declare are taking the lunch money of grade, junior high, and high school students, must be moved from any store, café, or drug store where students usually congregate, Hoop decreed," the *Tribune* continued.

The college-professor-slash-police-commissioner found an avid supporter in Mayor Penney.

"I have received more complaints from the parents of children about these machines than any other one thing," the mayor postulated. "It seems even that prizes are offered for high scores!"

Following the mayor's lead, "We can show that they are gambling machines," Hoop declared. But he never really showed *how* they were gambling machines; he only stated that he *could* show it.

The metaphorical torches and pitchforks came out during a meeting of the Parent Teacher Association held later that same day at the First United Methodist Church. The PTA was demanding the machines' "complete removal in view of the recent tragedy in our city."

"It is not a case of marble machines and such being taken away only near the schools," one PTA delegate declared to nodding heads of approval. "Children can get a long ways from home as you know and they will find them any place. That is why we must remove them all!"

"In the face of the recent tragedy this particular bit of work comes within our realm of child welfare and if we don't take a stand on this now, we arent's (sic) good for anything," one middle-aged mother shouted.

"Not only is it the actual playing of the machines that is a corrupting influence," another mother stated, "but it is the atmosphere. My children can go into the places near their school, where these machines are, and they stay around and watch outsiders play and gamble, and I feel that they should not be subjected to this temptation."

But this was just the beginning. Whether they knew it or not at the time, they were steeling themselves up for a city-wide moral crusade. As Christian soldiers fighting for the salvation of their children, they would soon find the devil's influence in more than just arcade games.

A Timeline of Events, Chapters 1—10

Thursday, November 29	- Phil Kennamer shoots John Gorrell Jr. in the head twice sometime after 11 p.m.
Friday, November 30	- Gorrell's body is found at 12:05 a.m. - Early afternoon, Edward Larson contacts Richard Oliver who informs him about "Bob Wilson."
Saturday, December 1	- Richard Oliver arrives in Claremore, OK. - Mid-morning: Floyd Huff tells his story to KC Detective Higgins - At 2:40 p.m. Phil Kennamer surrenders. - Later that night, Ted Bath tells his story to investigators.
December 2-8	- Witnesses come forward to share their stories of what Phil Kennamer told them about his plans to murder John Gorrell Jr, and what he said and did after the murder. - The investigation continues with many thoughtless statements made by police and prosecutors.
Sunday, December 9	- Phil Kennamer's friend and key witness, Sydney Born, commits suicide.
December 9-16	- The story, and the investigation, is reinvigorated with wild rumors and frightened witnesses. On December 12, Phil tells his version of what happened to reporters.

Chapter Ten

PHIL KENNAMER LEANED FORWARD IN the matron's rocking chair, gripped a wooden match in his right hand, set his thumbnail on the head, and slid it to the left with enough friction to light it with one strike. It was a maneuver he practiced often, and as he squinted through the tobacco and phosphorous smoke at the reporters in the room, he returned their grins and smiles with his trademark smirk. He was in a good mood the morning of Wednesday, December 12, and he appeared comfortable in the furnished room that had been his "cell" for the last two weeks.

With *Tulsa World* and newswire reporters there, as well as some from several out-of-state large dailies, Kennamer was holding court and enjoying the moment.[1] By working his smooth charm and silver tongue, he was confident he could cod these twits into empathizing with his side of the story. After Born's death on Sunday, the narrative throughout the city had decidedly turned against him. Rumors that his friend was murdered to keep quiet steered the case away from the direction Kennamer needed it to go.

But there was another reason Kennamer wanted to get his story out: he hated the story his attorney was putting out. In an interview published Tuesday, the day before, Moss had laid the groundwork for an insanity defense. When Kennamer read that article, he was livid. An insanity defense discounted his heroics. It didn't tell the story of how he'd outsmarted a dangerous

---

[1] *Tribune* reporters were not allowed because Kennamer was angry with them for the stories they wrote about him and his turbulent youth.

criminal like John Gorrell Jr. and saved Virginia's life. Why couldn't they see that?

Besides placing blame back on the victim, and reinforcing their claims of self-defense, Moss also said during his interview that Kennamer's infatuation for Virginia Wilcox had become obsessive, and that he had mental health issues because he told people he was going to kill John Gorrell.

"Possibly, he was suffering from heroics and this may have added to his desire to join Gorrell, expose him at the opportune moment and incidentally redeem himself in the eyes of Miss Wilcox," Moss theorized. "If Kennamer had not been abnormal, he would not have told several friends that he intended on killing Gorrell, as well as discuss various fantastic and imaginary [scenarios] with him as the hero."

He also pointed to several of Kennamer's youthful transgressions as incidents in his life that should lead one to question the boy's sanity. In spite of this, the lawyer had no doubt in the boy's claim of self-defense. After all, Gorrell was the one who brought the gun, and they were prepared to show it was his handwriting on the famed extortion note that no one had seen.

In a three-hour interview with reporters, Kennamer gave his own version of events that conveniently weaved in and around the witness statements published in the newspapers. He had nearly two weeks to put together his account of what had happened, and by the time of the interview, he had a logical explanation for everything, as well as counterarguments that were impossible to prove or disprove.

Kennamer prefaced his story by saying that he had first heard of the plot to kidnap Virginia in September and had then formed a one-man conspiracy to enter into the scheme and frustrate it from the inside. "His sole idea, he said, was to prevent harm to Miss Wilcox or embarrassment to any member of the Wilcox family," the *World* reported. The same newspaper also pointed out that Kennamer "scoffed at many questions plied to him as well [as] at several of the police theories."

He then recounted how he met Born at 10:30 Thanksgiving night at the Quaker Drug Store.

"Sidney told me to take his car but I said I'd rather have him drive me. I told him I was going to meet Gorrell. We drove to a point near St. John's Hospital. We saw Gorrell's car parked near 19th Street and Utica Avenue. Sid remarked that Gorrell was in the car. I got out of Born's car and he left, but before he did, he warned me that it would be dangerous to reveal to Gorrell that the Wilcox plot was not going through.

"I got into Gorrell's car and we started driving toward the Forest Hills addition. We were driving about thirty or forty miles an hour. Gorrell asked me 'how the shake was coming along.' I told him 'it wasn't coming along at all.'

"'What's the matter, didn't you mail that letter?'" Kennamer quoted Gorrell as saying.

"I told him it was not mailed and that I never intended to mail it. I told him I had the note right here in my pocket. Gorrell asked me what the idea was. I told him I was going to stop this thing. I told him the reason I got into it was to stop it.

"'You just think you are,'" Gorrell answered, according to Kennamer.

"Did you ever hear of the double-cross?" I asked Gorrell. "I told him he was getting the double-cross now. Gorrell asked me how I was going to stop the plot. If in no other way I can turn this note over to the authorities, I told him."

At about the same moment, Kennamer said the car slowed down to ten to fifteen miles per hour as Gorrell reached down at his left side, jerked out a pistol, pointed it at Kennamer's head and pulled the trigger. Twice.

"It didn't go off and I grabbed it," he said. "We both had our hands on it. I struck at him and we struggled. I remember the gun was pointing at Gorrell's head. He may have pulled the trigger again or I may have, but it went off. The second shot came almost instantly, just as the car hit the curb.

"I was panicky. I guess I was almost hysterical. I put the gun back into the holster. I remembered when Gorrell jerked out the gun the holster flew off.[2] I placed the gun beside his body. I got out of the car and walked to the Owl Tavern. I guess it was about two miles away.

"I stayed there a few minutes and then went to the Quaker Drug Store where I met Robert Thomas. I told him I just killed Gorrell and explained the reason was the extortion note.

"That's the way it happened. It was just his life or mine. I had to do it," Kennamer said with a smarmy shrug of his shoulders.

"Gorrell was stronger than you and shouldn't have had much trouble in overpowering you in the fight," a reporter asked Kennamer. "How did you manage to turn the gun on him?"

"I don't know," Kennamer replied. "It happened so fast."

"When did this kidnapping plot, later changed to one of extortion, originate?" a reporter asked.

"It was last September that I met two other Tulsa young men[3] who told me of the plot Gorrell was working on, and how they had refused to enter into such a scheme. I decided I would try and find out more about it. I was not going to allow any harm to come to the Wilcox family when, after all, I am very fond of Miss Wilcox and could not see her harmed in any way. I

---

[2] Besides getting to the weapon before John returned from the hospital, claiming "the holster flew off" was the only logical way he could account for putting the gun back inside and leaving it on the seat. Leaning across John's body to retrieve it would have begged the question: Why?

[3] This turned out to be Preston Cochrane and Pat Burgess. Burgess was a young reporter for the *Tulsa World*, and Cochrane was an ex-employee of the paper. Burgess introduced Kennamer to Gorrell in September, when Burgess sought out Gorrell for repayment of a small loan, and Kennamer tagged along.

then conceived the idea of joining in the scheme," Kennamer answered before he lit another cigarette.

"I learned from one of these two Tulsans, who incidentally are not involved in any way, that the plot was to kidnap Miss Wilcox. An airplane was to be waiting near Tulsa and the girl was to be flown to Kansas City," Kennamer said. She was then to be tucked away and guarded in a suburban hideaway until the ransom was paid.

"After my investigation, I went to Kansas City about the middle of November and found Gorrell," Kennamer began again as he moved from the rocking chair to the bed. "We talked a bit and then I remarked how I heard something was coming against the Wilcox family. When Gorrell discovered I was interested, he said he did not know that I would be interested in anything like this."

At this point, the nineteen-year-old began to crack a smile as he told of how he had outsmarted his adversary.

"I replied I was in for anything that had easy money connected with it. We talked over the original plot and I told him it was way too complicated. I said it had too many people in it and that the better way was merely to write Homer Wilcox an extortion note.

"I told him I'd discussed extortion news with Mr. Wilcox and that I *knew* he would pay off. Actually, I've seen Mr. Wilcox only twice in my life and have never discussed extortion or anything else with him," Kennamer said with some animation.

"All we had to do was write an extortion note and Wilcox would pay off. We agreed to this plot. I suggested that Gorrell write a letter but we decided to wait awhile. My idea was to get that letter as evidence of the plot."

Since Oliver had reported seeing rubber gloves, Kennamer had to explain the rubber gloves. He also had to explain the hunting knife. Why would a young man go to Kansas City and buy rubber gloves and a hunting knife as soon as he got there? His reason for purchasing them was to fool his co-conspirator into thinking he could write the letter without leaving evidence behind. Kennamer's cleverness, he pointed out to reporters, was in knowing full well the handwriting could be matched to Gorrell.

"I knew it wouldn't make any difference whether there were fingerprints or not," he confidently declared. "The science of handwriting detection is sufficient to incriminate him."

It was a good story, but he forgot about one small thing: that he had told Huff he planned on wearing the rubber gloves "when he stabbed his friend."

Kennamer then explained to the reporters that Gorrell had been too drunk to write the letter that night of November 20, and it was put off until the next day.

"We went to bed and the first thing Gorrell said in the morning was a suggestion about writing the letter. I stood over him while he wrote the letter. It threatened harm to members of the Wilcox family if the amount demanded, $20,000, was not paid. I was to take the letter and mail it. It was addressed to H. F. Wilcox and marked 'Personal' and 'Air Mail.'

"Gorrell was so anxious to write the letter that when he woke up, I remarked that it wasn't so important that he would have to get me out of bed."

Even if Gorrell did write the extortion note, Kennamer never explained why he didn't turn it over to police when he returned from Kansas City. As for the knife, he told them, it was purchased in anticipation of the deer hunting season. But as for why it was in his bag, Kennamer would not talk about that, either.

Although he had put responsibility for Gorrell's death back on Gorrell, Kennamer had more explaining to do. Huff would be a star witness against him in the preliminary hearing next week, and he had to chip away at his account of their inebriated car ride to Tulsa.

"Later that day, with the letter in my pocket, we contacted an aviator to obtain passage to Tulsa. We talked to Floyd Huff,"

Kennamer said. "Due to the weather Huff refused to fly but offered to drive me to Tulsa. Later that day, I started to Tulsa with Huff. We had a few drinks and he made some remark about Gorrell and a deal he had been trying to make in the purchase of a plane."

According to Kennamer, Huff was angry with Gorrell for pretending to be financially capable of buying an airplane from him and suggested that Gorrell was "crazy."

"'I'll show you how crazy he really is,'" Kennamer said he told him.

"Then I showed him the note," he said. "But I made no threats against the life of Gorrell. When we reached Pittsburg, Kansas, we stopped at a hotel and got a room. I took my [bag] to the room. When I opened it, Huff saw the dagger now in possession of the sheriff's office. I had a pair of rubber surgical gloves also. I told him that I often had a knife like that which I used when I went deer hunting.

"I doubt if I get to go deer hunting this year, though," Kennamer said as his voice trailed off in thought for a moment.

Returning to his story, he said, "I bought the rubber gloves so that Gorrell could write the letter without leaving any fingerprints on the letter," Kennamer repeated. "Then we continued to Tulsa and I told Huff that I was going to wait for Gorrell to come to Tulsa and then stop the extortion plot."

Kennamer's account skirted Huff's claim that Kennamer described to him a daring plan to get the dental student up in an airplane and "crack Gorrell over the head with a wrench and then bail out in a parachute." It was a point Huff clearly recalled to investigators because if it had worked, he'd have lost his $8,000 airplane.

When a reporter asked him about Huff's claim, Kennamer denied it.

"I didn't tell Huff that I planned to stab Gorrell or of a plot to get him in an airplane, slug him in the head and then bail out of the plane with a parachute while Gorrell crashed."

But in giving his account of his time with Huff, Kennamer forgot one fine point. It was a point confirmed the next day by a *Tribune* report that the field manager of the Fairfax Airport in Kansas City recalled that Kennamer had questioned him closely as to whether the plane would carry parachutes or not.

The death of his friend Sidney Born was a hot-button issue for Phil, and when he was asked about it by a reporter, Kennamer used his friend's death to his advantage with new claims that could not be confirmed or denied by his dead friend.

"There isn't a person in Tulsa that will say that Sidney was the type who would take his own life," Kennamer said as he lit another cigarette. "He was murdered and I KNOW IT! They bungled the job when they found Born dying in his car and destroyed any evidence that might have offered a clue to the murder.

"Born could have testified at my trial and blown up the state's evidence that I hid in Gorrell's car and deliberately killed Gorrell. The second motive could have been someone feared Born knew too much about the case and his testimony might involve others on the information he had," Kennamer explained.

Kennamer then went on to name three young men who had motive to kill Born and that any one or all of them were responsible. He said he had given these names to Sheriff Charles Price and that Price knew the young men.

"You can't take that fellow's story at its face value," Price said when he was asked about it. "We haven't got enough on any of those fellows to arrest them."

Their names were wisely left out of the newspapers.

Returning to the extortion plot that was on everyone's mind, a reporter asked the chain-smoking prisoner, "Why did you show the extortion note to so many people?"

"I had no reason to fear anything in the case. When I heard of the plot last September, I set out to stop it. I went about it carefully and when I had obtained the written note from

Gorrell, I had the evidence to show of the plot and didn't care who knew it," Kennamer said.

He was then asked about why he told Robert Thomas he had killed Gorrell. "Thomas thought I was joking," Kennamer replied. "I didn't offer to show the body. Thomas asked to see it. I told him I had to kill Gorrell, that it was too bad, but that it was his life or mine and that the trouble was over the extortion note."

Kennamer then told of how Tommy Taylor had given him a ride home and that the next morning he went to his father's farm in Chelsea to hunt quail. Saturday morning, he got back on the train to return to Tulsa to see his attorney, "and make a clean breast of the whole thing."

With humor, he recalled how he accidentally ran into Richard Oliver.

"I got on the train and walked to the front of the smoker car. I sat down and then decided to move further back in the car. I looked at the other passengers and noticed the man, later known to be Oliver, and thought he looked familiar," Kennamer said as he held back his laughter. "His eyes looked as if they were about to pop out of his head!"

He couldn't hold it in anymore and paused to laugh, with the reporters joining in. "I—I started to ask him if he was going the wrong direction for the insane asylum! I looked at him closely and he covered his face with his hands."

Despite the poor boy's being scared out of his mind, the reporters were laughing with Kennamer. The *World* reminded its readers of Oliver's first words to police that morning. "Protect me! The killer is on this train and is trying to kill me!"

Kennamer continued laughing and remarked, "That is just another strange coincidence in this case." The other strange coincidence Kennamer acknowledged was Homer Junior, Bill Padon, and their dates shooting out the streetlights near the crime scene.

The day before Kennamer gave his version of the truth to reporters, the *World* published a story which quoted the anonymous police official. Since the start of the investigation, the *World* had quoted only two people with the Tulsa Police Department when it came to their coverage of the investigation: Police Chief Carr and Sgt. Maddux. Within their December 12 story, the same unnamed police official hinted that the photos and negatives, which had never been connected with the case but were the subject of city-wide gossip, "probably will be produced at trial." For Tulsans—and scandal-hungry tabloids nationwide—this was another explosive angle to the case. With all the other problems their children had supposedly gotten themselves into, now there were naked pictures of them doing things they weren't supposed to do until they got married.

"Do you know, for a fact, that the negatives and photographs figuring in street rumors in connection with the Gorrell slaying exist?" the police official was asked.

"I can't deny that they do exist," the police official answered, in a puzzling reply.

"Will they be introduced during the preliminary hearing?"

"I wouldn't be surprised. If the state finds it necessary to introduce them, I believe they will be available."

"Do you have them?"

"No."

"Are they in possession of Dr. Gorrell?"

"I can't say, I don't know."

Exasperated with getting nowhere, the reporter finally asked this anonymous source, "Where are they?"

"I understand that they are in a safety deposit vault in a certain downtown bank," the police official said.

In the paragraphs that came directly before that exchange, the newspaper is quoting Sgt. Maddux. Later on in the story, Sgt. Maddux is the next person quoted. If Sgt. Maddux came before and after the unnamed police official, it wasn't hard for many to know who it was.

Including Phil Kennamer.

When the subject of marijuana and dirty pictures came up, Kennamer unleashed a verbal broadside at Sgt. Maddux.

"The efforts of Mr. Maddux to conceal the facts of this case are little short of criminal," Kennamer began. "He has consistently hinted at the existence of salacious pictures involving girls of prominent families, when he knew that no such pictures existed, in order to perfect the pattern of the case he has attempted to build around me. He has considered it necessary to vilify and slander the name of Sidney Born and others.

"I'm morally certain Gorrell had no such photographs. I know I did not. If anyone has them, they acquired them by the process known as super-imposition."

When reporters challenged Sgt. Maddux about the photographs the next day, he denied knowing anything about them and added that, as far as he was concerned, the investigation was over.

As for the rumored drug use that was going on around town, Kennamer denied that he or any of his friends used drugs and asserted that "narcotics entered in the case in no way."

But when pressed for why Born might have been murdered, according to *his* version, Kennamer answered that he was convinced that someone representing himself to speak for Phil Kennamer telephoned Born on Sunday morning and made a date for Born to meet at the spot where he was fatally wounded. When Born went to the drugstore to try to telephone Kennamer, he was attempting to verify the message. Unable to do so, Born went to the meeting and was shot in the head by one of the three boys from Gorrell's "gang," who then staged the scene to look like a suicide.

However, Josey Henderson told police the family only received one telephone call that morning, and it was for her, which made Kennamer's story impossible.

The interview came to a halt when it was time to serve Kennamer his evening meal. In his own mind, he had just talked himself out of a murder trial. In spite of the sanctimonious confidence he had in his performance, some of his answers actually seemed plausible. And the prosecution had a major hurdle with the fact that Gorrell was killed with his own gun. Kennamer didn't go to the meeting armed with a weapon; Gorrell did. And if Kennamer didn't go to the meeting armed, it would be hard to prove premeditation. Coupled with the possibility that Gorrell may have actually written the note, Kennamer's lawyers had a good defense.

Judging by all the crazy stories being told around town, Tulsans, it seemed, were capable of believing anything. And if they believed even half of his story, that could give a jury enough reasonable doubt to let him go free.

When the judge's son went to bed that night, he was confident he'd done the right thing. He had told the truth, and the truth would exonerate him. Everyone would read his side of the story in tomorrow's newspaper, and perhaps they would even let him go free after Monday's preliminary hearing. In his mind, Phil Kennamer had just won his own case.

Chapter Eleven

PHIL KENNAMER MAY HAVE JUST blown his own case. When Flint Moss read his client's story the next morning, he got sick, went home, and didn't get out of bed for two days. One of his assistants told reporters he was resting from "a nervous condition."

The fifty-four-year-old attorney liked to play his cards close to his chest. He didn't want prosecutors to know about his defense until the trial. At the preliminary hearing scheduled for Monday, he had no plans to call any defense witnesses, or to put on any defense at all, for that matter. Doing so would have shown Anderson and King which cards he intended to play at trial. But now, his client had given away almost everything. The prosecution would be adequately prepared to counterattack valid arguments the defense wanted to preserve for the trial.

In thirty-four years of practicing law, Moss had never had a client quite like Phil Kennamer. Judge Kennamer shared in his frustration, but he'd also grown accustomed to his son's impulsive behavior. After a long talk with the boy, Judge Kennamer had a long talk with Sheriff Price.

"Judge Kennamer conferred with Sheriff Price yesterday [Thursday, December 13] and requested that his son not be permitted any visitors unless they were approved by him or the youth's attorneys," the *World* reported the day after the story was published. "Kennamer told the sheriff that since his son was a minor, he would exercise his privilege as a father and not permit the boy visitors unless they are sanctioned. The sheriff agreed to the request."

In other words, he couldn't trust his son to keep his mouth shut.

Local excitement about Monday's preliminary hearing soared exponentially over the weekend. Newspapers gave their readers in-depth speculation on the strategies of both sides as if it were a sporting match. The lineup of players was announced and dissected. Both the *World* and *Tribune* listed all of the nearly two dozen state witnesses and reminded their readers of the role each had played in the events leading to the moment.

For the prosecution, County Attorney Anderson would lead while his assistant, Tom Wallace, would provide backup. Wallace was much older than Anderson and had far more experience in the courtroom trying murder cases. State Attorney General J. Berry King was invited into the case as a special prosecutor, and his involvement sent a powerful message.

"The state is in this case to give vigorous assistance to local authorities," King declared to reporters on Saturday. "It should be understood that the state is primarily interested in seeing that criminal laws are enforced, and it is not interested in idle rumors and the talk of common gossip."

What King was alluding to was a startling new development that came from Sgt. Maddux, who had informed his superiors he was offered $25,000 to "drop certain phases of his investigation." It was also insinuated that Maddux might receive bodily harm if he didn't do so. Maddux was careful not to reveal the source of the bribe, but declared it was made to him while he was away from Tulsa interviewing another blind-alley witness. When Chief Carr and Police Commissioner Hoop were asked about the bribe, they neither confirmed nor denied it. King would not elaborate on his statement, and Maddux himself would say very little except to note that a record of his investigation and evidence of the bribe had been locked away in a safe deposit box.

It was a peculiar claim by Maddux, one that would take on a life of its own in the months ahead. Its peculiarity dwelt in the notion that a bribe to drop certain phases of the investigation, as he said it was, was even possible. It had seemingly come way too late. The entire case was heavily reported on in newspapers throughout the country. The cat was already out of the bag. How could Sgt. Maddux be expected to put a screaming, clawing cat back in the bag without arousing suspicions?

It was an inflammatory accusation that, if true, made the Kennamer family look suspect and could negatively influence the jury pool. But Maddux wasn't the only one throwing mud at the Kennamer defense. Colonel Hoop, with more verbal ambiguity, softly intimated to both Tulsa newspapers that he was also in physical danger from the same men who had tried to bribe Maddux. When asked about both the bribe and the implied threats, he gave reporters an evasive answer that only seemed to confirm the rumor.

"I can't say as to that," he told them.

There was more to the story, but Tulsa would have to wait to hear it all. For now, it was just the latest in a long line of sensational proclamations from authorities. The day before, J. Berry King had succumbed to the trend when he told a United Press reporter, "The real facts in the Gorrell slaying case have never yet been permitted to come to light. The trial of Philip Kennamer will prove a series of sensations undisclosed at present."

There were more sensations? His careless comment seemed to confirm that the wild rumors flying around town might actually be true.

Ruth Sheldon, a feature writer for the *Tribune* declared, ". . . he set tongues wagging again in Tulsa." The public, already keyed up and on edge, were vulnerable to that kind of tantalizing statement. When the Oklahoma Attorney General said there was more to the case, folks believed him. King, like many other officials involved in the case, was fueling the machine that drove public excitement and jeopardized Kennamer's chances for a fair trial.

And Flint Moss was taking note of it.

Despite all the hype and preparation, the task before the state on Monday was simple. They only had to show Court of Common Pleas Judge Bradford Williams three things: that Gorrell was slain on the night of November 29, that a crime was committed, and that there was probable cause to believe that Phil Kennamer had committed that crime. If the judge ruled in the prosecution's favor, Kennamer would be bound over, and his murder trial would be set for the January term of district court. Due to an idiosyncrasy in the law at that time, it was unlikely that he would be allowed bail.

At first, Anderson said he would only put on a prima facie case—just enough to have Kennamer bound over. Later on, he seemed to waffle on this strategy out of concern that many of the state's witnesses were in hiding and could disappear completely before the trial date. If he called them in at Monday's hearing, their testimony would be on the record, which could then be used at the trial.

Over-excited from a nonstop assault of rumors and revelations, many hoped the preliminary hearing could give Tulsans the answers to all their questions. Who gave Kennamer a ride to the Owl Tavern after he murdered Gorrell? Was it Sidney Born? And who was Born's killer, and will his death affect the prosecution? What role did marijuana play in all this? Will the extortion note be presented? Did Gorrell really write it? Where are the salacious pictures of Tulsa debutantes, and who was in them? Is Wade Thomas the leader of a criminal gang of rich kids? Why did Floyd Huff serve three sentences in prison? Is he a marijuana smuggler? What was that Wilcox boy really up to that night? And the marble machines—what about the marble machines?

Veteran *Tribune* editor Harmon Phillips played into the public's demand for answers when he raised their expectations in the lead paragraph of a front-page story published the afternoon before the December 17 hearing. "The hysterical theories and fantastic rumors which have swept the city the past two weeks in connection with the deaths of John Gorrell, Jr., and Sidney Born, will be reduced to reality Monday when Phil Kennamer, 19, sits in a courtroom to hear the state, for the first time officially, reveal the facts upon which it prosecutes him for the murder of Gorrell."

However, further down in that same article, Harmon hedged against his over-promise in the lead when he wrote, "The preliminary trial may prove sensational or it may assume the plane of simple formality."

Floyd Huff, the state's star witness, arrived Saturday, and reporters were cautioned not to interview him or ask questions. Prosecutors were taking no chances in the final hours. After a one-hour meeting with the nervous man, Anderson said they were merely "brushing up on his testimony."

A big deal was made in the papers about how Born's statement to police—that he gave Kennamer a ride to meet with Gorrell—could not be used at trial. It was an observation used to introduce the fact that witness statements given at the hearing could be used later at trial "should any state witness die a natural death, disappear, commit suicide or be murdered." As intimated by Anderson earlier, this was a true concern of many.

In anticipation of an insanity defense hinted at by Moss, Anderson requested that Dr. Felix Adams, superintendent of the Northeastern Oklahoma Hospital for the Insane in Vinita, be in attendance to observe the defendant. "At this time, Doctor Adams will begin his official observation of Kennamer to offset any defense plan [to plead insanity] at the subsequent trial," the *World* reported early Monday morning.

The psychiatrist rumored to be snagged by the defense was one of the biggest names in his field at the time, Dr. Karl Menninger of Wichita, Kansas. Menninger's book, *The Human Mind*, published four years earlier, had made him and the Menninger Clinic famous. For the next few decades, he enjoyed a successful secondary career as an expert witness for defense attorneys with clients facing the death penalty. He was their go-to psychiatrist when they needed to have a client declared insane, and Karl Menninger declared nearly all of them "insane." During a 1951 competency hearing of a spree-killer in federal court in Oklahoma City, evidence was produced that Menninger had been a long-term but secret member of a national anti-death-penalty group.

Accurately gauging the public's interest in the case, Judge Williams moved the preliminary hearing from his relatively small courtroom to the more accommodating courtroom of a district court judge. A large crowd was anticipated. In their Monday morning issue, released before the hearing began, the *World* accurately revealed what was in store for that day.

"Indications that a throng will pack the courtroom and overflow in the corridors were seen yesterday with continuous demands upon officials for seats. Throughout the day, county and city officials were besieged at their homes with telephone calls from hundreds of friends and acquaintances desirous of getting in the courtroom. No official who has been even remotely mentioned in connection with the Gorrell-Kennamer case escaped the avalanche of calls."

In spite of the city-wide excitement, Anderson and King were cautioning Tulsans that there was likely to be no sensational testimony or other developments during the hearing. It was a statement that showed Anderson had finally decided to put forth only the minimum necessary to have Kennamer held for trial.

"The public apparently does not understand the significance of a preliminary hearing trial, which is meant only to present sufficient evidence and testimony to justify the holding of the defendant for jury trial," King explained to both *World* and *Tribune* readers. But nobody was listening, and King's own relatives in Tulsa reported they were flooded with telephone inquiries from those hoping to get seats via their connection with the attorney general.

In addition to the four regular bailiffs, six deputies were called in that morning to "herd the human horde." Despite the nine o'clock starting time, a large mob was already present when the courthouse opened at 6:45 that morning. Forty-five minutes later, the normally spacious Division Two courtroom on the second floor was packed with hundreds of seated and standing spectators. Several hundred more who were too late to get inside massed together in the second-floor corridors, flowed down a wide stairwell with two wings, and spilled out all over the first-floor lobby, in a line that kept on going out the front door. Outside, more people gathered around the large granite steps and along the sidewalk. Anyone with regular business at the courthouse that morning discovered it was impossible to park a car within a reasonable distance.

Photographs taken from the second-floor landing that day reveal folks of all ages, races, and levels of society. The pressure of this crowd to get inside became so great that the courtroom had to be locked one hour before the hearing started. The eight-foot, wooden, double doors banged and creaked and moaned under the stress of the excited mob.

For the two deputies tasked with escorting Kennamer to court, the only way down from the third floor was the elevator. When the doors opened, the hallways leading to the hearing were so clogged with the morbidly curious that Kennamer had to be rerouted and brought in through the judge's chamber. When he emerged into the room, reporters were careful to note the time, 9:07 a.m., and the dark blue-grey suit with grey tie he wore. His face was solemn and serious, and he kept his gaze from the crowd.

"As he calmly walked to a chair at the defense table, the murmur of voices from the spectators developed into a crescendo of tongue wagging," senior *World* journalist Walter Biscup noted. He shared the jury box with nearly twenty other local, state, and national reporters. No photographers or cameras were allowed, and the visually dynamic scene had to be painted with words. "Kennamer sat upright and had his arms crossed against his chest. His face was expressionless. During the two weeks that he was held in the county jail, the prisoner's complexion has assumed the 'prison pallor.'"

In addition to the hundreds of curious spectators observing his every move, Kennamer was scrutinized by the careful gaze of Dr. Felix Adams, who was tasked with discerning any signs of abnormality.

One man noticeably absent was Judge Kennamer, who was in his chambers at the federal building. However, other members of the Kennamer family were present, including the defendant's older brother, Franklin Jr., a young attorney working in Oklahoma City, and his sisters, Juanita Hayes and Opal.

A few minutes later, thirty-one-year-old Judge Bradford Williams took his seat with a call to order. He wasted no time in getting down to business. "If there are any schoolchildren here, including those of high school age, I want them out of the courtroom and back in their classes," he ordered.

When Assistant County Attorney Tom Wallace called for the state's eleven witnesses, only five answered. The other six were trapped on the first floor behind a sea of people. Five deputies were dispatched to escort them to the courtroom. "This they did by means of the old-fashioned wedge formation used in football games two decades ago," the *World* reported.

The first witness called to the stand was Dr. Gorrell, who had been seated at the prosecution table next to Dr. Adams.

"Did you know John F. Gorrell Jr.?" County Attorney Anderson asked him.

"Yes."

"How long did you know him?"

"All my life."

"Is he living or dead?"

Tears welled in the doctor's eyes, and he appeared to be struggling with his emotions. "Dead," he said with a tremor.

The second witness was coroner Dr. Carl Simpson who testified that he saw Gorrell's body at the Tulsa Undertaking Home, that he had been killed, and that there were two gunshot wounds to his head. He also noted there was a swelling over the right eye and a discoloration of the lips, indicators he'd been punched or struck with an object.

Wesley Cunningham, sleek-haired and serious, took the stand to tell how he had discovered Gorrell dead at five minutes after midnight on the morning of November 30. His testimony closely resembled what he had already told investigators: that he was driving south, coming from downtown Tulsa, and he had discovered Gorrell's car, which was facing him with the left front wheel over the curb.

Anderson then called his star witness, Floyd Huff, and secretly hoped the agitated man would hold it together on the stand. The story he told that day was similar to what he had first told Chief of Detectives Thomas Higgins in Kansas City and had later told Tulsa investigators. The airplane mechanic and parts dealer was suffering from a cold, and when Anderson led him through his introductory questions, his replies were little more than a whisper. Moss, who had been leaning forward in his chair, struggling to hear the witness, called out to Huff to speak louder.

"Can't," a defiant Huff said. "I got a cold."

"I can't hear well so we make a bad combination," Moss countered.

Huff smiled nervously and swung his head back toward Anderson who asked him if he knew Gorrell before November 21.

"I had met him twice before at Fairfax Airport in Kansas City," Huff answered. He was wringing his hands in a clear sign he was anxious. "Our acquaintance was casual."

Oblivious to the banging and creaking coming from the lobby outside the courtroom, Anderson continued. "When did you first meet Kennamer?"

"I met him at the Fairfax Airport the morning of November twen—"

BOOOM! The latch bolt and faceplate to the locked wooden doors holding back the horde cracked and broke apart, causing a surging tide of bewildered men and women to flow into the courtroom, crashing forward, screaming, falling over themselves, and sweeping aside two bailiffs who were powerless to stop it all.

Huff, possibly expecting an assassin, jumped several inches out of his chair and stared wild-eyed at the melee. The dam had broken, and one of the doors hung askew, a hinge pulled partially out. Judge Williams pounded his gavel viciously as nine other uniformed lawmen ran forward to force the mob back and restore order. Angered that his proceedings could turn into a circus, the judge threatened to clear out the entire courtroom unless calm prevailed.

Returning to his story, Huff told how Gorrell and Kennamer had arrived that morning, looking to rent an airplane, but were turned away because of bad weather. Then, for reasons not made clear, Huff said he drove the duo to the municipal airport in Kansas City where Kennamer left the return portion of his Braniff Airways ticket for safekeeping.

"Kennamer said he might get drunk and lose it," Huff told the prosecutor. "He then sent two telegrams. I didn't get to see them."

He paused for a moment to blow his nose. Smiling sheepishly, he put the white handkerchief back in his pocket. Huff then told the court how their car ride to Tulsa had been arranged, and how Kennamer's return ticket was sold to Gorrell's friend, Everett Gartner.

When Huff and Kennamer left Gorrell at Gartner's apartment, it was the last time Huff ever saw the young dental student. He then told how he and Kennamer first stopped at his house, and then at a Kansas City hotel where Kennamer bought a quart of whisky, a fact that did not surprise many Tulsans who were now aware the judge's son had a drinking problem.

"During the ride, do you remember any startling conversation?" Anderson asked.

"Yes, he told me he was going to kill Gorrell," Huff answered before correcting himself. "Well, he asked me if I knew why he came to Kansas City and I said I didn't. He said he'd come up to kill Gorrell.

"'You don't believe me, do you?' he said."

"'Well,' I said. 'I don't know.'

"Then he reached back into his bag and brought out a dagger about eight or nine inches long and said he planned to kill Gorrell with it. He showed me, too, some rubber gloves and said he brought them with a view to not showing fingerprints."

"What other conversation was there?" Anderson inquired.

"Well, he told me he thought a lot of this Wilcox girl, Miss Virginia Wilcox, daughter of Homer F. Wilcox, head of the Wilcox Oil and Gas Company, and that he was going to kill Gorrell because of a note.

"He said he went to Kansas City to get him, but that he missed connections and didn't meet him until midnight the night before, which was too late. He told me then he had a plan to rent an airplane and to hit him on the head when they were above the clouds."

"On the trip from Pittsburg to Tulsa, did Kennamer say anything else concerning Gorrell?" Anderson asked.

"He said that Gorrell was going to Tulsa the following week and that he'd get him then. Kennamer told me he would leave his car in some isolated spot and have Gorrell drive him out there. Then, he said, he would get out of the car and let him have it and drive away in his own machine."

"Did he show you anything else besides the dagger and gloves?"

"I never saw the gloves," Huff replied.

"Did he show you anything else?"

"Yes, it was an extortion note as he called it. He said he and Gorrell were in on it but he wasn't going to mail it. It was addressed to Wilcox."

Before he dropped Kennamer off at the Philtower Building in downtown Tulsa, Huff said he asked for Kennamer's name and number in order to continue their acquaintance. The scrap of paper Kennamer wrote on was introduced as state's exhibit one.

"When did you first learn Gorrell was killed?" Anderson asked.

"I think a week to the day that I left Kennamer here," Huff answered.

"And then you related the facts to authorities?"

"Yes."

"I have no more questions for this witness."

Now, it was Moss's turn, and as he carefully cross-examined the state's star witness against his client, he zeroed in on how intoxicated everyone was, and the alleged threats against Gorrell.

"When you first saw these boys, they were drinking?" Moss asked.

"Evidently," Huff said as he held up three fingers pressed together. "They had this much liquor in a bottle."

"When did Kennamer first tell you about Gorrell?"

"About two hours after we left Kansas City."

"What sort of liquor did Kennamer buy?"

"Pretty good liquor," Huff replied, while the crowd laughed with him and Kennamer grinned. "It cost $4.50 a quart. A Canadian Scotch."

"How many drinks did he have before the first statement was about Gorrell?"

"About three or four."

"Was he tight [inebriated]?"

"Oh no."

"Were you?"

"No."

"There had not been an unpleasant act or word between Kennamer and Gorrell, had there?" Moss queried.

"No."

"They gave you to understand they were acquainted and friends?"

"I didn't know they were anything but friends until Kennamer made those statements," Huff said.

"Of course, you were surprised to hear such violent talk?"

"Sure, wouldn't you have been?"

"Yes, I would," Moss chuckled. He could sense Huff was getting agitated, and he wanted to encourage that to discredit him.

"Did you ever before hear of any such scheme for murder as this airplane plan?"

"I never did," Huff said.

Although his questions, at first, seemed only to reinforce the prosecution's line of inquiry, when broken down, they served to reinforce the defense attorney's theory that his client was insane. After all, what sane person would clobber a man and then jump out of an airplane?

"Did Kennamer ever tell you that he had bailed out of a plane in a parachute before?"

"No."

"How long did it take Kennamer to tell you this story?"

"Twenty or thirty minutes."

"Quite naturally, you didn't talk. He just talked constantly?"

"I didn't know what to think," Huff said with a bit of cockiness. Moss's questions were taking longer than he imagined, and they seemed focused on the mundane.

"At Pittsburg that night, there was no further conversation on this topic?"

"No."

"The next morning, did he talk of it again?" Moss pressed.

"Yes sir, he told it to me all over again except that last part."

After a long discussion that seemed to go in circles, Huff clarified several times for Moss "that last part" referred to Kennamer's plan to get Gorrell to a lonely spot and kill him there.

Sensing Huff's frustration growing, Moss pressed him again. "What part did he tell you?"

"I've told you for the fourth time, Kennamer told me he was going to get Gorrell in a car and let him have it."

"Did he say what he was going to let him have it with, was it the knife or a gun or what?"

"I don't know."

"What was he going to use—knife or gun?"

"He didn't say," Huff answered.

"Now, just a minute ago, you said—" Moss began.

"Look at the record," Huff shouted, while pointing his finger at the court reporter. Moss tried to reply, and Huff interrupted him again. "Retrace your statement and you'll see what I said."

"Thank you."

"I didn't come down here to get mixed up," the ex-convict said as he glared at Moss. "I want to tell what Kennamer said. I'm not going to answer to you."

Judge Williams called him to order and told him to be more mindful of the duties of a witness.

"Now please, for God's sake, don't get mad," Moss teased. It was a comment that broke the tension, sparking nervous laughter throughout the courtroom, where even the judge smiled broadly.

"You didn't believe any of the stuff Kennamer told you?"

"No."

"Where did he show you the note?"

"We were driving, at night. Kennamer turned on the dome light."

"Did he tell you what was in the note?"

"He said it was a demand for $20,000 to be left in twenties, tens and five dollar bills."

"Did he tell you what would occur to the Wilcox family if the money wasn't delivered?"

"He didn't go that far into detail," Huff answered.

"Did he tell you what he intended to do with the letter?"

"No, but I advised him to turn it over to the police," Huff answered. "He did say something in regards to the letter. He said he thought an awful lot of the Wilcox girl, and would keep the letter on her behalf."

"Did he tell you he was going to disrupt the plot?" Moss asked.

"Yes, he did say something to that general effect."

Moss concluded his cross-examination, and Huff was dismissed. His testimony had the crowd sitting at the edge of their seats, straining to hear every word. One more witness was called, and if they were hoping for confirmation of scandalous rumors, they were disappointed. Deputy Sheriff Nathan Martin merely recalled the moment that Saturday afternoon when Kennamer surrendered and said, "I shot Gorrell."

State Attorney General King was right. Besides Huff's testimony, there were no sensational discoveries. No new names mentioned. No rumors put to rest.

Almost immediately, Judge Williams rendered his judgment. "I order the defendant, Phil Kennamer, bound over for jury trial on a charge of first-degree murder, at the January term of district court."

There was a surge of the crowd toward the door and deputies had difficulty pressing Kennamer through the massive crowd to get him to the elevator that returned him to the matron's quarters. During the slow procession, he managed to remain quiet and answered no questions.

Judge Thurman Hurst of district four was slated to receive the case. Court watchers predicted the trial would start on January 28. Tulsa would have to wait six weeks until all the wild rumors they knew to be true were finally confirmed as factual. And in that moment, filled with both disappointment over the bland hearing and eagerness to learn more, it seemed as though hundreds of city residents would wait those six weeks right there in the courthouse.

"The hundreds of spectators who could not obtain access to the courtroom refused to leave the building," the *Tulsa World* reported. "They believed that a recess had been called and bailiffs were attempting to trick them into leaving the building in order to lessen the number of spectators."

It took another three to four hours for the most obstinate of the crowd to admit defeat and go home.

Chapter Twelve

FOR THE FIRST THREE CENTURIES after Columbus "discovered" America, not much had happened in the region that would later become Oklahoma. The area was largely occupied by Indians of the Caddo, Wichita, and Pawnee tribes, and later, the Kiowa and Apache. With the Louisiana Purchase of 1803, America acquired 828,000 acres of territory from France at three cents an acre, for a total cost of $15 million. This area would eventually yield fifteen states and a small portion of two Canadian provinces.

Three territories, Missouri, Orleans, and Arkansas, were named from this purchase by the time the Indian Removal Act was approved in 1830. This act paved the way for the federal government to forcibly relocate Indians from the Five Civilized Tribes of the Chickasaw, Choctaw, Muscogee-Creek, Seminole, and Cherokee Nations from their homes in the Southeastern United States to what would become known as Indian Territory. Tens of thousands of Indians were marched halfway across the country in a forced mass migration that would eventually be called the "Trail of Tears," a reference to the thousands of Indians who died along the way.

At their destination, the five tribes received large allotments of land, formed their own governments, and were encouraged to become farmers, trappers, and ranchers. But over the next five decades, numerous acts and treaties reduced their holdings and made generous allowances for white settlers.

When the Muscogee-Creek Indians from Alabama moved into their new lands, the Turtle Clan settled down underneath a large oak tree near the corner of what is now Cheyenne Avenue and 18th Street in Tulsa.[1] They named their new settlement "Tulasi," which meant "old town" in their language. The Civil War largely postponed economic development in the region, while the Reconstruction era contributed only slightly to the area's growth. The first post office for a village that now called itself "Tulsa" wasn't built until 1879.

In 1882, a railroad spur was extended to Tulsa to serve the growing cattle business. Seven years later, when the city was incorporated on January 18, 1898, the population had grown from two hundred to eleven hundred settlers. By the 1900 census, it had increased by three hundred more people.

In 1901, oil was discovered a short distance from Tulsa, across the Arkansas River in a small area known as Red Fork. Although oil had been found decades before in other areas of what would later become Oklahoma, this discovery was "the first major commercial field developed in Indian Territory," reports author Kenny Franks in his book, *Oklahoma: The Land and Its People*. Within a month, one thousand people had moved into the area. But it was the 1905 discovery of the large Glenn Pool oil reserve fourteen miles southwest of downtown Tulsa that changed everything for the city.

"It was Oklahoma's first major oil field—and the richest field the world had yet seen," wrote Norman Hyne in 2008. "Unlike the thick, sour oil from Spindletop, the famed 1901 Texas discovery that had already played out, this oil was light and sweet—just right to refine into gasoline and kerosene.

"The reservoir was shallow, less than 1,500 feet deep, well within the range of the cable tool drilling rigs of that day," the professor of petroleum geology at the University of Tulsa continued. "It is said that more money was made on the Glenn Pool oil field than the California gold rush and Colorado silver rush combined."

---

[1] The oak tree is still there and is called the Creek Council Oak Tree.

After this discovery, Tulsa became known as the "Oil Capital of the World," and its population exploded. When Oklahoma became a state in 1907, the population was 7,300. Three years later, it had grown to 18,182. "Tulsa became a mecca for oilmen such as Henry F. Sinclair, J. Paul Getty, William K. Skelly, and Waite Phillips," Franks declared in his book.

More wells in the area were discovered, two refineries were built, and a major construction boom took place. By 1920, the population was 72,000. Men like Homer Wilcox, worth $20 million in 1922, more than a quarter of a billion dollars in today's money, were not even in the top echelon and are all but forgotten today. Fourteen years later, the city's population had doubled to 150,000. That kind of economic boom, exponential growth, and money attracted both good Christian folk and those untamed men who worked the oil fields—and a criminal element that followed them.

Tulsa developed a dual personality.

The Kennamer case was by no means Tulsa's first taste of hysteria or mob behavior. On Memorial Day, May 31, 1921, a minor incident in a hotel elevator between a black shoe-shiner and a young, white, female elevator operator was misinterpreted and blown far out of proportion in an unfortunate series of escalating events that began as vigilante "justice" and led to sixteen hours of racial violence. The unrest then morphed into economic envy by whites who were jealous of the success achieved by blacks in their segregated but financially prosperous Greenwood District. When it was over, Greenwood, the wealthiest black community in the United States, which included "Black Wall Street," was obliterated. More than twelve hundred black-owned residences spread out over thirty-five city blocks were destroyed, leaving ten thousand people homeless. The official number of black fatalities given at the time was thirty-nine, but that was the sanitized version. Later estimates place it closer to three hundred, and others go far higher.

Although it was an atrocity of historic proportions and without comparison in American history, vigilante justice by white Tulsans wasn't limited to just blacks; they also murdered white men as well. A year before the race riot, nineteen-year-old Tom Owens, alias Roy Belton, was lynched by an armed mob that stormed the county courthouse after he shot and killed a popular taxicab driver during a botched robbery. The hot-tempered pack of revenge-seekers intimidated Sheriff Jim Wooley easily enough, and he surrendered his prisoner without resistance. Owens was then loaded into the victim's own taxi, and during the nine-mile journey to a favored lynching tree outside of town, more than a hundred cars formed a death parade behind the taxi. Newspapers at the time estimated the crowd in attendance to be north of a thousand.

Many notable outlaws of the era called Tulsa home. The most famous criminals belonged to the Barker-Karpis gang, including Ma Barker herself. She and her son, Fred, would die in a shootout with FBI agents in Florida approximately one month after Kennamer's preliminary hearing. Before they formed the Barker gang, many were members of Tulsa's notorious Central Park Gang of the 1920s, which included Volney Davis and Harry Campbell.

"I can remember the principal of Longfellow told me at one time that there were more graduates of Longfellow grade school in Alcatraz Prison than any other elementary school in the United States," recalled *Tribune* reporter, Bob Foreman, during a 1980 interview. Those graduates included Davis, Campbell, and Arthur "Doc" Barker.

Ruby Floyd, the wife of Charles "Pretty Boy" Floyd, lived in Tulsa, and her house was often under surveillance. Alvin "Creepy" Karpis's ex-wife, Dorothy Slayman, was also from Tulsa and worked as a waitress at Bishop's Waffle House. Other notable Tulsa crime figures of the day were bank robber Coney Coffey and local gangster Johnny Mayo.

Mayo was once part of the gang that participated in the infamous Osage Indian murders of 1920. His wife also worked at Bishop's Waffle House—one of the most popular restaurants in Tulsa. The marriage took a left turn when he heard his wife was running around on him while he was a trustee at the Tulsa County Jail. For this and other reasons, Mayo stole a submachine gun and a pistol, locked up the night jailer, took the elevator to the first floor, walked out of the courthouse, and hailed a taxi to take him to the Drexel Hotel. When the night clerk refused to tell him what room his wife was in, he was persuaded to change his mind when Mayo shoved the Tommy gun in his face. Mayo grabbed the key, went up to the room, and caught his wife *in flagrante delicto* with her paramour. After considerable begging on their part, he eventually let them go.

The next day, Mayo called up *World* police reporter Walter Biscup, told him the whole story, and said he was on his way to Mexico. But it didn't work out the way Mayo planned, and he was captured four days later.

Coming late in the year, the Kennamer-Gorrell case was notable in one of the decade's most notable years for crime. First, Raymond Hamilton, who ran with Bonnie Parker and Clyde Barrow, was captured on April 25. One month later, the two outlaw lovers were ambushed and killed on a rural stretch of road in Louisiana. John Dillinger was also ambushed and shot to death on July 22 in Chicago. Then, Bruno Hauptmann was arrested on September 17, two years after the Lindbergh kidnapping, when federal investigators and state police got a break in the case.

Pretty Boy Floyd was the next to go, when he was killed in Ohio on October 22, followed by Baby Face Nelson, on November 27. Texas outlaw Irvin "Blackie" Thompson, who had robbed banks all over Oklahoma, was killed in a shootout on December 6. He had escaped from Texas death row that summer after fellow gang members on the outside bribed a guard to slip him and his partner, "Whitey" Walker, a gun.

Whitey was shot and killed by a guard when he was halfway over the prison wall. Blackie was killed by officers in a hail of bullets near Amarillo. To cap off a historic year for the end of infamous criminals, the end came for the most sadistic killer in American history when New York City detectives announced they had arrested child killer and cannibal, Albert Fish. Most of the gruesome story he would later give to a psychiatrist was unprintable in newspapers.

THE MORAL CRUSADE TO SAVE the souls of Tulsa's wayward youth continued after the preliminary hearing, with a two-pronged attack to remove the purveyors of evil influence and redirect their attention toward more wholesome activities supervised by adults. The front-line soldiers came from a cross-section of the most influential groups in Tulsa: city leaders, law enforcement, school officials, church pastors, the Parent Teachers Association, and the newspapers. The *World* didn't just cover these efforts, they took the initiative by using an undercover reporter to produce an exposé on a fairly new problem—marijuana.

Under a grammatically confusing headline, "Thrill-Seeking Tulsa Youths Blamed for Marijuana Evils," an unnamed *World* reporter went undercover to buy marijuana cigarettes with the intent to connect dope with "thrill-seeking youths" and the Kennamer case. But by the end of his story, the problem of marijuana use seemed to be more prevalent among adults than high school kids.

"It is the stimulant that builds a super-superiority complex and excites sex instinct. It is the stuff upon which hijackers whet their nerves for robbery and murder," the writer boldly began. "It is the drug that feeds on brain cells and ultimately transforms human beings into raging maniacs."

Ten years before, marijuana was completely unknown by Tulsans, the author reported. It first appeared on Tulsa streets around 1930, and had grown in popularity ever since. But as the writer quickly discovered, marijuana was hard to come by, thanks to the hysteria whipped up by the Gorrell murder.

"Events of the last two weeks—whether marijuana is involved with disclosures in the Kennamer case or not—have made the weed difficult for the novice to obtain, and peddlers who made from $6 to $10[2] a day have lost their aggressiveness [with] which they formerly plied their trade."

The article carefully explained to the uninitiated what marijuana was (a fast-growing weed reaching heights of four to sixteen feet), where it came from (India to Mexico to the southwestern United States), where it was grown (some locally, but the higher quality coming from Mexico), who was selling it ("mostly Mexicans, some Negroes"), how it was being used (rolled into cigarettes or filtered to make tea), and how much it cost (three cigarettes for 25¢ before the Kennamer-Gorrell case erupted, but double that price by the time the reporter went undercover, or a tobacco can full enough to make sixty cigarettes for a median $4.75), and who had laws against it (states most affected by that time, which were only Texas, Oklahoma, and Kansas, and there were no federal statutes). The problem was bad enough that the Tulsa police department had its own narcotics squad led by spectacle-and bow-tie-adorned Sgt. Francis McMillen.

When the reporter made the rounds of local peddlers to make his undercover purchases, he didn't get quite the sensationalistic results promised from the headline. At his first stop, to allay the seller's suspicion, the reporter was "forced to smoke part of it on the spot."

Unfamiliar with this new buyer, other skittish dope dealers wouldn't sell to him, or even admit they had any, and they sent him "from one place to another and in his rounds, [he] ended up at the source [where] he started." At one dealer, he arrived too late because a local orchestra, which played for one of the

---

2 The 2014 equivalent of $106 to $176, when adjusted for inflation.

many country-music dance halls in town, had bought up the entire supply.

With no connection in his story as yet made between marijuana and high school boys, he next went to Central High School and then the University of Tulsa, hoping to find stronger evidence of his premise. But it wasn't there. Officials at both schools were proactively working against the problem. Staff members at the 4,300-student high school, along with undercover investigators who'd been brought in, had found no evidence of the weed being sold or used in the building. To familiarize themselves with its distinctive smell, relevant members of the school staff fired up a joint obtained from the narcotics squad.

Principal Eli Foster admitted he had heard stories of wild conduct by high school students but dismissed them as nonsense. With the exception of some peddlers being arrested near the high school that spring of 1934, the rumor mill had painted another false picture.

"I have run down any number of these stories, and they are all just about as ridiculous as the one that was circulated to the effect that anyone who wanted it could buy liquor on the third floor of the high school building," Principal Foster told the reporter. "And I want to say, with some heat, that although I have heard any number of such stories I have yet to find anyone who can offer one iota of proof of those that have been circulated."

At the University of Tulsa, a problem had existed there until the crackdown came that spring on peddlers dealing to high school students. After that, the dealers avoided the university, as well as any other school.

Undaunted by his inability to find direct evidence between dope peddlers and teenagers, the reporter ended his article with narcotics squad Sgt. Francis McMillen's theory that "marijuana only became a problem when peddlers began to find a new market among young men." Apparently, adults didn't have a problem with it; they weren't the ones overcome with sexual excitement and raging madness. Despite all the public interest with the Kennamer-Gorrell case, and the far-out rumors in its orbit, it all came back to an out-of-control youth and a writer who ended his story with an unproven hypothesis: "Young men and boys, looking for a new expression for modern youth hysteria—a new thrill—that, says the sergeant, is the big problem."

The earlier campaign to drive marble machines away from schools met with success when operators, sensing public opinion was against them, voluntarily agreed to move them away. But the precursor to the pinball machine wasn't the only demon that needed to be exorcised. More were named, and new battalions came forward to join the fight.

The county-wide Christian Endeavor League took direct aim at what one headline called "Tulsa's Lax Morals." The group led a meeting that began with a strong message: "We declare open warfare upon the vicious narcotic ring closing in upon the youth and the red coterie of bootleggers who are peddling hard liquor."

The meeting, which included one hundred young people in attendance, adopted the slogan, "Make Tulsa Youth Christian," and planned to print up and distribute ten thousand windshield stickers with the new message. They, like the *World*'s article on marijuana, connected their "war" with the Kennamer-Gorrell case. "We are alarmed at the lack of moral and spiritual sensibilities among the youth of our generation, as revealed in general by the common, every day observations and in particular *by recent developments*," the group proclaimed in a new covenant.

Emboldened by their success at moving marble machines away from schools, the PTA focused next on: "Salacious magazines, gambling, marble machines (complete banning), firearms, and burlesque theaters and taverns."

Their fixation on firearms had about as much to do with John Gorrell's murder as it did with a campaign by the National PTA that year "to take murder out of the nursery" by banning toy guns. "We must do away with pernicious games of 'cops and robbers,'" declared one officer of the organization. To accomplish this, the group sought pledges from schoolchildren to stop playing the make-believe game, and surrender their toy weapons peacefully.

As amusing as that might seem, it had ironic relevance for Tulsans in December of 1934, which saw a rash of headline-making deaths after Born's suicide, one of which was caused by children playing with guns. Carl Pulliam, seventeen, was playing poker with sixteen-year-old Paul Lumary and three other boys in a vacant building the young gang frequented, when a quarrel erupted. Lumary started waving a pistol around. Claiming that he "didn't know the pistol was loaded," Lumary said the gun "accidentally" fired a bullet into Pulliam's neck, mortally wounding him. Both he and Pulliam were on parole for a burglary conviction, and two of the other three young teenage boys were also parolees from juvenile court.

Other deaths, all coming within a few short days of each other, unsettled Tulsans. These included a farmer who died in a fight, the suicide of a prominent real estate man, the murder of a wealthy Claremore café owner by a twenty-year-old ex-convict, and the mysterious murder of Robert Sample, a forty-year-old, unemployed, department-store clerk, who was found face-down in a pool of water in an abandoned coal mine a few miles west of Tulsa. Rumors quickly tried to connect Sample's death with the Kennamer case, but this was sharply denied by authorities, who discovered Sample had just recently moved to Tulsa from Texas to live with his sisters after losing his job. His murder was never solved.

Motivated by all the recent deaths caused by guns, Oscar Hoop proposed that city commissioners pass local gun registration laws, and he also drafted an ordinance himself for mandatory licensing of bicycles. The bicycle licenses, just like the gun registrations, would require fees, which seems to be what Hoop was really after.

"If such a plan can be financed, I will put on eight or ten additional men to stamp out both juvenile and adult crime," Hoop told city leaders. But few in local government were listening to him by that time. He'd already lowered the salaries of many police officers when he divided them into three tiers based on an intelligence test, and that had made him very unpopular.

A month after he made the proposal to license guns and bicycles, Hoop's desire to prevent local dance halls from serving beer was shot down when it was pointed out that beer licenses were governed by the state. He then reversed his proposal and asked city leaders to reject applicants who applied for dance hall permits while holding a state beer license. That idea was also quickly dismissed, despite his public temper tantrum during the meeting.

In spite of his failures, police were already cracking down on illegal gambling joints, as well as establishments that sold beer to minors. Densil West, proprietor of the Sunset Café in the heart of the Jelly Bean Center, was arrested for that same reason. He was given a sixty-day jail sentence and fined one hundred dollars for selling beer to kids under eighteen. Other highly publicized raids by police and deputies showed the crackdown was having the desired effect.

As eager as everyone was to wage war on perceived outlets of evil influence, a few also recognized that banning something wasn't always the answer. On Thursday afternoon of December 20, a teen dance was held at Central High School for the first time in fourteen years.

"It was the answer of the school authorities to the beer halls, honky-tonks, and the places where students have learned to spend leisure time among companions of questionable character," the *Tribune* reported. By offering dances at the schools, parents and educators saw they could control a social activity their children enjoyed. When the school board banned them in 1920, it had never stopped young people from dancing; it only forced them to hold their own dances somewhere else, which is exactly why the Hy-Hat Club was formed in the first place.

The Central High dance was wildly popular. One hundred fifty tickets were handed out for an estimated one thousand requests. Two days later, a *Tribune* columnist applauded the "courageous step" with high praise, and revealed the backward prejudices that had led to the logic behind banning them in the first place.

"There has been, in this town, for a number of years, a bigoted prejudice on the part of a small percentage of the population against dancing in general," the writer began. "They hold to the ancient idea, inherited from the time of Pilgrims, that dancing is evil. The idea belongs to the same era as the belief that it is a sin to kiss your wife on Sunday, or own a deck of cards, or eat pasty-cake without first shaking it to get the devils out of it."

Other clubs and churches saw the wisdom behind this new thinking and began sponsoring social events for young people and planning dances of their own.

But the *Tribune* wasn't the only newspaper with an opinion. Across the country, newspaper editors observed what was occurring in Tulsa, and the reviews were not good. The editors of the *World* read these sanctimonious articles and editorials and saw what was happening. They looked out over their city, and it began to dawn on them that things were getting out hand. Rumor had replaced fact. Hysteria had replaced common sense. The city was besieged by an overreaction of its own making.

During the latter half of December, the *World* published several opinion pieces calling for a return to normalcy. The first of these appeared the day of Kennamer's preliminary hearing under the title, "Denouncing Tulsa."

"In consequence of the Kennamer-Gorrell-Born case, we notice a rather prevalent newspaper disposition to include all Tulsa in denunciations. . . . The indirect intimations are that Tulsa society as a whole, and youth in particular, are corrupt."

The editorial went on to point out that Tulsa kids were probably no worse than the children anywhere else. "The 'gilded youth' idea is naturally played up [by other newspapers] in this Tulsa upheaval. We would call attention to the fact that bad conditions are likely to develop anywhere, in any grade of society . . . it is to the credit of Tulsa youth that its general moral and intellectual average is high."

On December 28, the *World* published two more opinion pieces that highlighted the public's hysteria, and cautioned against it. The first editorial, "Tulsa Youth," revisited the 'gilded youth' idea and called for a fair and balanced examination of the entire case.

"When all the facts are in, and the whole episode is calmly analyzed, most of us will be surprised at the smallness of the number of young people who actually have been contaminated or damaged by a few."

The paper then went on to admit that despite its own investigative report that attempted to connect widespread marijuana usage among young people, most of them "know very little about these dope cigarettes."

On that same page, the *World* devoted a separate editorial to "Rumors." "In the last three weeks, Tulsa has developed the rumor habit; it is a bad and disagreeable habit. The mortality list of Dame Rumor has been very large and almost anyone can start a 'sensation' about something."

Tulsa citizens were asked to be more careful about judging the rumors they heard, and not to pass them on or embellish them. "There is a strange weakness in human nature, which makes the peddling of bad news a delight to many people, and many are not any too particular how they get their sensational fodder," the editorial keenly pointed out.

But Phil Kennamer was the gift that that kept on giving. His unrelenting desire to manipulate, communicate, and influence events would once again backfire on him—just as it would for Sgt. Maddux. And as the police would soon discover, their chief investigator had a dirty little secret of his own.

Chapter Thirteen

A FEW DAYS AFTER KENNAMER surrendered, *Tulsa World* photographer Lee Krupnick took several photographs of him that appeared in newspapers across the country. The wire services, as well as the *World*, were clamoring for photos of the federal judge's son charged with first degree murder. Always friendly and personable, Krupnick chatted with Kennamer not as a man in jail, but as a contemporary and fellow newsman since, as a cub reporter for the *Daily Oklahoman*, Kennamer had gotten to know *World* reporter Pat Burgess and was an intimate friend of ex-reporter Preston Cochrane.

"I had never known Phil until then," Krupnick later said, "although I had photographed him. But we wanted some better pictures. Phil asked me to bring the prints back and show them to him so he could pick the ones he liked."

After visiting with Kennamer a second time, the two had another long and friendly discussion. At the end of their conversation, Kennamer asked Krupnick if he would obtain for him a photograph of his friend, Homer Wilcox Jr. This simple appeal by Kennamer was the genesis for a series of events that would bring intrigue, coded messages, and secret meetings to the case. For Kennamer, the request was a test of his capacity to enlist Krupnick into his confidence, and if he would respond to his manipulation.

Krupnick was not one to take chances. After agreeing to bring the photograph, he took the elevator to the first floor, walked into Sheriff Charlie Price's office, and told him what his star prisoner requested. "They told me to go ahead, but to put a pin hole in the picture so it would be identified in [the] event Kennamer might tamper with it," Krupnick continued.

When Krupnick returned with the photograph on December 17, he and Kennamer had another long chat. They talked about Sidney Born's death, and Kennamer confided to Krupnick the name of a Tulsa boy whom he believed had murdered his friend and witness in the case. Krupnick, privy to the police investigators' theories, and the coroner, who steadfastly maintained it had been a suicide, asked Kennamer: why that boy? Why would he murder Born?

"Phil was silent for a moment, [and] then he made a jump at me and I was scared. But he only grabbed my pencil out of my pocket and went to the corner of the room.

"'You stay over there, Lee,' he said. 'Leave me alone for a few minutes.'

"Pretty soon he came over and gave me a folded piece of paper. 'Give that to Cochrane,' he said. 'Tell him I said 3-2. Don't forget to tell him I said 3-2.'"

In the elevator, Krupnick unfolded the note and saw it was a coded message:

FCQYHFHRHQGQQSDV

Once again, Krupnick found himself in the sheriff's office. There, deputies copied the message, and later that night Krupnick deciphered it.

Can we depend on Pat?

When Kennamer said "3-2," he was giving away the key to decode the message. The 3-2 system was a code developed by Cochrane while he was a student in Vienna, Austria, in 1933. At the time, the Nazi uprising in Germany had created tension there. Fearing their messages to each other would be read by authorities, Preston and Phil used the numerical code to communicate with each other. To decipher the first letter, the coded message's receiver would substitute the letter three places before it in the alphabet. To decipher the second letter, one would count two spaces back. Then, the decipher repeats again as three before the intended letter, and then two, and so on.

The "Pat" the message referred to was *Tulsa World* newspaper reporter Pat Burgess, who had introduced Kennamer to John Gorrell in late August. Cochrane also once worked with Burgess and Krupnick but quit the *World* that October. Kennamer was insisting that Gorrell had made the kidnapping proposal to Burgess and Cochrane *before* he had ever met Gorrell. As part of his defense, Kennamer wanted them to testify that the kidnapping plan was all Gorrell's idea.

Realizing Kennamer may have created a trap for himself, Sheriff Price took this information to Anderson, who then called for a secret midnight meeting at the Mayo Hotel. With Anderson, Price, two deputies, and Krupnick in attendance, a plot was hatched for the photographer to continue operating as a secret courier for Kennamer and Cochrane in the hopes that it might reveal valuable information that could be used at Kennamer's trial. Anderson told Krupnick that his participation in their scheme would "render the state a valuable service by following Kennamer's wishes in the matter." Anderson then informed J. Berry King, who approved of the operation, and the *World* backed their photographer, knowing they might get the best scoop of the entire case.

Once again, Kennamer chose to forgo his lawyer's advice, and authorities dismissed his father's request that only attorneys and family could see his son. In spite of this, it was still Sheriff Price's jail—the same Sheriff Price that Judge Kennamer had locked up several years before during Prohibition.

Preston Cochrane was the son of a corporate attorney for one of the local oil companies. He was a handsome young man, with high cheekbones, a strong jawline, and a full head of hair he parted on the left. He wore fashionable glasses and dressed in expensive clothes that rested stylishly on his slender frame. He enjoyed poetry and read many books, and although he was extremely intelligent, his soft and agreeable manner was no match for the domineering personality of Phil Kennamer. And with many of those same characteristics, neither were Sidney Born or Homer Wilcox Jr., who was just seventeen. Phil Kennamer had a unique way of selecting friends who were passive and pliable. Applying these criteria, he seemed to believe Krupnick was the same sort.

Together, Kennamer and Cochrane started an advertising agency, but like many of Phil's endeavors, he quickly grew tired of it, and they later sold their accounts to another agency. Before Cochrane went to work with the *Tulsa World*, the two traveled parts of the United States together and stayed in hotels under aliases. Cochrane was known as "Douglas Montgomery Blair," while Kennamer traveled as "Richard Barnard."

On December 20, Krupnick delivered the note to Cochrane. At first, Cochrane wanted the photographer to deliver his message orally, but Krupnick convinced him to put the message in writing "because Phil will know your writing."

Cautious, Cochrane replied to Kennamer:

BGVKVCITDKGJHYLNOIHVLPLVEUUPWJLU

This translated to: "Yes, is afraid he [Pat Burgess] will get mixed in this. Burn this."

Embracing his new secret-agent role, Krupnick was a master manipulator himself and persuaded Cochrane, that very day, to write another note to Kennamer, and to mark it with his signature.

"I'm for you, you know that," Cochrane wrote in code. "Would have been up to see you but Moss says not now. Law thinks I know something and are [watching] me. (GJE)."

The initials *GJE* stood for *DMB*, or *Douglas Montgomery Blair*, which Cochrane reluctantly added after he was persuaded to do so by Krupnick. If the notes later made it into evidence at trial, authorities wanted there to be no doubt who was behind them.[1]

To ensure the secrecy of their little conspiracy, the sheriff's department took an active role by posing as lookouts. When Krupnick was with Kennamer, Sheriff Price positioned himself near the elevator doors on the ground floor, where he kept an eye on anyone going up to the jail. In the sheriff's office, Chief Deputy John Evans watched for Price's signal. If one of the defense attorneys or a family member was going up to see Kennamer, Evans was ready to transmit a signal using the jail buzzer. Upstairs, jailer Tony Benson was ready to receive the signal. Benson would then knock on Kennamer's door, which was the signal to Krupnick, to advise him that a visitor was coming up to see him. Knowing that this was potential evidence, they also took photostatic copies of all the correspondence.

The fourth note passed, from Kennamer to Cochrane, turned into an all-out forgery by the crafty Krupnick. When pressed to write it, Kennamer also wanted Krupnick to deliver it orally since he too believed the exchange of notes was getting too risky. In order to continue the sham, Krupnick typed out Kennamer's message on his typewriter at *World* offices. But instead of passing along Kennamer's caution, he removed those statements and substituted phrases that encouraged continuance of the whole note-passing affair:

> Stay away from reporters. Lee is okay. Other birds are swine. Give me more facts. Don't worry I will burn your answers. I am doubtful about Pat. He might talk. Give me actual low-down. I have lots to confide you. Tell me all. Be sure and typewrite. Don't ever write. We sure can

---

[1] *GJE* doesn't follow the 3-2 pattern. However, *GJE* was the code used for his alias, Douglas Montgomery Blair, on prior occasions, but with a different cipher. Cochrane was hoping to obfuscate his connection to the notes, and he knew Kennamer would understand *GJE*.

depend on Lee. A real pal. What's doing? You know what I mean. Hurry with your answer. Keep your chin up fellow.

When the note was delivered on December 21, Cochrane was naturally suspicious because it had been typed instead of written. Krupnick explained that a typewriter was available in the room adjoining Kennamer's, which was actually true. When the two met up again in a downtown café on December 22, paranoid that he was being watched, Cochrane put his reply in a matchbox that he passed to Krupnick under the table. It read:

> These better stop for few days. Am being watched. Pat won't talk but won't go on stand for defense. Wants to stay clear out of it. Who is trying to spot me? Why, I am for you Sweetheart. We'll win in the end.

But that's not the note Krupnick delivered. Instead, he substituted a typewritten note in which the phrase "these better stop for few days. Am being watched," was eliminated.

After delivering Cochrane's message, he returned to the matron's room on the morning of December 23 to find Kennamer still in bed, sleeping.

"Lee, bring me my trousers," Kennamer said when he woke. "Tell Cochrane 3-5." From one of the pockets, he handed Krupnick a typewritten note that read:

> I know you are with me. Don't think I'll forget it. After I am sprung we are going to sue every paper in the United States. Forget it now though. Vital Pat takes stand. You received a letter from Gorrell in November. Keep your chin up, Sweetheart.[2]

---

[2] Kennamer would later assert that it was the *Tulsa World* who inserted the word *Sweetheart* in both messages "to inject an element of eroticism into the case."

When Cochrane was ready with his reply, they met once again at the café on the evening of December 24.

> Merry Christmas. Don't understand about Snedden except that he tried to frame me. Same one, I know who. My chin's up. How's yours? - XXXXXXXXXX

According to Krupnick's account of the whole affair he later explained in a newspaper article, *Snedden* referred to Jack Snedden, and was a reference to a conversation between Cochrane and the photographer.

"Cochrane told me he didn't like Snedden, and that Snedden didn't like him," Krupnick later explained. "I thought I might get some information by mentioning Snedden, so I told Cochrane that Phil said 'Snedden is talking too much, be careful,' but nothing came of it."

When Krupnick delivered the message to the prisoner later that Christmas Eve, Kennamer cautioned him not to come the next day because his family would be present. When he returned the day after, Krupnick came with the idea of unraveling the story behind the letter that Gorrell supposedly wrote Cochrane in November. When he got there, he told Kennamer that Cochrane was worried about the letter from Gorrell.

"I was sitting on the bed and Phil was sitting in the rocker," Krupnick later recalled. "Phil became very quiet and for at least three minutes he sat with his head on his hands, saying nothing. Then he looked at me in the eye and said, 'Listen, you tell him not to worry about that Gorrell letter, that I will say that he lost it. Be sure to tell him Pat must take the stand.'"

Krupnick then tried to convince Kennamer to put that in writing but he refused, and instead the photographer received an eighth message that was not in code.

> Skip matter of epistle [referring to Gorrell's letter], find out if Pat hasn't been 'contacted' by someone from the

gang which is out to get me. Keep your chin up and don't worry.—K

But Krupnick didn't deliver that message, and once again, he concocted a different one, with the knowledge of county authorities and his bosses at the newspaper. "Don't worry about Gorrell letter. I will say you lost it. You and Pat be sure and take the stand."

It was the last note that would ever be delivered after Kennamer let something slip to his chief counsel, who put a stop to it. On January 3, a small portion of the entire affair appeared in the *Tulsa World* when Moss, seeking to do damage control, spoke of it to reporters. Moss said it was further proof that his client "was not entirely responsible for his 'whimsical actions,'" the paper reported. It supported the defense's theory, Moss added, that Kennamer was unbalanced.

"I have not seen the notes but Phil told me about them Sunday [December 30] in a way that indicated he was boasting of his shrewdness," Moss said. "As far as I have been able to learn, these notes contained nothing incriminating or of any relevance [where] the slaying proper is concerned. Kennamer is entirely out of hand."

He was right that the whole scheme had not produced anything that would incriminate his client, and even the county attorney had to agree. For those who still believed Kennamer had an accomplice on the outside who would have been revealed in the notes, that ghostly figure remained elusive.

Within that same article was confirmation by Fire and Police Commissioner Oscar Hoop during a public meeting with city commissioners that Sgt. Maddux was offered a bribe for the staggering amount of $25,000.[3] As he had already shown in the past, Maddux's proclamation inflamed the story line and fed into city-wide beliefs of a conspiracy. Or, at the very least, it

---

[3] The 2014 equivalent of $443,000, when adjusted for inflation.

insinuated that the Kennamer family was behind it, which they weren't.

"[In December], I was informed by Sergeant Maddux that he had been offered $25,000 to discontinue his investigation along certain lines in a criminal case, that he had declined, and that the person making the offer then said he would be obliged to use other means to stop further inquiry," Hoop said. Although he had been careful not to mention *which* criminal case it was during a public meeting, privately, everyone knew what he meant, and that it tied back to earlier bribe reports in the newspapers. Hoop also told city leaders that Maddux claimed only a little more evidence was needed before he could make an arrest.

"I directed Maddux to submit this statement to me in writing," Hoop continued, "and I have filed his written statement with my own affidavit in a safe deposit box. In case of an 'accident,' these papers and others relating to the case in question will be sufficient for the police to place in custody the persons involved, although the case is not yet complete."

But it is what Hoop said next that was most intriguing to reporters and commissioners, and if the newspapers knew what it was, they didn't dare report on it.

"A few days later, letters and papers alleging misconduct by Maddux in another part of the country some years before were turned over to me by Mayor Penney," Hoop said. "It is evident that every effort will be made to discredit this officer and secure his removal from further participation in the work in which he is now engaged. These facts are submitted to you so you may be fully informed in case further efforts are made to prejudice the commission against Maddux, and also as a distinct warning to others of our purpose."

And there it was. Maddux's past had come back to haunt him. In 1924 he was employed as a deputy state game warden in northern Texas. That was the year the twenty-five-year-old began a love affair with Annabelle Barker, a twenty-three-year-old divorcée from Elk City, Oklahoma. In late August, the two lovebirds embarked on a romantic getaway that took them through southeastern Oklahoma and down to the Texas Panhandle. While in Elk City, the happy couple told Annabelle's sister they were going to Shamrock, Texas.

But there was just one problem Annabelle didn't know about. Henry Bailess Maddux had a wife and three young children in Decatur, Texas. During her husband's romantic escapade, his wife Clara got word of the affair, left town on Wednesday, September 3, and traveled to Elk City to confront her husband's mistress. When she arrived, she spoke with Annabelle's sister, who told her the couple had already left for Shamrock. Furious, twenty-six-year-old Clara bought a .32-caliber, hammerless pistol before leaving town. But when she got to Shamrock, she was told that her husband and his female companion had driven farther south to Childress.

Clara rented a car and drove from Shamrock fifty-seven miles southwest to Memphis, Texas, where she boarded a train that took her the last thirty-one miles to Childress.

After walking two blocks from the railroad station down Second Street, Clara saw her husband leaning against his car, reading a letter in front of the Nave Hotel. Sitting in the passenger's seat was his mistress. Neither one of them saw her coming.

Recognizing the woman from a photograph she had obtained, Clara walked up to the driver's-side window, pointed the pistol at her husband's mistress, and shot her twice at point-blank range. The first bullet entered Annabelle's left temple and came out two inches behind her right ear. The second entered her body from the left and tore through her heart. Maddux acted fast and ripped the pistol out of his wife's grip before she could take another shot. He then carried his unsuspecting lover into the hotel. She died without saying a word or even knowing why it had happened.

Clara was quickly arrested but was released the next day on a $2,000 bond paid by family and friends who came to her aid. The Childress County prosecutor had Maddux arrested and charged with violation of the Mann Act, which made it a federal crime to cross state lines with "any woman or girl for the purpose of prostitution or debauchery, or for any other immoral purpose."

He was certainly guilty of that, and Maddux was immediately fired from his job. The outcome of the charge against him is unclear. His soon-to-be ex-wife went on trial in late January 1925, and after three days of testimony and twenty-two minutes of deliberation, she was acquitted of murder. To escape the mess he'd left, the former Marine Corps private moved to Colorado, where he joined the National Guard and was promoted to captain. Later, he attended Northwestern University, where he studied criminology for two years. He then took a job as an assistant criminologist in Phoenix, before he was hired in January 1934 by Hoop, who made it his mission to hire intelligent new officers. While living in Tulsa, the 1935 city directory indicates he was married to a woman named Eleanor. His three children remained with their mother, who eventually remarried.

Maddux had apparently left that whole wife-killing-his-mistress business out of the hiring process, because it was news to both Mayor Penney and Hoop when it reached them ten years later. In spite of this, Hoop was still standing by his man. For now.

WHEN KENNAMER WAS BOUND OVER for trial in district court, his case was assigned to Judge Thurman Hurst. Then as now, rural Pawnee County was included with Tulsa County to make up the Twenty-First District Court of Oklahoma.[4] Hurst was born in Cassville, Missouri, in 1889 and

---

[4] Now the 14th District.

moved to Oklahoma in 1892 with his parents, who later settled on a farm five miles south of Pawnee, the seat of Pawnee County. After high school, he enrolled at the University of Oklahoma's law school in 1909, graduated in 1911, and was admitted to the bar in 1912, without having to finish the bar exam due to a state supreme court decision which came while he and other students were in the middle of taking the test. Halfway through the exam, the announcement was made, and every student in the room got up and walked out.

After receiving his license to practice law, Hurst worked both in private practice and as a county attorney. He was elected district judge for Pawnee County in 1930 and was just beginning his second term in January 1935.

Judge Hurst was small-statured, and it appeared to others as if his black robe had swallowed him. He had a reputation for being fair and honest, but also stern, and he was held in high esteem by his colleagues and by attorneys who tried cases before him.

"Around the courthouse," the *Tribune* reported, "you will learn that Judge Hurst gets all the 'dirty work.' By that, they mean, that because he lives in Pawnee, he tries almost all the cases involving Tulsa governmental questions and important business interests."

Tasked with hearing cases both in Tulsa County and in the new $125,000 courthouse recently completed in Pawnee, Judge Hurst spent a lot of his time traveling the nearly sixty miles each way. He was often late to arrive for his own hearings and proceedings in Tulsa.

And so it was on January 5, when he arrived forty minutes late for an arraignment of thirty-nine prisoners, which included Kennamer and five other accused murderers. Once again, "a record throng of spectators [was] in the courtroom, all straining for a sight of the prisoner and principal in Tulsa's most startling slaying," the *World* reported. Two large officers had to push and shove onlookers aside so Judge Hurst could make his way into his own courtroom. While the thirty-eight other prisoners were all marched in and out together, Kennamer was escorted in by himself.

Dr. Gorrell was there, as he had been in every proceeding, a guardian of justice for his murdered son. No one from Kennamer's family attended his second arraignment. Reporters noted that he appeared more "pallid" and stoic, and had lost that cocksure attitude displayed previously. By looking at him, those in attendance could tell he was a special case; he was the only one wearing a clean, newly pressed suit. A small white tissue with a spot of red revealed that he had just shaved prior to coming to court.

In spite of rumors published the day before that Kennamer would plead guilty and seek an insanity hearing, he was sticking to *his* story, not his attorneys. He wasn't guilty of anything—it was self-defense.

As the other defendants remained, two guards escorted him out of the courtroom and back up to his quarters. Later that day, his court date was announced by Anderson. Phil Kennamer would go on trial for the murder of John Gorrell on Monday, January 28. Moss had three weeks left to prepare for a case made more difficult by his inability to reach Phil's friends who didn't want to talk to his legal team.

He wasn't prepared.

Chapter Fourteen

BY LATE DECEMBER AND EARLY January, Tulsa's high-profile murder case was just starting to get traction in newspapers around the world. Four days before Christmas, the *Tribune* received an urgent teletype from the head offices of the International News Services.

"ANYTHING NEW LATEST TULSA SHOOTING? EUROPEAN CABLES PRESSING."

Newspapers in Australia, England, Germany, and France were reporting on the case, some of them emphasizing the more titillating aspects to their readers, as well as getting many of the simplest facts wrong or inventing new ones. One Australian newspaper, which came to the story late, titled their article, "Sinister Orgy." But this was not just any kind of orgy Tulsa youth were involved in, the paper reported, but a "Bacchanalian Orgy."

In Flemington, New Jersey, Bruno Richard Hauptmann's trial got underway on January 3, 1935, and would last until February 13. Newspapers across the country, including the *World* and the *Tribune*, devoted hundreds of column inches each day to the story, with trial coverage that quoted participants, comparable to an official trial transcript. Very little was left out, and readers soaked it up. Everywhere but Tulsa, the Phil Kennamer story was pushed into the background. If his was Tulsa's "most sensational case in more than a decade," then the Hauptmann trial was being deemed America's "Trial of the Century."

The gossip and rumors never went away, and the murder was still a topic of conversation in homes and barber shops, in taxicabs and rotary club meetings. Although the story had lost its initial fervor, everyone had an opinion and freely expressed it when asked. The secondary narrative of wild, out-of-control, rich kids was slowly melting away locally but continued to be played up nationally by the likes of International News Service and King Features, which published sensational stories that hinted at unmentionable goings-on, with a *wink-wink* from writers crafting a story that met with modesty standards for 1935.

All of the social events and hanging out after movies for members of the Hy-Hat Club and their contemporaries came to a crashing halt after Born committed suicide. An Associated Press article dated January 16 summed up the situation best.

> Tulsa—In casual meetings and through the sittings of social and other clubs, hundreds of questions fly to and fro, causing dissension and enmity in some but testifying to the nervousness that remains, particularly in the wealthy south side, where the principals and most of the witnesses live.
>
> Out at Eighteenth Street and Boston Avenue, known as the "Jelly Bean Center" for years, the youths no longer gather in the evenings. The Quaker Drug Store closes early. Uniformed waitresses no longer answer yodeling horns on the automobiles of sons and daughters of the wealthy, parked at the curb before, after and between movie performances and dances. Tulsa's sons and daughters are staying pretty close to home.
>
> Next door at the Owl Tavern, the lights stay on fairly late, but the customers are few and they do not linger around the beer bar and the cigar counter as of old. And a block away, the Sunset Café feeds a few customers, and then is barred for the night.
>
> Those places swarmed with youngsters two months ago.

It was a similar story when the new sheriff, Garland Marrs, grabbed some deputies and raided all the nightclubs on "Roadhouse Row." Before taking office, he had publicly announced that he was giving all roadhouse operators a "fair chance to get within the law before arrests were made." They took his advice. The gambling tables were put in storage, the liquor hidden, and the dancing girls, some of them advertised as wearing only cellophane, were sent home.

The moral crusade had been a success.

It was true that most of Tulsa's young society set were keeping a low profile. Their parents were anxious to keep the family name out of what they saw as a corrosive scandal. To support his defense strategy that Kennamer was insane, Moss wanted to gather up all the wacky stories on the boy that he could. To do this, he had to talk to all the young people that knew him.

"There must be anywhere from thirty to fifty in the younger set who can testify about Kennamer's actions, some of the crazy things that fellow did, but they won't come in. They say, 'See my attorney,'" Moss told the Associated Press. "And some of those lawyers won't let them talk to me. They don't want their names mixed up in a murder case."

This blockade led Moss to hint that he was not prepared for trial, and he might be forced to request a postponement. His tactic to reach them had been simple; he hired key witness Robert Thomas as his ambassador to persuade his contemporaries to come in. "I wanted Robert to bring in the young folks to help build up the defense case," Moss said. Even though he was paid four dollars a day, Thomas wasn't very successful in finding anyone who wanted to come to Kennamer's defense. Whether they liked him or hated him, Phil was poison.

Although Moss couldn't gather as much anecdotal evidence as he sought, he did get what he wanted from two psychiatrists. During that second week of January, they sat down with

Kennamer and interviewed him over several sessions. Doctor Karl Menninger was able to make it in and out of town with hardly anyone knowing he'd been there. But his opinion of Kennamer found its way into newspapers, where he was quoted as saying that Kennamer was "legally insane." However, "legally insane" wasn't necessarily a medical diagnosis. The terminology Dr. Menninger would use to describe Kennamer's mental affliction would have to wait until the trial.

But Oklahoma City psychiatrist and Kennamer family friend, Dr. Eugen Werner, was not shy about expressing his medical opinion. Judge Kennamer personally requested he examine his son. After several interviews with Phil that took place that same week, Dr. Werner shed some light on the thinking process of John Gorrell Jr's killer.

"He thinks he is right and everyone else is wrong and has it in for him. . . . Under the definition that a man is demented unless he knows right from wrong, Phil is legally insane. He thinks he is right and everyone else is wrong," Werner told reporters.

Something seemed to have changed in the prosecution's attitude immediately after the defense psychiatrists' opinions were published. When County Attorney Holly Anderson read the AP story, he scoffed and grunted. "A very interesting hypothesis," he said of Dr. Werner's judgment. "We will show that there is no legal or medical basis for such a finding."

He might have been feeling outgunned. Moss was a gifted attorney with more than thirty years of experience. He knew all the tricks of both the prosecution and defense, having worked both sides. He was a powerful presence in the local legal community and had successfully defended several high-profile murder defendants. In a 1979 interview, former court reporter Sadie Gelfand described him as a gentleman who walked tall and proud. During a difficult part of any case he was involved in, he had a peculiar habit he employed to irritate his adversaries.

"He had some coins in his pocket and [would] jiggle them," Gelfand recalled. "He'd sit at the counsel table and play with the coins. That was a trademark of his. I guess he did it more to confuse than anything else."

In a one-on-one contest in the courtroom, Anderson was no match for Moss. Anderson was a politician, not a trial lawyer. After serving as mayor of nearby Sand Springs for six years, he ran for and was elected county attorney, always a two-year term in Oklahoma during those days. He had just begun his second term that January. During his first term, he reportedly left the bulk of all trial cases to his assistants, who had far more criminal courtroom experience than he did.

But it was never going to come down to just those two men. Each side had assembled their own dream team of courtroom brawlers. Anderson's chief assistant was old veteran Tom Wallace, an attorney with thirty years of experience, seventeen of them in the CA's office. By his estimate, he had tried more than one hundred murder cases, more than any other lawyer for either side. He'd gone up against Moss in a murder trial before and beat him. Wallace had secured one of the few death sentences in Tulsa courts up to that time when he sent James Hargus to the chair for killing a city detective, and he'd also sent Arthur "Doc" Barker to prison for life for killing a hospital security guard in 1922, only to see him paroled ten years later.

Anderson was undoubtedly grateful to have former state Attorney General J. Berry King on board. Although he was a lawyer turned politician, and the state's top prosecutor for five years, he was a force to be reckoned with as special prosecutor.

However, even with Wallace and King, the prosecution was still outmatched. Assisting Moss, with an even bigger legal reputation than his, or King's, or Wallace's, was Charles Stuart, with fifty-six years of practicing law. From 1893 to 1895, Stuart served as a federal judge for Indian Territory.

But the defense team didn't stop there. It also included Judge Kennamer's old law partner, Charles Coakley, who had four decades of legal experience, and Herman Young, with nearly twenty years of experience working both sides of the courtroom.

Anderson was likely cognizant of the fact that the integrity of courtroom justice in his time was questionable. Juries were different too, often taking a direct middle road, judging fairly but also sometimes leaning toward the defendant in many instances, depending on the crime. They often viewed them as misguided men who had stumbled accidentally into crime and were worthy of forgiveness and a second chance. And when it came to female defendants, acquittals were notoriously common, even when there was no reasonable doubt. If they were convicted, their sentences were exceptionally light.

It was also the era of long sentences by stern judges and early releases enabled by parole brokers who negotiated paroles, pardons, and clemency under often-corrupt circumstances. By December 28, a few weeks before he left office, Governor William Murray's clemency count was more than 2,400 criminals, which included 372 murderers, 324 robbers, and 813 liquor violators.[1] The *Tulsa World*, a Republican-leaning newspaper at the time, was keeping track.

Aware of all this, and possibly intimidated by the defense team and the boy's father, Anderson launched a misguided attack against Moss with a public accusation of witness tampering. After a conference with King, Anderson told newspaper reporters in mid-January that "efforts had been made to tamper with Floyd Huff." In addition to this claim, Anderson said he had proof that "approaches" had been made to two other state witnesses.

With pumped-up outrage and ambiguity, Anderson claimed, "We are not, at this time, going to make full public disclosure of

---

[1] An Associated Press article from 1939 gave a much lower figure for Murray, with 920 pardons and paroles. Without knowing the methodology that was used, it's hard to know which figure is accurate.

these 'tampering' movements. We are not mistaken and neither is Huff. We are positive that overtures have been made to Huff, who promptly refused to have anything do with this lawyer."

In his next statement, Anderson contradicted himself within two sentences. "We have not yet learned the reactions of these other two witnesses. We are not indulging in any guesswork and won't stand for any more nonsense of this sort. If this doesn't stop immediately, someone is going to be arrested and prosecuted."

Like Maddux, King, and Hoop before him, Anderson had thrown gasoline on the fire of public perception of the defense. New excitement was injected into the local gossip.

As inflammatory as it was, there were problems with his statement. The incident with Huff took place before the preliminary hearing and was no incident at all. Two unidentified attorneys from Tulsa, working for the defense, traveled to Kansas City to interview Huff about his time with Kennamer. A Kansas City paper falsely reported that Huff claimed the two men asked him to change his testimony. When Anderson questioned him about it after the preliminary hearing, Huff said it wasn't true, and that the men talked with him about his upcoming testimony, but had not asked him to change it. The conversation was short. "Huff says he did not talk with them long enough to give them any information," Anderson said after the December 17 hearing to reporters.

Fast-forward one month, and Anderson used that incident as the basis for his witness-tampering allegation. He also refused to name the other two individuals, and oddly claimed that although there was no guesswork about it, he didn't know the reactions of these two other witnesses to the alleged tampering.

Naturally, reporters ran to Moss to get his reaction, and he immediately backed Anderson into a corner with a challenge to prosecute.

"I don't want any mystery in this case," Moss declared. "If anyone has approached Huff [to change his testimony] that person was guilty of a crime and I challenge Anderson to arrest him and prosecute him."

He then dared Anderson to name the other two witnesses. The following day, Anderson's published reply to Moss was to name Sgt. Maddux and Robert Thomas, and he repeated his threat to prosecute.

"So that's it?" Moss replied when he heard about it. "Mr. Anderson's conduct in this case is wretched and contemptible." The purported bribe-offer claim by Sgt. Maddux, and the violence he alluded to, was a pot that hadn't yet boiled over. Naming Robert Thomas as the other witness was just an outright lie, Moss declared. He wasn't "tampering" with Robert Thomas, he had hired the young man to act as a liaison between the defense team and Phil's friends who didn't want to get involved.

"Two days before I hired Thomas I went to Anderson and told him I wanted to employ the boy to talk to young witnesses and bring them to my office," Moss told reporters in his law office. "I suggested to Anderson that we have him make a sworn statement with each side retaining a copy.

"So I subsequently employed Thomas at $4 per diem to check witnesses. But before I employed him, I took a sworn statement from him, wrote Anderson a letter explaining the situation, and had Thomas deliver them in person to Anderson.

"Thomas stood in Anderson's office while the county attorney read them and when Anderson said 'All right,' Thomas left."

For Moss, who had endured hyperbolic proclamations and embellishments from Maddux, King, Hoop, and now Anderson, as well as yellow journalism, one-sided editorials, and an entire city that was trying to connect the Gorrell slaying with marijuana, naked pictures, bootleg liquor, marble machines, and illegal gambling, the witness-tampering nonsense was the last straw. He was furious, and determined to push back the tide.

Tulsa would soon learn why he was the city's number one defense attorney.

As Moss retreated into a huddle with his team over the weekend, Anderson carried on. He'd already mailed out subpoenas to twenty witnesses in the case, and after his tampering accusations, certified a list for twenty-three more. The names on his first list had been published, and he announced his intention to question them all to learn if they had been "approached." When it came to his second list of twenty-three, Anderson was keeping his mouth shut in some kind of noble effort to secure them from the evil defense team. With ten days to trial, his office sent jury notifications to one hundred fifty residents to serve as jurors in the upcoming district-court session. Twelve of them would go to the Kennamer case.

Even with all the local and national interest in the story, Anderson did not see what was coming next. Flint Moss's announcement on Monday, January 21, that the defense would file a change-of-venue motion the following day, was explosive. If the motion were granted, it would not only move the trial to Pawnee, it would also delay it, since jury notices had not gone out yet for their term of district court. The announcement also upset thousands of Tulsa County residents aiming to get a courtroom seat for the most important trial in city history. Pawnee was sixty miles away, and the locals there would get the best seats. Although it would change everything, the motion had to be considered. To settle the issue, Judge Hurst scheduled the venue hearing for Thursday, January 24.

Long before the motion, Moss had privately told reporters he would not seek a change of venue. But when the Maddux bribery story came out, again, followed by the fictitious witness-tampering allegation by Anderson, all bets were off. The defense motion filed the next day was a two-pronged attack against both Tulsa newspapers and the prosecution's team, including Anderson, King, Hoop, and Maddux, who were all specifically named and subpoenaed to testify.

"There has been undue publicity in this case and the defense doesn't think a fair trial can be obtained in Tulsa County," Moss told reporters outside the courthouse the morning he announced he would seek the venue change. "We think newspaper editorials have been unfair to our client. Equally unfair have been the statements of the county attorney that state witnesses have been tampered with."

In his motion, Moss specifically attacked editorials in both newspapers that belittled the testimony of so-called expert witnesses—especially psychiatrists. He also argued that both papers published "pretended statements of facts, which are false and untrue, which resulted in arousing in the minds of all qualified jurors of Tulsa County feelings of prejudice against the defendant."

Farther on, he left no doubt which officials were behind those pretended statements of fact when the petition named Anderson—for his false witness-tampering allegations, Maddux—for his dubious bribe story and for claiming Kennamer telephoned Born the morning of his suicide, and Oscar Hoop—for talking about the bribe and physical threats during a meeting of city commissioners.

Submitted as evidence were all local newspaper articles on the case, including those issues which publicized false allegations against the defense, and editorials and columns from both papers. When they discussed the bribe-and-threat claim with reporters, Moss and Hoop gallantly declared that in case of their demise, the investigative file and affidavits that would lead others to the man who made the offer were locked away safely. Justice would carry on, with or without these heroic men.

Moss subpoenaed those documents as well. It was time to put up or shut up.

"This bribe story has been talked around so much that we are going to bring it out in the open," Moss said. "It will be part of our proof that Kennamer should be granted a change of venue."

And just for good measure, Moss subpoenaed forty other witnesses from all over the county, and from all walks of life, who would testify that Kennamer, in their opinion, could not receive a fair trial. His subpoena list also included the circulation managers from both newspapers, with cause to show how circulation increased during its coverage of the case.

Anderson's reaction was to claim he was at a loss to explain the defense's move, and their true motive was to stall for a postponement. As for him, he truly could not understand how Moss came to his conclusion. He grumbled that he had already subpoenaed forty-three witnesses and sent out jury notices, and that moving the trial would cost the county more money. He was stunned that Moss would try to put him on the stand, and he vowed to fight back, arguing there was no law that allowed the defense to subpoena prosecution documents in a change-of-venue motion.

"We will oppose rigidly the introduction of the bribe testimony," Anderson said. The contention for his argument, which came from commissioner Hoop, was that those documents were "personal property," and were now, somehow, not part of the investigation. Facing the possibility that those documents could be presented in court, Hoop minimized the bribe-and-threat story to reporters, and backpedaled on his earlier claims.

"The bribe attempt directed at Sgt. Maddux involved one phase of the Gorrell slaying investigation, and has but an indirect bearing on the Kennamer case as a whole," Hoop said the day before the hearing. "I may go so far as to have the affidavits with me in person tomorrow, but I will combat with every resource any effort made by Kennamer's attorneys to make me produce them in court."

Although he never shied away from making a statement to the press in December, Maddux suddenly stopped talking. If Moss got his way in the hearing, he would have to reveal everything.

Even with his two-pronged attack and his thorough list of county citizens ready to testify in support of his argument, Moss was leaving nothing to chance. But his greatest weapon was legal precedent. When ex-convict Earl Quinn brutally raped and murdered the Griffith sisters, Zexie and Jesse, a few days after Christmas 1930 in Kay County, the local community was outraged. The girls were beautiful, popular, and successful. They were the daughters of a Blackwell police captain and had everything going for them. After he was captured the following year, Quinn was tried in Kay County and sentenced to death, the first death sentence in that county's history. His lawyer argued successfully to set aside his conviction on the grounds that the defendant could not have obtained a fair trial because of local sentiment, and a change of venue was required. Quinn then received a new trial in nearby Garfield County, where he was again sentenced to death.

Thursday's hearing opened with a long parade of defense witnesses expressing their opinion that, for one reason or another, it was impossible for Kennamer to receive a fair trial in Tulsa County. It was a day that started out civilly, but would end with yelling, jibes, soaring tempers, and snarky facial expressions. As faithfully as always, Dr. Gorrell was in the courtroom. Kennamer, this time, was supported by his two sisters.

Among the first from Moss's long list to be called up were six attorneys, including a former county attorney, who all testified that in their opinion, Kennamer could not receive a fair trial in Tulsa due to the publicity, and because it was all locals could talk about.

Added to this group of witnesses was former district judge Saul Yager, who was wandering around the courthouse that day when he casually stepped into Judge Hurst's courtroom during the venue hearing to see what was going on. He was just about to leave when Moss spontaneously called him to the stand. His statement turned out to be one of the strongest in defense of Moss's argument.

"The air in Tulsa is permeated with the Kennamer case," Judge Yager told the court. "Everyone talks about it. The many people I've discussed it with would not make fair and impartial jurors."

A former Tulsa Mayor, a banker, an oil operator, and a shoe cobbler testified that most of the people they talked to had fixed opinions one way or the other. They were followed by a movie theater operator from nearby Broken Arrow, whom Moss asked if he had ever talked to anyone who did not have a fixed opinion of the case.

"No, I haven't," he answered.

"Were you promised any compensation for coming here?" Anderson asked next.

"Yeah! He was offered twenty-five thousand bucks!" Moss interrupted as he roared with laughter.

And so it went on. Following the afternoon recess, Moss's parade of witnesses was relentless and continued with a mechanic, a barber, a grocer, and an insurance man, all backing his argument. Charles Parker from Sand Springs testified that the case was the most frequent topic of conversation at Rotary Club meetings. "Two or more people cannot meet or have not met in Tulsa County since this happened without discussing the situation," he told the court.

After more than thirty defense witnesses had made similar statements, Judge Hurst got the point and halted the defense's line of attack, saying it was needlessly repetitive.

Moss then began a new offensive directed at the state's bribery claim. His subordinate, Herman Young, read into the record newspaper articles from the *Tulsa World* that quoted King, Hoop, Maddux, and Anderson, to the effect that a $25,000 bribe had been offered to the detective.

First up to the stand was King. "Are you the Mr. King referred to in these articles?" Moss asked.

"I may be but I cannot be held responsible or accountable for what appears about me in Tulsa newspapers," King responded.

"I wish you would then relate to the court something about this bribe offer."

And with that, Anderson objected on the grounds it was immaterial and irrelevant to the issue now before the court. Although it was sustained, King answered anyway. "At the proper time and at the proper trial we will prove the bribery offer."

"I don't believe that!" Moss shouted.

"We're not interested in whether you believe it or not but we'll prove it at the right time," King retorted.

"I challenge you to prove that because I don't believe you," Moss threw back, which was then followed by a rap of the gavel from the judge.

Sergeant Maddux was called up next, but Moss could only get as far as "Who offered you a $25,000 bribe?" before Judge Hurst sustained Anderson's objection. As Maddux stepped down, Moss challenged him, "I don't believe there was any offer." His remark was answered with a cocky smile.

Moss got about the same distance with Commissioner Hoop, and when he was being excused, the frustrated attorney blurted out, "Was anyone offered a bribe?"

This time, both King and Anderson roared in objection, which initiated a fierce round of bickering before everyone could settle down. Having made his point through the back door, Moss rested. Anderson then questioned seven witnesses and presented thirty-one affidavits asserting the belief that Kennamer *could* receive a fair trial in Tulsa County.

But in the end, it wasn't the witnesses or affidavits or circulation figures or the bribe story; it was the appellate court decision that gave Judge Hurst the foundation for his decision.

"In view of that decision [the Quinn decision], my judgment is that if I denied a change of venue in this case, there would probably be a reversal," Hurst told the attorneys. "Basing my judgment on the evidence submitted, I think it will be very difficult to get a fair jury here and in this case."

The State of Oklahoma v. Philip Kennamer would begin in Pawnee in nineteen days.

Chapter Fifteen

GETTING THE TRIAL MOVED TO Pawnee was just one part of the defense's pre-trial strategy. Two days later, the infamous extortion note was shown to *Tribune* reporter Harmon Phillips. Now it was Moss's turn to use the press to sway the jury pool over to defense claims in a one-sided interview. With a straight face, Moss told the reporter he was releasing the contents "to definitely inform the state prosecutors that there is such a note."

They already knew that.

Admittedly, he would not allow a photostatic copy of the note to be made because he didn't want the prosecution to examine it with their own expert witnesses. If the jury was going to hear from a handwriting expert, it was going to be *his* handwriting expert. Phillips could copy the contents and describe its physical appearance, but that was it.

The letter was written on two pages of inexpensive, ruled paper concealed in an unstamped envelope addressed to H. F. Wilcox, 1351 East 27th Place, Tulsa, Okla. In the lower left corner was written "Personal," and "Air Mail," underlined twice, was written on the right side.

> Dear Sir: You will secure $20,000 (twenty thousand dollars) in bills of the following amounts—ten thousand in $5 (five) dollar bills, five thousand in $10 (ten) dollar bills, and five thousand in one dollar bills. You will be given further instructions at later either by phone or mail by an operator who will identify himself by the Symbol at the close of this letter. Failure to comply with our demands will result in certain and painful "DEATH" for one or more of your children.

Keep the said sum in your immediate house, for a moment's notice.

You must secure the money, not later than Friday noon. You will keep the money on hand, so that if you are notified in two days or two weeks, you will save us lots of trouble, and yourself lots of misery.

Yours in expectation—

John Doe.

Symbol-This is H.F.W. speaking

Strict silence, even in your family, must be observed.

In the same article, defense experts matched the note to Gorrell by comparing it with known samples of his handwriting, and observing how the tails of his *y*'s and *g*'s appeared to come straight down. Moss then tried to establish a connection with how the note was signed, "John Doe," to John Gorrell's first name, as well as the *D*, which looked like a *G* that had been scribbled over.

Gorrell's father continued to tell reporters his son was killed because he refused to participate in Kennamer's plot, and he would not say John wrote the note until he saw it for himself. But Anderson didn't even want to see it, and he downplayed its importance. "It is their duty to deliver the note to us if it is essential to the state's case," he told reporters.

"Ho, ho," King laughed when he heard about the *Tribune* article. "They're just trying to build up sentiment for that boy. It's ludicrous. Their 'exposing' it is part of a buildup that will continue all week.

"They're just out to paint the boy as a character deserving sympathy for a chivalrous deed. They've swung to the lawyer's idea of pleading temporary insanity. He acts goofy for anyone who goes in to see him now."

That last sentence was a jab at the final part of the defense's pretrial strategy: let Phil tell his bizarre story to the press. Again. But where the *Tribune* was left out the last time, they got the exclusive on this one. After the coded-message imbroglio, the defense team established an embargo against the *World* in general, and Lee Krupnick in particular.

There was no way Moss was ever going to agree to let Kennamer take the stand, where Anderson, Wallace, and King would pound the boy to dust under cross-examination. However, he still wanted potential jurors to discover what he and defense psychiatrists had observed. And where Kennamer thought this was another opportunity to take control and talk his way out of trouble, Moss knew what it really was: a perfect occasion for Phil to show potential jurors just how nuts he really was. This new and improved version of what happened that night was a feint against the prosecution, and a trap for his own client.

As before, the interview took place in Kennamer's private quarters. The cabinet radio and rocking chair had been removed by newly elected Sheriff Garland Marrs, who left the boy with a bed, the dresser, and the portrait of Governor Martin Trapp.

At first, Kennamer chose his words with careful deliberation, but this would wash away when the story reached its melodramatic moments. By the end of it, Phillips wrote, he was swearing and laughing as he ridiculed someone else's version of what had happened. At no time did Kennamer ever express remorse for his victim, whom he blamed for everything.

"Why did you kill Gorrell?" Phillips asked.

"In order to defend my own life," Kennamer answered quietly. He then plunged into an evolved version of his one-man crusade to save Virginia.

"I met Gorrell last August through Preston Cochrane.[1] At the time I met him, the conversation was almost a monologue on the part of Gorrell, dealing with various crimes, hijackings, kidnappings. I didn't pay much attention to him. It was an incident of another meeting with Gorrell which made me pay more attention and to change my mind about him."

Kennamer had an interesting new take on who said what during the September 13 meeting with Gorrell and Ted Bath. It was a complete reversal of what Bath had told authorities. He never proposed robbing the Idle Hour, or kidnapping Gorrell family friend Barbara Boyle, or having Bath seduce Virginia Wilcox to get naked pictures of her—those were all John Gorrell's ideas. And when it came to the honor of Barbara Boyle, well, he was her protector.

"It was at that meeting that Gorrell mentioned hijacking someone. I was propositioned to join in and I turned it down. Then the proposal to obtain some compromising photographs of girls was mentioned. The idea was that I was to put up the money and arrange for a party. At the time, I said the affair did not sound right and especially regarding one of the girls mentioned, I said I would not be interested."

In this new version, all of the things Ted Bath told police Kennamer had said in that meeting were actually what Gorrell had said. And all the things Gorrell had said were what he, Phil Kennamer, had said.

Ted Bath was simply confused.

"Later on, Cochrane told me that Gorrell had approached him with a kidnap plot in which either Homer Wilcox Jr. or Virginia Wilcox was to be the victim. He had turned down the proposition, as had Pat Burgess."

After Kennamer claimed he had discussed Gorrell's alleged plot with Burgess, Cochrane, and Jack Snedden, the group

---

[1] Earlier, he had said he met him through Pat Burgess, but since Burgess was unlikely to testify, he now said it was Cochrane who had introduced him.

decided that Kennamer should be the one to travel to Kansas City to see if Gorrell was serious.[2]

Kennamer then wove his story into a bad gangster movie that portrayed Gorrell as a Kansas City crime lord. Although he had enrolled in dental school just two months before, and worked in the hotel as a telephone operator on the graveyard shift three nights a week, Gorrell had plenty of time, along with attending his classes, to form a dangerous, well-armed gang. This was about as far away as one could get from the nervous boy who spoke of his fears to his roommates and Dean Rinehart, and then borrowed a .22-caliber pop-gun for protection but couldn't scrape more than three bullets together.

"Knowing that if Gorrell expected any treachery on my part, it might be dangerous, I bought a knife in Kansas City. I had it in my possession when I met him in the lobby of the hotel. There were several with him. He introduced me as Bob Wilson.

"Gorrell and I went up to his apartment and talked awhile. A man and another fellow came in and asked Gorrell 'Is this fellow ok?' Gorrell said 'yes.' The man asked again, 'are you sure?' and again Gorrell said 'yes.'

"Then this man asked 'do you have plenty of heat?' and Gorrell pointed to a pistol saying 'yes.'

"'If you haven't, I've plenty at my place,' said the man. Gorrell replied 'yes' and the man left with the words, 'OK boss.'

"I asked Gorrell what it was all about, 'Just a couple of my boys,' he replied.[3]

"I said, 'What do you mean?' and he replied, 'They do damn well what I tell them to!'

"Gorrell then told me that they had been working some petty hijackings and were now ready for 'a big deal.'

---

[2] Burgess, Cochrane, and Snedden later denied this meeting ever took place.

[3] Richard Oliver told police the only people in the apartment at that time were himself and Jess Harris.

"I said, 'what have you lined up?' He asked me what I had come to Kansas City for.

"'The matter you were talking about before you left.' I told him.

"He said, 'you mean the Wilcox deal?' and I said 'yes.'

"He asked me how I knew about it and I told him Cochrane and Burgess told me. He said 'Where do you figure in it?' and I said 'I figure in it all the way.'

"I believe it was at [my hotel room], rather than at his apartment, that he divulged the exact nature of his plan. Three or four of the chaps to whom I had been introduced were to come to Tulsa and lure one of the Wilcox children into a thinly populated district, crowd their car over, kidnap the boy or the girl, take him or her to a flying field outside of Tulsa where a plane would be waiting. Then the victim would be taken to Kansas City to a house in a suburban district. The details of securing the ransom were to be left to us in Tulsa. The ransom specified by Gorrell was $100,000.

"He asked me what I thought of the plan and I answered 'very little.' I told him it was too complicated, involved too many people and made possible too many contingencies. I then offered the counter suggestion that Gorrell write an extortion note asking for a more reasonable sum and obviating the handicaps presented by the other plan.

"He wrote the note the following morning and gave it to me to mail. Then I met Floyd Huff . . . and later [we] started back to Tulsa.

"Huff began to ask me about Gorrell, as to whether he had any money. It seems Gorrell had planned to buy an interest in Huff's airplane salvage.[4] I finally told Huff, 'Well, I'll show you how crazy he is' and showed him the extortion note Gorrell had given to me.

---

[4] In his previous story, Kennamer said Gorrell had wanted to buy an airplane from Huff.

"Huff asked me if I were going to turn it over to the authorities. I told him no, that when Gorrell came to Tulsa on Thanksgiving, I was going to tell him if he attempted to go through with the plot that I would turn it over to the authorities. I did not tell Huff that I was going to kill Gorrell.

"On Thanksgiving Day, I called Gorrell several times without getting him and about 7:00 p.m. he called me and asked 'How's the shake coming along?' I told him I couldn't talk about it. He asked me to meet him at 7:30 p.m. at a drug store near St. John's Hospital. When we met he again asked 'How's things coming along?' I said I would see him later. He finally suggested I meet him on the corner near the hospital at 11:00 p.m., after he had a date with one of the nurses."

Kennamer then explained how he met up with Jack Snedden and "Beebe" Morton at the Owl Tavern, and after he told them of the meeting he was to have that night with Gorrell, Morton had taken the knife away from him. At no time, he stressed, did he ever tell Morton and Snedden he was going to kill the dental student. He then caught a ride to the hospital with Sidney Born, where he found Gorrell sitting in his car waiting for him.

"We drove down South Utica Avenue. We talked in general for a while and then he said 'Have you sent that letter?' and I said 'No.'

"'Why not?' he asked. I told him I had no intention of mailing it. He wanted to know 'what's the idea?'

"'Simply this, John,' I answered. 'The only reason I went into this was because I thought you might try and go through with it. I've got the letter here.'

"Then I knew I had made a mistake in saying that. He said 'By God, you'll never do anything with that letter,' and drew a gun. He almost threw it at me. The holster falling off, he stuck it in my face and pulled the trigger. It snapped. I grabbed it and twisted it back. I was pushing his face with my left hand. The car had slowed up. My finger was inside the trigger guard. There was a shot. I have no distinct recollection of the second shot but it came immediately. The car hit the curbing. I put the gun in the holster and sat there a moment. I do not remember wiping off the fingerprints. Then I got out and walked to the Owl Tavern."

Although his new story was similar, it had changed in many places from the account he gave in December. His description of how he was pushing on Gorrell's face when the gun went off would later become one of the strongest clues that it was not self-defense. Since Moss had already announced Kennamer would not take the stand in his own defense, Anderson's team would find it hard to cast doubt on both stories. But they did have witnesses to call who could shred it to pieces—and nearly everything he'd just said was contradicted by witness statements to police.

AS PART OF THEIR BUILDUP to the trial, the *World* published a running account of witnesses set to testify. Two days before the February 11 start date, the list had topped out at 108, and was almost evenly divided between the defense and the prosecution. Nineteen were set to testify for each side.

At the top of Anderson's roll call were the names of all the major witnesses who had come forward in December and with whom Tulsans were already familiar. Over the last few weeks, two new names had floated to the top and were leaked to the press. Hanley "Cadillac" Booth was an Oklahoma City bail bondsman and former bootlegger who said that during the summer of 1934, while Kennamer was a rookie reporter for the *Daily Oklahoman*, the boy had brought up the Wilcox name and proposed crimes similar to what Ted Bath had reported.

The other star witness came forward just a few days before the trial would begin, and what she had to say was a bit of a mystery. Mrs. Edna Harman was an apartment-building manager with a story in which she allegedly overheard Kennamer saying something incriminating to another boy while in the process of renting a room. She had reached out to Dr.

Gorrell, who took her to see Anderson and Wallace. But what neither prosecutor realized at the time was that Edna Harman was a little unbalanced and histrionic, and that she had inserted herself as a witness in other murder cases before. Without knowing it, when Anderson signed her up to testify for the state, he was taking the single biggest gamble of the entire case.

Many of the names on the defense list consisted of classmates and friends who had Phil Kennamer stories to share that supported the defense's theory of insanity. The list also included Judge Kennamer and Phil's sister Juanita Hayes. The only star witnesses they had were their handwriting expert and Dr. Karl Menninger, the celebrated psychiatrist.

Kennamer's friends on the list were members of the Hy-Hat Club. With just a few days to go before the trial began, the often-ridiculed and maligned club of young men from prominent families, the subject of sensational journalism from out-of-state metropolitan newspapers for the last two months, finally received some vindication. A cooler, more rational mindset prevailed in the minds of local adults who had once looked upon them so critically. The mission statement of the club turned out to be more altruistic than getting drunk and holding parties, and professed: ". . . the promotion of good fellowship among its members, the promotion of good sportsmanship, and the advancement of society in the best interest of humanity."

Members paid dues and ended every meeting with the club prayer: "Most Holy and Gracious Father in Heaven, we who are gathered here in Thy name ask that Thou accompany each of us as we depart from this meeting, that we may neither fail nor weaken in the ideals of our creed, and Thy love, that becomes stronger and better each day in the sight of God and man. Amen."

This exoneration was further supported by an announcement on February 1 that both state and defense investigators finally admitted there were absolutely no naked pictures of high-society girls in existence anywhere. It confirmed what Ted Bath had told them, if they had actually listened to him. Bath merely said Kennamer had proposed the idea of seducing a girl to get compromising photos of her that *could* be used for blackmail. But at no time did anyone claim to have seen such photos. As in their overreaction to everything else, authorities and residents just assumed the photos existed because it was too thrilling to think otherwise.

WHEN THE FOLKS IN PAWNEE heard the Kennamer trial was coming to their city, it was an immediate source of pride for the community of 2,800 people.

"This town is ready for the trial and welcomes it," said the publisher of the local newspaper. "Everyone, including the defendant, will be treated with fairness, courtesy and hospitality here. After discussing the change of venue with numerous people here, I am safe in saying that there will not be prejudice in this community."

They cast their eyes 1,400 miles to the east to where the Bruno Hauptmann trial brought robust commerce to the merchants of Flemington, New Jersey. The Pawnee Chamber of Commerce estimated $10,000[5] would be spent in their community during the course of the Kennamer trial. Within the first twenty-four hours, half the rooms at the only two hotels in town were booked, and the rates doubled. The defense would take up residence at the Graham Hotel, while the state prepared to move into the Pawnee Hotel. Both of them were strategically placed across the street from the courthouse. The chamber president also assembled a list of local homeowners willing to rent out rooms. The Kennamer family rented out an entire cottage for themselves four blocks from the courthouse.

When a local hamburger vendor read in the papers that a hot-dog stand operator in Flemington had cleared $2,000 in one

---

[5] The 2014 equivalent of $173,000, when adjusted for inflation.

week, and then learned the Kennamer trial was coming to his town, "Friends say he almost hit the ceiling and rushed out of his shop, down the street, and spent a quarter for a new haircut."

The news also called for hurried preparations to the courthouse itself for a trial that would be the biggest in Pawnee history. Construction on the four-story, sand-colored, brick building had begun three years before, and it was put into use one year before the trial began. It featured a neoclassical, art-deco style common for the era. A floral crown adorned the parapet and stood above inlaid, carved Indians in full headdress standing watch over all who entered. Thirty feet below them, closer to the eye, hard-edged, low-relief sculptures depicted scenes of early Pawnee County life that included Indians, cowboys, farmers, and pioneer settlers. Three-story-high, fluted pilasters on the exterior were complemented by fluted woodwork for the judge's bench. To get to the third-story, solitary courtroom that ran east to west, participants and spectators walked on a polished, chipped-stone, composite floor.[6]

It was an impressive building for such a small community, and it was well suited for a trial that would be featured in a newsreel shown in movie houses throughout the country. The building sat in the middle of an entire city block, and with the tiny business district facing it on all four sides, it was effectively the town square. The courtroom itself was much larger than any in Tulsa. In the gallery, lawyers, jurors, newsmen, teletype operators, and court personnel could be squeezed together behind the railing. Behind them, another four hundred spectators could sit tightly on eighteen church-pew-style benches.

---

[6] The flooring, judge's bench, gallery benches, attorney tables, juror chairs, wall clock, and door molding are all the same today as they were in 1935.

Within days of the announcement, telegraph-and-telephone-company construction crews were stringing wires to two improvised press rooms that were hastily assembled near Judge Hurst's chambers. They were equipped with ten typewriters, two teletype transmitters, and three telegraph-sending sets, spread over four tables and twelve chairs in two rooms that together, "most housewives would say [were] too small for a bedroom," the *World* declared. Tulsa radio station KTUL also set up shop in Pawnee with remote-transmitting equipment that was cutting-edge for 1935 Oklahoma.

When it was designed, the fourth floor of the courthouse was intended for use as the new county jail. However, commissioners ran out of money to outfit it by the start of the Kennamer trial. Prisoners were still being kept in the old, two-story, rough-cut sandstone jail built in 1899. Pawnee residents seemed to take particular delight in the fact that Kennamer would be locked up in a bona fide jail cell complete with flat-iron-barred doors and windows, and shelf-like beds made of steel. His only comfort would be a thin mattress, and he would have to live with nearly a dozen other prisoners, some of whom had prior run-ins with his father.

Judge Thurst and Pawnee officials were anxious to avoid a repeat of what happened at Kennamer's preliminary hearing. Extra security precautions were planned and stricter rules drawn up. Tulsa County Deputies John Evans and Tony Benson would be sworn in as Pawnee deputies and tasked with escorting Kennamer to and from the courthouse. The courthouse doors would remain locked until 8:00 a.m., and no passes would be issued for spectators.[7] All trial-watchers would be required to sit on one of the gallery benches, but there was to be no standing along the walls. They also had until 10:30 a.m.

---

[7] In reality, this did not happen, and the rich and the politically connected were able to obtain seats in the first two rows. It is unclear how they were able to do this.

to find a seat or clear out. After 10:30, only jurors, attorneys, newsmen, courthouse employees, and other people with business related to the trial would be allowed to roam freely over the third-floor corridor while court was in session. Witnesses would have to wait in the district attorney's offices until their names were called.

No photographs would be permitted in the courtroom during the trial. Those who violated these rules would be barred from the building, and the reporters associated with their newspaper would also be invited to leave.

Since the fourth floor was mostly empty, the jury deliberation room was situated there. Once twelve men had been selected,[8] they would be sequestered in a house one block south of the courthouse, where guards would keep the public and press away.

BECAUSE THIS WAS NO ORDINARY CASE, the transfer of Phil Kennamer to the Pawnee County Jail on Sunday, February 10, was bound to be anything but ordinary.

"Hundreds of curious persons had thronged the [Pawnee] courthouse grounds at noon in anticipation of Kennamer's arrival," the *World* reported. "Peanut and pop vendors hawked their wares to the matinee crowd. The eleven prisoners in the rough-cut sandstone jail, all serving minor sentences, also were affected by the holiday spirit. They wore freshly laundered clothing for the occasion."

The crowd consisted of women dressed in their best attire, men in business suits, Indians wrapped in blankets, cowboys on

---

[8] At that time, the Oklahoma Legislature's interpretation of the 1907 state constitution gave them the legal means to prohibit women from serving on juries because it specifically stated that juries were to consist of "twelve men." In 1942, a constitutional amendment was passed that allowed women to hold state office. However, they would have to wait another nine years, until 1951, before they earned the right to serve as jurors. Instead of "men," section 19 now calls for juries to consist of "persons."

horses, and uniformed Boy Scouts, as well as the local high-school football team, which, for some reason, also wore their uniforms. Standing out in this stand-out crowd was the town's most famous resident, Wild West showman and entertainer Gordon William Lillie, otherwise known as "Pawnee Bill." His long, gray hair, worn in the style of George Custer and Buffalo Bill, was of extreme interest to eastern newspaper reporters who were already migrating to Pawnee, which was being referred to as the "Flemington, New Jersey, of Oklahoma." These were the newshawks who had already covered a large portion of the case, as well as a few who had just left the Hauptmann trial behind, where jury deliberations would soon begin.

As a courtesy, deputies Evans and Benson permitted Kennamer a ten-minute visit with his ailing mother, Lillie, whom he had not seen since he surrendered on December 1. When he left, he appeared unaffected by the visit with the woman who had worried the most about him. As he got closer to trial, Kennamer had grown surly and foul-tempered. Word had gotten back that the prosecution would qualify jurors on only one question: their opinion of the death penalty.

His first stop in Pawnee was the county clerk's office, where papers were signed that officially transferred him to Sheriff Charlie Burkdoll's custody. As they did so, newspaper photographers strained to take his picture.

"He roundly berated them, cursed the publishers of the Tulsa newspapers, and generally vented his wrath on a score of acquaintances," the *World* reported. But it was the sight of their own Lee Krupnick, the double agent behind the note-passing embarrassment, which sent him into an apoplectic fit.

"Do I have to stay in the same room as that son-of-a-bitch rat, Krupnick?" Kennamer cried out to Sheriff Burkdoll inside the clerk's office.

"What's the matter with you, Phil?" Krupnick toyed with him. "Don't you know when a friend is trying to help you?"

"Aw, you rat!" Kennamer screamed as he unleashed another volley of curse words.

"What happened to all your friends, Phil? None of them came up to the jail to see you." Still thinking that Kennamer had unknown accomplices, Krupnick unsuccessfully tried to lure him into revealing their names. "You're just trying to be a hero and take the rap for the other fellows."

"I guess I know how I killed him," Kennamer answered sarcastically.

"I mean the extortion note."

"Well, that's my affair. And I want it understood that anybody can take pictures of me except that rat, Krupnick," Kennamer told the sheriff.

Every time Krupnick tried to get a photograph of Kennamer, Kennamer would turn his back or dodge behind someone. Krupnick only managed to take a few photos for Monday's morning edition by waiting patiently, acting like he was engrossed in something else, and then hurriedly snapping a picture. This battle with Krupnick would last throughout the trial and would involve the entire Kennamer family and defense team. But it wasn't just Krupnick; Judge Kennamer was lashing out against any photographer who snapped a picture of him, or his three children, without his permission.

The entire case had turned into a circus, a Roman holiday, and Judge Kennamer was just as gruff as Phil. His reputation as a strict judge who handed down long sentences was coming back to haunt him, now that his own son would be tried for murder. A week before the trial, Charles Stuart reported that the judge had been the target of anonymous gibes from criminals, who saw the whole affair as poetic justice.

"Judge Kennamer has been stern and severe on law violators," Stuart admitted to the *Tribune*. "Now, members of the underworld, and especially those who were sentenced by him, have telephoned and said they are glad his son is in jail."

The judge would have a front-row seat at the defense table during his son's trial, while his wife, Lillie, remained at home, too ill to travel. His son and two daughters would support their brother from a bench directly behind him in the gallery. As with most women with important ties to the trial, the daughters' clothing and accessories would be described in great detail by newspapers.

Lost in the fervor of it all was the grief of a father and mother whose eldest son was murdered by another boy who wanted to impress a girl and her family. Never without a cigar clenched in his mouth, the stoic fifty-four-year-old Dr. Gorrell kept his composure while he endured the slander of his namesake. Newspapers steered clear of interviewing the doctor, not because he was ill-tempered like Judge Kennamer, but because he didn't believe in showcasing his grief and anger to the public. According to his grandson and the victim's nephew, John Robert Gorrell, he kept that quiet, dignified demeanor for the rest of his life.

"It was a sore spot for them, my father and grandfather," the sixty-three-year-old said in 2014. "They never talked about it much. They just told me my uncle John was murdered, but they never said who or why." John had to learn about his uncle in bits and pieces, from cousins and friends, and still has the aviator helmet John Jr. had once so proudly worn.

Like Judge Kennamer, Dr. Gorrell and his wife Alice would be seated with the legal team who represented their son, and while the case had become so much more to everyone else, to the Gorrell family, it was only about one thing.

PHOTOGRAPHS

John Gorrell Jr. (*Courtesy of Family*)

Crime Scene as it looks today. Search "Philbrook Museum
Tulsa" on Google Earth to see more.

Phil Kennamer (*Courtesy of Tulsa World*)

Phil Kennamer (*Courtesy of Tulsa World*)

Virginia Wilcox (*Courtesy of Family*)

Sidney Born Jr.

Floyd Huff (*Courtesy of Tulsa World*)

Tom Wallace with Ted Bath (*Courtesy of Tulsa World*)

J. Berry King and William "Dixie" Gilmer

Defense Team: A. Flint Moss, Herman Young, and Charles Stuart. Not pictured is Charles Coakley. (*Courtesy of Tulsa World*)

Judge Thurman Hurst *(Courtesy of Oklahoma Historical Society*

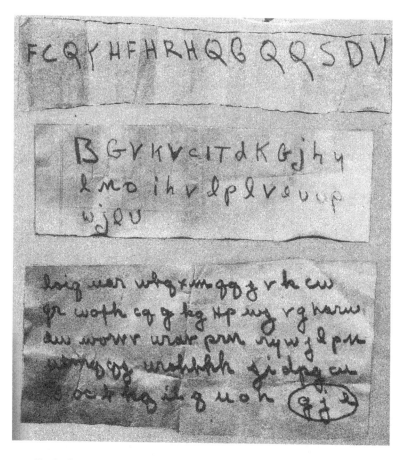

Coded messages exchanged between Phil Kennamer and
Preston Cochrane (*Courtesy of Tulsa World*)

Preston Cochrane

More photos are available for viewing by going to:
HistoricalCrimeDetective.com *(Courtesy of Oklahoma Historical Society)*

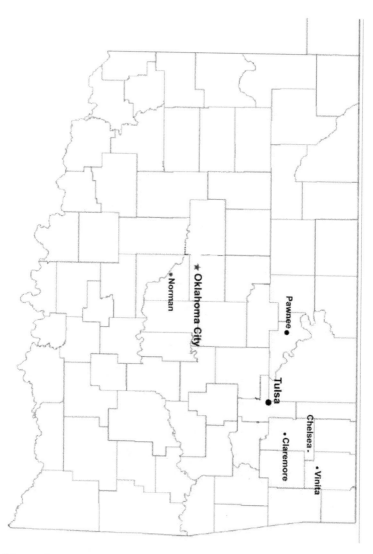

Map of Oklahoma showing Tulsa in relation to Pawnee and Chelsea.

Part Three: The Trial

It was a riot in miniature. They stampeded through the corridors, surged up the stairways four abreast, women and men alike. On the top floor all broke into a run for the last few yards of the race and those in the lead flung themselves elated into the seats of their choice.

Men and women shoved and elbowed alike. Women were knocked down on the stairs, clothes were disarranged, belongings were lost and forgotten in the scramble. There were shouts, laughter, squeals and some curses.

— *Tulsa Daily World*

Dramatis Personae

Prosecution Team	Defense Team
Holly Anderson	A. Flint Moss
Tom Wallace	Charles Stuart
Dixie Gilmer	Charles Coakley
J. Berry King	Herman Young
Prentis Rowe	J.D. McCollum
Lee Johnson	Paul Pinson

Prosecution Witnesses	**Defense Witnesses**
Dr. John Gorrell	Gorrell's flying instructor
Richard Oliver	Judge Kennamer
Floyd Huff	Handwriting Expert
Ted Bath	Jack Snedden, again
Mrs. Gorrell	Claude Wright
Eunice Word	Homer Wilcox Jr.
Jack Snedden	Virginia Wilcox
Edna Harman	Judge Kennamer, again
Randal Morton	Juanita Hayes
Two Unnamed Witnesses	Dr. Karl Menninger
Dr. Simpson (coroner)	Dr. Eugen Werner
Deputy Nathan Martin	Phil Kennamer
Sgt. Henry Maddux	

Rebuttal Witnesses

Dr. Felix Adams
Two unnamed psychiatrists
Hanley "Cadillac" Booth
Otto Kramer
Dr. Cecil Knoblock

Chapter Sixteen

Monday & Tuesday, February 11 & 12, 1935

THE CHANGE OF VENUE HEARING was a pregnancy that gave birth to more lawyers. In a rural county where neighbors relied on each other, and the reputation of a man followed him wherever he went, neither side wanted to take the chance of seating a plant on the jury. Well-known Pawnee attorneys John McCollum and Paul Pinson were brought in to guide the defense team through the selection process. The prosecution picked up Pawnee Assistant County Attorney Prentiss Rowe, and former county attorney Lee Johnson—a cool-headed tactician who would later prove himself invaluable to the entire coterie of thirteen counselors. County Attorney Carl McGee was also allied to the prosecution, but in name only. When the hoopla evaporated and the crowd of celebrity reporters, photographers, newsreel cameramen, aspiring authors, gossip magazine editors, criminologists, psychiatrists, state political bosses, Hy-Hat Club members, and one wacky witness left town, Pawnee would have its own lawbreakers to prosecute.

The owner of Pawnee's Katz Department Store found this unprecedented amount of local traffic to be the perfect time to throw a going out-of-business sale. And what better way to promote his low-low prices than to co-opt the very theme that had brought so much traffic to their little city? During that first day of jury selection, visitors were kept away from the courthouse to make room in the gallery for the pool of seventy veniremen eligible to serve. An afternoon recess brought a much-needed respite to the tedious process, and as the defense team stretched their legs in the third-floor corridor, Paul Pinson casually looked over his town through a window and to his horror discovered that the department store had erected a twenty-five-foot-wide banner that read:

YOU ARE GUILTY

Back in the courtroom, whispered outrage flowing through the defense team led to a conference with Judge Hurst, who then ordered Carl McGee and Sheriff Burkdoll to have the sign taken down. As it turned out, the twenty-five-foot banner was only half of it. The other twenty-five-foot section,

if You Don't Attend Katz Department Store Quit Business Sale!

was yet to be lifted into position. Bored photographers, anxious to send anything out of the ordinary back to their newspapers, pounced on this satirical opportunity. Thirty minutes after it first appeared, an apologetic store manager had it removed. The crackerjack sales promoter brought in from Oklahoma City who'd conceived the idea was criticized by both officials and citizens alike, and he quickly left town. Judge Hurst also ordered that no photographs of the sign be published in any newspaper.

The trial's first disaster was averted. There would be more.

The Pawnee attorneys working for both teams shortcut the selection process, and by Tuesday afternoon, fifty-one potential jurors were boiled down to twelve men who attested to their own impartiality. As predicted, the state qualified their choices on the death penalty, the defendant's youth, and whether it mattered to them that his father was a federal judge. The defense sought jurors who were open-minded to self-defense and insanity claims. By the end, both sides claimed to reporters that they were content with the outcome.

Those twelve stone-faced men became instant celebrities. A group photo and a short profile on each were published in newspapers throughout Oklahoma. Those who worked in the elements had the characteristic "hat tan" which gave them sun-darkened faces below their brows, while above, their white foreheads emphasized receding hairlines. They would spend the remainder of the trial sequestered together in a house rented just for the occasion. Deputies were tasked to watch over them and keep the outside world out. Radios were off-limits, newspapers were censored by cutting out trial coverage articles, and even their meals were delivered.

With an hour and a half left to go that Tuesday afternoon, veteran prosecutor Tom Wallace presented the state's opening remarks. A short man with thinning hair, Wallace looked as if he would be more at home as a bookkeeper with an insurance firm. The only color on his pasty-white face was from the round, thin-framed glasses he wore. But this was the man who had put Doc Barker away. This was the man who had once beaten the most intimidating lawyer in the courtroom, Flint Moss. This docile-looking man had one hundred murder trials under his belt—far more than anyone else.

With little room inside the crowded railing to maneuver, Wallace stood up from his chair, holding a stack of well-worn papers in his hand. "Your Honor, and gentlemen of the jury," he began in a commanding voice that surprised many, "I will read to you this information and make a statement as to what the evidence will be on behalf of the State."

With the jury seated, the gallery was opened to the public, and the long benches were half-filled with spectators who had waited patiently for the moment they could storm the courthouse. Their excitement at the promise of what was to come was reflected in the whispered voices and shuffling about as they settled in. But when Wallace began to speak, the quiet roar suddenly stopped as they strained to consume every provocative word.

"Now, the evidence will show on behalf of the State that on the 29th of November, 1934," Wallace said as he turned to look at Kennamer and point his finger, "the defendant, Phil Kennamer, SHOT AND KILLED JOHN GORRELL!"

His rise in volume seemed to wake the sleepy defendant.

Wallace then recounted the entire story, from beginning to end, of all the major events in the case. He gave biographical sketches of the important players in a drama in which he claimed Kennamer not only planned Gorrell's murder in advance, but was the architect of the entire kidnapping and extortion plot. He praised John's character and pointed out that he had graduated from the Missouri Military Academy in Mexico, Missouri—a subtle jab at Phil, who never completed secondary school at all and had run away from a military academy in New Mexico. John had then taken classes at both the University of Tulsa and Oklahoma A&M before enrolling at Spartan Air Academy to fulfill a childhood dream of learning how to fly. He succeeded there as well and proudly earned his government-issued pilot's license in the spring of '34. Within two weeks of meeting Phil Kennamer, he began dental school in Kansas City on September 15. The industrious twenty-one-year-old worked three nights a week as a telephone operator in the hotel, where he shared a room with two other Oklahoma boys.

His read-between-the-lines message was simple: John Gorrell was on the road to success. He was disciplined, ambitious, and able to finish what he started—a good boy who was doing all the right things to become a valuable member of society. And if they didn't know it then, the jury would soon learn: Phil Kennamer was none of those things.

Wallace spoke of the meeting Kennamer had had with Gorrell and Ted Bath, and of the armed robbery Kennamer had proposed, of first targeting Barbara Boyle, and then switching to a plan to get compromising photos of the woman he professed to love, Virginia Wilcox. He told them of how Jack

Snedden had driven Kennamer to the airport and of the events that happened in Kansas City as related by Dick Oliver and others. Wallace gave special attention to the car ride with Huff, and to the intricate murder plot Kennamer had planned for the dental student.

The events he spoke of, and what was said and who said it, were all familiar to Tulsans, but were most likely new to the minds of the jurors of Pawnee, who had not followed the case so closely. But it was what Wallace spoke of next that was news to everyone in the courtroom.

"A few days before Kennamer went to Kansas City, he and another boy went to Mrs. Edna Harman and asked her if she had an apartment to rent."

When Charles Stuart heard Mrs. Harman's name, he perked up and shared a knowing smile with Moss. This ticking time bomb of a woman may have been a prosecution witness, but she was their secret weapon who would explode in Anderson's face after Moss cross-examined her. Edna Harman and her husband managed an apartment building, and the story she told Anderson allegedly took place there a few days before Kennamer flew to Kansas City. However, she had waited two months to tell prosecutors her story. They heard it for the first time just a few days before the trial began.

"She said, 'I only have this small one, and maybe that wouldn't suit you. Over here are some nicer apartments.'

"Kennamer, doing all the talking, said 'No, this [one] suits us, we will take this one.'

"After they went out she got to thinking about the good-looking fellows wanting an apartment, and wondering about their business. So she goes around the house on the south side. She saw Kennamer sitting at a desk or table with a pencil and tablet, and Kennamer says to the boy who was there in the apartment with him, he says: 'That fellow has got yellow. He has backed out. I am going to Kansas City and I am going to put the skids under him.'"

In the buildup before the trial, reporters pressed Kennamer for news about this mysterious new witness who had recently come forward. "You can say this for me about Mrs. Harman, I never heard of her," he told them.

When they told Anderson what Kennamer had said, the county attorney snapped back that he didn't care what anyone thought of Mrs. Harman's testimony because he was mighty impressed with it. "Her testimony is the most important yet uncovered," he proclaimed.

Wallace returned to his speech by showing graphic photographs of the two bullet wounds to Gorrell's head, taking great care to give a vivid explanation of how the second bullet was fired a minute or more after the first shot. The jury, one reporter noted, "was visibly impressed."

"The first bullet wound, the blood ran straight down this way, filled his ear, ran down the back of his neck and collar," Wallace explained. Pointing to where the second bullet had struck, Wallace detailed the path the blood from that wound traveled, crossing over the blood streak from the first wound.

For Mrs. Gorrell, this was too much, and she escaped to the corridor where a water fountain would cool her cotton mouth.

"You can see from this photograph where the blood flowed from. Not only that, the body of John Gorrell showed bruised spots as though hurt with a blunt something-or-other. The bump raised up right here where he had been struck," Wallace declared as he pointed to the spot on the enlarged photograph the coroner had taken at the funeral home.

On top of all that, the victim's clothes were smooth, his hair unruffled, his foot was still on the gas, and the ignition was still on; Gorrell had been shot *while* he was driving, Wallace explained.

"When we have shown this," Wallace said to the jury as he brought his statement to a close, "we shall expect a verdict of guilty at your hands with the extreme penalty."

The state of Oklahoma wanted to see Phil Kennamer dead.

Wednesday, February 13, 1935

OVERNIGHT, A HEAVY RAIN PASSED through Pawnee that soaked into the red soil Oklahoma is known for, creating jagged ruts and furrows in the dirt roads leading to the small community. Automobiles carrying travelers into town with business that morning brought the clay-heavy earth with them, their slender tires pounding and flipping it out in all directions as they circled the square looking for a place to park.

Inside the medieval-looking jail a few hundred yards to the northwest of the courthouse, Kennamer was laughing and joking with the eleven other inmates as they ate their oatmeal and toast. They washed their food down with coffee and smoked cigarettes Kennamer had purchased for all of them after a Kangaroo Court was convened by the other prisoners to fine the new occupant three dollars on his very first day. It was his initiation, and he took it well—better than his first impression of his new quarters, when his jaw dropped and sagged there for several moments as he scrutinized the tiny cell with its flat-iron door and steel-frame bed.

But Phil quickly adapted, and his gregarious personality won him friends among the other prisoners. Bitter over the treatment he'd received in Tulsa, where newspapers bashed him as the perennial problem child, and Sheriff Price set him up to be double-crossed by Lee Krupnick, he was anxious to sing the praises of the Pawnee Jail to anyone who'd listen.

"He seems to be a pretty nice fellow," said pack leader Everett Hargraves, who was serving a ninety-day sentence on a liquor violation. "The boys seem to like him and he said right out that he likes it here a lot better than he liked staying in the Tulsa County Jail."

Kennamer also welcomed the new reporters from Oklahoma City, Kansas City, New York City, and Chicago, who were now swarming around him. When the press wasn't out to get him, as the Tulsa reporters had been, he turned up the charm and loved to talk about himself and all the flaws in the case against him.

"I have nothing to worry about," Kennamer boasted. His confidence was based on one reason—he was going to tell his story on the stand. This was news to Tulsa writers who were under the impression Moss would not let him testify. But whispered remarks from other members of the defense team that weekend indicated their client *would* tell his story. The only evidence they had to support their self-defense claim was what Phil said. If they wanted to sell the jury on self-defense, Kennamer would have to tell them about it.

And true to his ego, the nineteen-year-old was "confident he has an excellent chance to be acquitted and that his own story of the student dentist's death will improve his chances materially," wrote a *World* reporter, who was mixed in with the out-of-town journalists. Kennamer discussed the case freely with them and enjoyed the attention while reporters played to his ego to get quotes for their stories.

"I feel much better about my chances now that I know I am going to testify," Kennamer professed. "I know I will have a much better chance to get a fair trial here than I would in Tulsa," he declared, in a voice that sounded more like a seasoned criminal lawyer than a nineteen-year-old on trial for murder. "The biggest obstacle I have to overcome in this case is the jaundiced public opinion of statements created by persons who know nothing of the case."

Holly Anderson was the first to arrive at the courthouse Wednesday morning, and he was confident that he was the obstacle that Flint Moss and the defense team would not be able to overcome. As he sat there quietly by himself that morning, going over his questions, he knew that if he was ever going to advance his political career, he had to give his best performance in the one case everyone in Oklahoma and the rest of the country was watching. This was Oklahoma's biggest trial since George "Machine Gun" Kelly. Comparisons between that case, as well as the one in New Jersey, which would end that same day with a verdict from the jury, were being made by enthusiastic observers and reporters.

Today, more than any other day in his life, the former mayor of Sand Springs had to make a good showing.

His first witness to the stand that morning was the victim's newspaper-shy father, Dr. John Gorrell, who had sat at the prosecution table this whole time with his wife, Alice, just four feet away from Judge Kennamer. Somehow, the two fathers had managed to avoid eye contact the entire time. Both had gained the right to privileged seating, right up front, where each could closely monitor what was in their own best interests: justice for one, freedom for the other.

After taking Dr. Gorrell through a brief history of the high points in his son's short life, Anderson got to the reason why they were all there.

"When did you last see your son alive?"

"At 7:30 Thanksgiving night last year."

"Is your son now living or dead?"

"He is dead," Dr. Gorrell said in a slow and clear voice as Judge Kennamer and his son stared at him intently. Not once in the two-and-one-half months since the Gorrell's son was killed had the judge ever said one kind word to the newspapers for the victim's family. The only tears he was ever known to have shed were on the day his son surrendered.

Richard Oliver took the stand next. In the months since he'd accidentally met up with "Bob Wilson" on the southbound Frisco train, he had steeled himself up for this moment. After taking the young, baby-faced, dental student through his short history as Gorrell's roommate and his experience with Bob Wilson, Anderson got right to the point.

"Is the man who was introduced to you as Bob Wilson in the courtroom today?"

"Yes," Oliver responded, and he pointed his arm straight and steady at Phil Kennamer.

In his first cross-examination of the day, Moss's questions indicated that part of his strategy was to attack the victim's character.

"Gorrell was supposed to work at a switchboard in your hotel at Kansas City, wasn't he?" Moss asked, which got him an affirmative answer.

"Wasn't he so drunk that you had to work there for him?"

Anderson roared his objection, which forced Moss to ask the same question, repeatedly, in less provocative language, but he was blocked each time.

"How many nights had you worked the switchboard after the middle of October when you three [Gorrell, Oliver, and Jess Harris] began rooming together?"

"Well, we changed a lot—"

"I didn't ask you that," Moss snapped. "How many nights had you worked in John Gorrell's place?" he repeated as he raised his voice.

"Possibly three or four times," Oliver responded.

"Why?"

"Because he wanted to go to a dance."

He wanted the boy to say Gorrell was too drunk, but when he couldn't get that, Moss switched course. "Did Gorrell introduce Kennamer as Bob Wilson?"

"Yes sir."

"He told you that he was from Chicago?"

"I don't remember."

"IN FACT," Moss began by raising his voice again, "he told you that he was a gangster!"

"He did not."

"What had he told you about the circumstances?"

"You want me to tell?"

"Tell me," Moss said confidently. "I won't cringe about the facts."

"He said that 'when this fellow comes, I want you to get a good look at him. If I am ever killed he will be the one to kill me.'"

Tulsa's most highly esteemed defense attorney was off to a bad start.

When Floyd Huff sat in the witness chair, Anderson led him through his entire account of everything Phil Kennamer had said in that now-famous car ride to Tulsa. His story had not changed since he'd told it to Kansas City Chief of Detectives Thomas Higgins and during the preliminary hearing in December.

"What did he tell you of his plan to kill John Gorrell?"

"He said he would kill Gorrell next week in Tulsa. Take him out on some by-road, as I would call it, after dark, make out like he had a flat tire, and when they got out, he would let Gorrell have it then."

Huff's statement was important, and it supported what Jack Snedden had told police: that the murder of John Gorrell Jr. was premeditated. However, the middle-aged, bald man had a past that could discredit him. Before he ended, Anderson felt the need to stave off a potential disaster with this witness, and it was better the jury heard it from him first—before Moss sunk his teeth into Huff.

"Mr. Huff, have you ever been convicted of a felony?"

"Yes. Twice."

"In jail on any other offense?"

"Once."

On cross-examination, Moss took Huff back through his story of the car ride, with careful attention applied to the extortion note. He probed and prodded for holes and weak spots in Huff's story but was unable to churn up anything substantial. He then tried to steer the witness to discuss his client's state of mind, in an attempt to lay the groundwork for his insanity defense.

"Didn't you tell Kansas City police that you thought Kennamer was crazy?"

Before he could answer, the young gun of the prosecution, Dixie Gilmer, fired off another one of his many objections that day. He was determined to go up against the old hand, the veteran defense attorney, and beat him.

"Do you think he's crazy?" Moss tried once more, only to watch as Gilmer flew out of his seat and blasted another objection with a speed that stunned even him.

"You didn't tell Gorrell that Kennamer had threatened his life?"

"No."

"Because you thought Kennamer was crazy?"

Gilmer objected once again but Moss didn't care; by then, he'd made his point to the jury three times.

For his part, Huff was clearly more amicable than he had been during the preliminary hearing, where his aggressiveness had played into Moss's hands. The prosecution, it seems, had cautioned their witness. Even when Moss forced him to talk about his prison record, Huff sounded more embarrassed than angry, and anxious to explain himself, which he did, but only after Moss thoroughly humiliated him over his minor criminal record.

During the Great War, Huff was stationed at Fort Bliss in El Paso, Texas, and had gone AWOL, an offense that earned him a short stint at Alcatraz, which was a military prison at the time. In 1920, he had served six months in jail on a vague charge of larceny, followed by a violation of the Mann Act in 1922 that also got him nine months in prison. In the latter case, the unmarried woman he'd transported across state lines later became his wife. As bad as it made Huff look, some courtroom observers thought he was being bullied by Moss, who purposely made all the charges sound worse than they really were.

Anderson's next witness was a strong one. Ted Bath was a tall, clean-cut, handsome, young man with thick, black hair and angular features. He possessed a quiet confidence that made him all the more believable, and his voice was steady and calm. But it was what he had to say about Phil Kennamer that would leave an impression on the minds of the jury. Bath's account of his time with Gorrell and Kennamer in the Brown Derby Café on September 13 was rich in detail. He spoke of how the judge's son had proposed the armed robbery of a beer joint that would yield them three or four hundred dollars, but that he, Bath, had dismissed that idea because someone could get killed. He then told the jury of how Kennamer had proposed blackmailing a girl named Barbara Boyle, but had then put forth Virginia Wilcox's name after Gorrell told Kennamer to leave Barbara out of it.

"He suggested that he would defray my expenses if I would ingratiate myself with Virginia Wilcox so as to be able to get her into a compromising position so that some pictures could be taken of her. I said I would not be interested."

Kennamer didn't like hearing this. He didn't want anyone to hear it. For the first time during his trial, his body language betrayed his emotion. As he listened to Bath talk about his plans to seduce Virginia to get naked pictures of her, Kennamer put on a show that was meant to be noticed—clenching and opening his fists, his mouth quivering, and his hate-filled eyes piercing into Ted Bath. When he saw this, Dixie Gilmer's face melted into contempt and disgust.

But after the next witness took the stand, all the attorneys would be disgusted, and one of them would put his career in jeopardy.

Chapter Seventeen

HARMON PHILLIPS KNEW SOMETHING BIG was about to happen. The lunch recess had ended, and by 1:15, the reporters, attorneys, and court personnel were settling back down in the courtroom. Most of the spectators brought sack lunches with them and hadn't even left—not wanting to lose their seats to others waiting outside to get in. When the trial resumed, Anderson's "mystery witness" would take the stand. Earlier that morning, the *Tribune* reporter caught up with forty-two-year-old Edna Harman and carefully prodded her with questions. Although matronly and plump, it was obvious that she was once a very attractive woman, with a strong jawline that supported a wide face, high cheekbones, and a small nose. Her blue eyes matched the blue dress she wore beneath a fashionable black coat with a fur-trimmed collar that came with a perky little hat. When she sat down to talk to Phillips, she looked nervously around the small lobby of the Pawnee Hotel and confided to the newspaper reporter her big secret—that ever since she'd told Anderson what she knew, her life had been threatened.

A lot.

"They've told me that it would happen within thirty days after the trial," she told him in an overly affected voice. "I know the men who came to see me, and if I am asked, I shall tell their names from the witness stand."

But as a noble mother, she of course was not concerned for her own safety, but that of her children. She had the way it would happen all figured out. "The threats have mostly been toward my eighteen-year-old son who carries the mail," she whispered. "It would be awfully easy some dark night for there to be an accident on the road from Tulsa to Ponca City."[1]

When Phillips queried her for concrete details, she dodged his question with a vague answer. "Some of the threats have been of kidnapping and others of death." They were, she added, meant to keep her off the stand.

The apartment-building manager had informed the prosecution about the threats, and at her insistence, they assigned county investigator Jack Bonham to be her bodyguard. He was sitting just a few feet away, reading a newspaper, oblivious to all the assassins targeting this poor woman.

Phillips immediately sensed something was off with Mrs. Harman and raised a question about some interesting facts leaked by the defense team. "Are you the same Mrs. Harman that appeared as a witness in the Birl Shepherd murder trial five years ago?"

Mrs. Harman's face dropped when Phillips mentioned Shepherd's name, but she recovered and manufactured a coy little smile. "What's your next question please?"

"Are you not the same Mrs. Harman who offered evidence in another trial in Tulsa some years before that case?"

Again, she smiled, and repeated, "What are your next questions?"

"What other trials have you appeared in?"

"I would rather not answer those questions until I reach the witness stand."

"The defense attorneys will ask you then," Phillips pointed out.

"Well, I'm not so sure I *will* take the stand," she replied haughtily. After a long pause as she studied a gruff-looking man walking out of the hotel, she changed the subject back to her favorite topic. "To tell you the truth I am afraid. I've had all

---

[1] Ponca City is one hundred miles northwest of Tulsa, with Pawnee approximately in the middle.

kinds of threats to keep me from the stand. Saturday, two men came to my house and suggested I leave town before the subpoena reached me."

As if all that weren't enough, she'd also received anonymous threats by telephone. Before Phillips could unravel that claim, Mrs. Harman quickly excused herself for "some royalty business," but said she would return that afternoon.

The afternoon had arrived.

When Anderson called Edna Harman to the stand, Phillips leaned forward from his perch and readied himself. Tomorrow's front-page headline was about to unfold.

"Do you know the defendant, Phil Kennamer?"

Mrs. Harman ignored the question and turned to face the bench, "Your Honor, I am afraid to testify in this case."

"Just answer the question," Judge Hurst replied.

"Let her testify and let the jury and everyone hear!" Moss shouted as encouragement.

"Honorable judge, I'm afraid to testify in this case. I want to be excused. My family has been threatened time after time during the last twenty-four hours. I—I can't do it!" she squawked. "My children—mean more to me—(sob)—than anything else on earth. I'll take the penalty. I won't testify!"

KA-BOOM! The ticking time-bomb of a witness had just exploded. Anderson froze. He couldn't think straight.

"Let her tell all—I have no secrets," Moss howled.

"Don't say anything, Mrs. Harman!" Anderson fired back. In the gallery, the quiet roar of excited whispers added to the chaos that was unfolding.

"Any witness who will make such a statement is a disgrace and I ask that she not talk like that," Moss yelled above the noise. "Your Honor, I demand that a mistrial be declared immediately on the grounds of prejudice."

Not knowing what to do, Anderson blamed Moss for telling the witness to "tell all," although it did come on the heels of Judge Hurst's order to answer the question.

Joining in, Charles Stuart stood up and pompously remarked, "It's a disgrace to the administration of justice!"

"It's the truth, Mr. Moss! It's the truth!" Mrs. Harman shrieked.

"It's Moss's own doing!" Anderson snapped back. How he came to that conclusion was unclear; but what was clear was that his political career was now in jeopardy.

The courtroom devolved into chaos: Judge Hurst was addressing the jury, saying something about "disregarding testimony"; the bailiff was rapping the gavel to quiet the gallery, where four hundred people were talking at once; Moss was still going on about a mistrial, and prejudice, and some other stuff Phillips couldn't make out; Anderson was calling for a ten-minute recess; and Mrs. Harman was still shaking her head in defiance of the defense attorneys who were attacking her character.

Kennamer found the entire outburst amusing. Carefully shielding his face from the jury with his hand, Kennamer turned to face his siblings directly behind him, flashed a knowing smile, and whispered a few words Phillips couldn't make out.

While the court reporter was reading back Mrs. Harman's statement to Judge Hurst, Moss leaned toward Anderson and whispered, "You're nuts." When the stenographer finished, Judge Hurst zeroed in on a sly comment Moss had made. "Now, Mr. Moss, you asked her to proceed," he pointed out.

Moss, well-known for his witty sarcasm in the courtroom, raised his hands in consternation, "Please, Your Honor, don't take advantage of my excitement."

This raised the ire of Dixie Gilmer, who was showing himself to be faster at caustic rejoinders than the sharp-tongued Flint Moss. "Your Honor, he never was excited in his life."

"What the hell, did you plan this?" Anderson whispered to Moss, loud enough for the first four rows in the gallery to hear. The defense attorney ignored both of them and instead glanced over at one of the Kennamer siblings, pointed his finger at

Anderson who'd turned his back on him, and made circles with his finger around his ear as if to say, *He's crazy*.

The trial was now personal.

"She endeavored to sell her testimony to the defendant," Moss said, getting back to business.

"Mr. Moss, you're a liar!" Mrs. Harman cried out.

"I can prove by attorneys Breckridge and Boorstin of Tulsa that Mrs. Harman attempted to sell her testimony to the defense in a case several years ago," Moss declared. Mrs. Harman wasn't scared from death threats, he would later tell Harmon Phillips. The woman sensed her career as a professional witness was about to be exposed by Moss on cross-examination. The defense had done their homework. He knew the state's witness better than they did.

"She asked for $2,500, and then $1,200, to sell her testimony to Judge Kennamer in this case. We can show some letters written to Judge Kennamer were written by her. In the last two weeks she called Wash Hudson [a criminal defense attorney] and sought to learn if she could obtain extra remuneration for testifying in an Oklahoma City manslaughter case."

Anderson felt as sick as he looked.

"There is no question but that the defense was ready for her appearance on the stand, and the state was not," Phillips wrote in his notepad.

"The state has already told the jury what she will testify," Moss said as he continued his attack. "Her statement is false. We never communicated with her or threatened her. We welcome her here. I want to tell what we know and then ask the county attorney to withdraw [from] the opening statement that part about her."

"It would be necessary if she didn't testify," Judge Hurst agreed.

"Your Honor, she told me two minutes before the session opened that she *would* testify," Gilmer contended.

"She has told me she was threatened," Wallace joined in. "At noon she got a telephone call. When she came back she was nervous. Two men warned her to get out of town."

"That's not the reason she's scared," Moss laughed. He was enjoying this moment. It was his revenge against Anderson, who had publicly attacked the defense with witness-tampering allegations merely because they had exercised their legal right to interview state witnesses before the trial started.

"Your Honor, [on] Saturday," Anderson began. "She told me a story that sounded plausible. I haven't had an opportunity to investigate her standing at home. If she's not telling the truth, I don't want her here."

"Mr. Wallace made a statement we want to challenge," Stuart protested. "He said this woman was approached by a lawyer she believed represented the defendant."

"I'll let her tell who he was," Wallace barked.

"She was visited by two representatives of the defendant after we were served with notice. We were entirely proper in doing so," Charles Coakley said, speaking for the first time that day.

"This is not a police court. It is a court of justice and I want my rights," Stuart demanded.

Judge Hurst had heard enough. Both sides were overheated, and he needed to restore order and facilitate a compromise. "Mr. Moss, if the court will admonish the jury to disregard her statement here, and [if] the state takes her out of her opening statement, will you waive your motion?"

"I'm not certain the case isn't prejudiced by what happened here," Moss replied. "I'm going to ask Mr. Anderson to investigate my charges and have him tell the jury that her proposed statement would be false."

"We'll recess for twenty minutes and Anderson can make an investigation. Jury dismissed."

Former Pawnee County Attorney Lee Johnson, who sat silent during the melee, sought out Moss and Stuart and worked diligently with them for a compromise. He would, they agreed, put together a strong statement for the jury. After that, Moss would withdraw his mistrial motion. Anderson, for his part, wasn't with that group and had disappeared with Mrs. Harman to investigate her claims of harassment and death threats. He was unaware of the compromise being worked out.

When court reconvened at 2:31 that afternoon, Lee Johnson explained how they had recently learned of Edna Harman without having time to vet her story, and he expressed regret for her outburst before bringing the prosecution's *mea culpa* to a close.

"Mrs. Harman voluntarily related her story and it was accepted in full faith. No one connected with the prosecution of this case knew or suspected that Mrs. Harman would make the scene she did. We have concluded she is unworthy of belief, and withdraw from the consideration of this jury her testimony," Johnson said. He then closed with a recommendation that Edna Harman should be arrested and charged with contempt of court.

Although Johnson had just saved the day for the prosecution, it didn't seem to matter to Anderson, who feared he had lost his case. He wanted a do-over.

"The scene just created in this courtroom a little while ago has undoubtedly left some influence on the minds of the jurors of this case. For that reason, I want to join the defense counsel in that this be considered a mistrial and that this witness be held."

Moss threw up his hands in disgust and another round of bickering, shouting, and finger-pointing flared up. But when Charles Stuart pointed out that this was not the first time in courtroom history that an outburst like this had taken place, and His Honor could simply tell the jury what to disregard, Judge Hurst seized upon that observation as his opportunity to put an end to the pandemonium that came courtesy of Mrs. Harman.

"Is there a man on the jury who is prejudiced on either side in this lawsuit by reason of what has happened in Mrs. Harman's testimony?" When all of the jurors gave negative replies, that they were not prejudiced, Hurst ordered the trial to proceed, and for Mrs. Harman to be arrested.

The woman who had come to Pawnee with a bodyguard to testify against Phil Kennamer would now reside in the same jail as Phil Kennamer.

WHEN THE VICTIM'S FIFTY-FOUR-YEAR-OLD mother took the stand, she did so with a sad expression that broke the hearts of every female in the gallery. Alice Gorrell was a well-dressed woman whose white hair contrasted nicely with the black hat she wore. She was dignified and well mannered, but the questions about her son's last night on earth were disturbing, and her voice sometimes wavered as she struggled to answer Anderson's questions as best she could. She told the jurors of how Phil Kennamer had called three times that night, looking for her son. Although she had met him previously and heard his voice before, and the voice on the telephone *told* her he was Phil Kennamer, Moss forced her to admit that she could not be certain the voice was actually Phil Kennamer, and he was able to block that portion of her testimony from entering the record.

When Eunice "Alabama" Word was sworn in and responded to Anderson's preliminary questions in her Deep South twang, it was painfully obvious why they called her Alabama.

"She may have uttered 'pardon my southern accent,'" Walter Biscup from the *World* wrote, but he really wasn't sure what she said. "She is a native of Huntsville and talks with a broad accent, which at times perplexed the jurors."

But as the county attorney led her through every single detail of that fateful night, the jurors grew accustomed to her voice. She told them everything that had happened from the time Gorrell picked her up—what they did and whom they were with—to the last moments she was with John. Anderson had shaken off the Harman disaster and was building up to something important.

"We got back to the hospital about 10:50 that night," she said. "I remember the time because I had to sign up when I came in because we had to be in by 11:00 that night." By Anderson's next questions, Alabama explained to the jury that the front entrance to the hospital was quite a distance away from the street where John had parked his car.

"How far was it, what distance?" Anderson quizzed.

"Well, about 100 yards, I guess."

"Did John go with you?"

"Yes."

"Now, when he left the car what condition did he leave it in?"

"He got out on his side and came around and opened the door for me. He left the motor running and the door open," Alabama said.

"He left the motor running?"

"It was raining and sleeting hard. There was frost on the windows," she explained.

"When he placed the gun in the pocket of the car, was any part of it visible?"

"Yes, the handle was sticking above the pocket," she specified.

"Ever see John touch the gun after he put it in the pocket at the pig stand where you ate a sandwich earlier that evening?"

"No, I did not."

As he had done with Oliver and Huff, Moss tried to discredit both the witness and the victim with questions about drinking. To his disappointment, Alabama told him they had consumed no alcohol that night.

He then pressed her with questions about how John was showing off the borrowed .22-caliber revolver and allegedly playing with it. As hard as he tried, he uncovered nothing other than that Gorrell must have been a novice at handling pistols since he seemed mildly fascinated by it. In spite of this, Moss did uncover one interesting fact: before they ate at the pig stand, they had gone to Cook's Court, a tourist camp with little bungalows for travelers.

"What did he do with the six-shooter when you were there [in one of the cabins]?"

"I don't know," she answered meekly.

"You weren't much interested in *that* six-shooter then?" Moss teased the poor girl.[2]

When Jack Snedden was called up and questioned by Anderson, the eighteen-year-old explained that he had been friends with Kennamer, had driven him to the airport, and for the last year, was Virginia Wilcox's boyfriend. Sitting less than ten feet away, Kennamer scowled at his former friend. His face was clenched tight and his eyes narrowed. He didn't know what the younger boy was going to say, but it really didn't matter.

"On the way to the airport, did you have any conversation with Kennamer about why he was going to Kansas City?" Anderson inquired.

"He said he was going up to see Gorrell and if he was going through with the extortion plot, he would kill him," Snedden said in a matter-of-fact tone.

When he didn't go through with it, Kennamer sent him a telegram: ". . . Keep your mouth shut. K." After he got back from Kansas City, one of the first things he did was to show Virginia's boyfriend the note, knowing Snedden would likely tell her, which is what Phil wanted.

But still, nobody took him seriously.

Snedden then told Anderson about the meeting at the Owl Tavern, where Kennamer showed him and Beebe Morton the knife he was going to use to kill Gorrell later that night.

---

[2] It was a nine-shot revolver, but that didn't sound as sexually suggestive as *six-shooter*.

"He told me he had a date with Gorrell and I asked him if he was going out there to kill Gorrell and he said 'Yes.' I talked to him about his mother and the Gorrell family and the trouble he would cause and he put his hands in his pockets and started whistling and he made a remark about, 'calm, cool, collected is me,' and so I left him."

"About what time in the evening was it that he left?" Anderson asked.

"There weren't any clocks in there but I imagine it was about 10:30 or a quarter of eleven."

Gilmer then led Snedden to recount an incident the previous summer when Phil Kennamer pressured him to telephone Virginia at her parent's Michigan vacation home and tell her that Phil was going to drink himself to death if Virginia didn't write him a letter. Although she agreed to write Phil a letter, she instead wrote Jack a sharp rebuke and called into question the sincerity of his feelings for her. In response to Virginia's letter reprimanding her boyfriend, Phil wrote a three-page apology letter to Virginia and gave it to Snedden to mail, which he never did. Introduced as evidence by Gilmer, Kennamer's own letter to Virginia discredited defense claims that his love for her motivated him to kill.

Phil began his letter by confirming Jack's loyalty and devotion to her, and asking that she maintain her relationship with Snedden. Kennamer ended with a melodramatic reassurance that he was no longer in love with her. As Gilmer slowly read out loud to the jury, the nineteen-year-old defendant lowered his head and covered his eyes with his right hand.

> The old feeling is dead, Virginia, whatever I said in my delirium came from the liquor and not from me. Towards you now I feel nothing but admiration, respect and friendship. It has been like that for some time and all I wish in regard to you is friendship. The old feeling is dead . . . it will assure you of absolute freedom from

annoyance from me. So long Virginia, if we meet again, I assure you it will be casually.

Moss's strategy for questioning Snedden was not to denigrate his character as he had attempted with previous witnesses, but to draw out graphic, firsthand accounts that exposed his own client's mental instability. He needed to paint a picture of an irrational, love-sick boy, who would do anything for Virginia Wilcox, even slay another human being.

"Now then, *JACK*, let me ask you this—shortly after you started dating Virginia, isn't it a fact that Phil came to you and told you that if you ever mistreated her in any way he would kill you? He told you that, didn't he, *JACK*? Did he tell you this too, *JACK*, that if you ever said anything about Virginia that was unfavorable, whether it was true or false, he would you kill you?"

"Yes."

Later on, Moss steered Snedden down the memory lane of another bizarre Kennamer story. "Have you known instances, *JACK*, when Phil would come to a gathering or a party where you and Virginia were and Phil had not had a drink that he would dash out and get a glass of beer and then pretend with the odor of the beer on his breath to be drunker than he was?"

"Yes, he would."

The reason for this was simple: Virginia had once written Phil a letter expressing her concern that he was drinking too much. Therefore, if he acted like he was drunk, he just might elicit more of her attention. Snedden further explained how Phil used his friendship to get closer to Virginia. Once, when the two had a date, Phil bought an impressive bouquet of flowers to be sent to Virginia, but with the instructions that Snedden not tell her who they were from. But of course, that's exactly what he did, and Kennamer knew he would, which is why he used the boy to drive him to the flower shop. Moss then got Snedden to reveal that during a Christmas dance at the Mayo

Hotel in 1933, Kennamer did not just crawl along the ledge outside the sixteenth floor—he ran along it.

Although Moss was laying the groundwork for an insanity defense, the embarrassing incidents revealed in court led his client to focus his anger on Snedden. During a recess, Kennamer unleashed his wrath on Virginia's boyfriend. In the third-floor corridor, the only place he and Dr. Gorrell and others were allowed to smoke, Kennamer's face reddened when he saw Snedden by the water fountain.

"YOU'RE A LYING DOG!" Kennamer shouted. "You don't remember what happened at the Owl Tavern Thanksgiving night! I don't think you can remember!"

Snedden grinned and walked away. He had told the jury that Kennamer had said he was going out to meet Gorrell that night to kill him. That was premeditation, not the actions of a hero, and Kennamer's anger for Snedden's testimony would last forever.

Back in the courtroom, Moss continued his cross-examination with a yardstick that he swung up and down and back and forth as he emphasized his points.

"Now, *JACK*, how many times did he tell you he was in love with Virginia Wilcox?" Moss asked as he pointed the stick at his own client.

"I did not count them."

"Now then, *JACK*, did he ever tell you there was no use of him living because Virginia didn't care for him?"

"Yes, he did."

"How many times did he tell you things like that, *JACK?*"

"Not more than two or three times," Snedden answered, seemingly unperturbed by the countless number of times Moss was enunciating his name.

"Did he tell you, *JACK*, that because Virginia would not care for him as he desired, that he thought he would commit suicide by taking poison?"

"He did not tell me he had done it. I took him to his home *to do it*!" Snedden blurted. However, when they got there, for some vague reason, Kennamer never went through with it while Snedden was there. Kennamer later told his friend that he *did* take poison that night, but that he had taken an overdose, and the poison did not work in that large of a quantity, and that was the reason he had not died.

After he carried Snedden through more of Kennamer's overly dramatic talk of suicide, Moss brought the boy around to the Hy-Hat Club, of which the witness and his client were once both members. The Hy-Hat Club was high on the list of salacious angles to the story that out-of-state newspaper reporters were hoping would be revealed. If drugs or sex or orgies or naked pictures or even petty crimes carried out by overprivileged brats were to come out of this trial, it would come by way of the Hy-Hat Club, and their ears perked up when they heard the club mentioned.

"Now, when the Hy-Hat Club gave a dance, how was it decided which boy would go with which girl?"

"A list was sent around to each sorority and the girls would write down the name of the boy they wanted to go with. Then, the club officers would meet and determine who was to go with who to the dance, [and] then pair them off," Snedden explained.

Okay, not yet, but it was coming . . .

"Now, *JACK*, do you know of any instances when Phil attempted to influence the Hy-Hat Club to let him go with Virginia?" Moss asked as he raised and lowered the yardstick that was getting on Anderson's nerves.

"He usually asked Virginia to go with him and she would usually tell him she had another date, that is, if she had one."

Hmmm, still nothing. Get to the good stuff . . .

"You do know that Phil did all he could within the Hy-Hat Club to arrange it so that he would be Virginia's escort to the dance."

"Every time I know of but once," Snedden recounted before being dismissed for the day.

That was it? Damn Hy-Hat Club.

Both sides had scored that day, but after the Mrs. Harman fiasco, the prosecution's case had lost its edge. In tomorrow's newspapers, writers would proclaim the state would likely rest its case later that day. But the big story that day wasn't Mrs. Harman or the scandalous revelations of any witnesses on the stand. Instead, it was the Bruno Hauptmann trial. The jury had found him guilty and sentenced him to die in the electric chair.

Was it a bad omen for Phil Kennamer?

Chapter Eighteen

PHIL KENNAMER WASN'T THE ONLY crazy person before the court that Thursday morning. The first order of business Judge Hurst attended to was a plea hearing for Edna Harman. Charged with contempt of court, her bond was set at $1,000, and her trial was scheduled for March 11. Instead of making money as a witness, she lost money as a prisoner. When Harmon Phillips tried to interview her again as she was being led back to jail, Edna Harman wasn't so talkative anymore.

"Although having discussed her appearance here and [her] reluctance to testify without hesitancy when she first appeared Wednesday morning, after the court ordered her held, she refused to discuss the matter with anyone."

The courtroom started filling rapidly as soon as the doors opened at 8:00 a.m., and the day began with Flint Moss recalling JACK Snedden to the stand. Many in the crowd that day were Tulsans attracted by all the Edna Harman drama and testimony summarized the night before in a remote broadcast by radio station KTUL.

Ever since he'd arrived in Pawnee, Moss had lived up to his reputation as "the smoothest man in the courtroom." His gabardine wool suits were tailor-made to fit, and he preferred dark colors with flashy silk ties and white pocket squares that shimmered. His deep-toned leather shoes were custom-made by a Tulsa shoemaker. Moss kept them clean by wiping them down as soon as he got into the building. As much as he wanted the jurors to think of him as one of them, he wasn't about to walk around in front of the jury box with red dirt on his shoes.

Despite some minor setbacks the morning before, he'd scored big with the Harman fiasco, and the momentum was on his side. The state would likely rest its case that day, and he looked forward to pushing the defense's double-pronged strategy before the jurors. But first he had to chip away some more from Anderson's witnesses. He began by introducing the most damning piece of evidence the defense had: that Gorrell was the mastermind of the extortion plot.

"Now Jack," he dropped the enunciation, "tell the court whether exhibit two is the handwriting of Phil Kennamer?" Defense exhibit two was the extortion note. Although Moss was showing it to Jack Snedden, a prosecution witness, he wasn't going to introduce it into evidence until the defense was allowed to present *their* case with *their* handwriting expert.

"This is not Phil's writing," Snedden said as he examined the note he'd first seen at the Quaker Drug Store.

"Jack, did the defendant ever tell you before he went to Kansas City that John Gorrell intended to kidnap Virginia Wilcox?"

"Yes sir."

"What did he tell you?"

"About this gang in Kansas City that was going to kidnap Virginia." It was the answer Moss wanted.

"Did he tell you what connection Gorrell had with the gang?"

"Gorrell," he said, "was the leader of the gang."

ANDERSON AND MOSS EXAMINED AND cross-examined six of the last seven prosecution witnesses in less than ninety minutes. The state's case had been reduced to the short-story version of what happened: Kennamer said he would kill Gorrell, then he shot him twice in the head, and then he confessed to it, claiming self-defense.

Anderson's next witness was Randal "Beebe" Morton, who testified about meeting Kennamer the night of the murder, and specifically, how he had relieved Kennamer of the knife—not once, but twice.

Hoping to show that his client surrendered the knife because he had no harmful intent, Moss asked him, "Now then, when you went to take it from Phil, he didn't protest or even resist you, did he?"

"No, not a bit," Morton said.

But there was a good reason for that. Beebe Morton was a very big boy—bigger than Kennamer. And when he took the knife away from him, it was not the first time he'd disarmed a killer. When Morton was just fourteen years old, he watched his neighbor Roy Freeman barge into his house and shoot both of his parents to death. Morton then attacked the crazed man, took the gun away, and called police. Freeman was sentenced to life in prison, and Morton and his brother inherited from their Osage Indian parents their oil-well rights granted by the federal government.

No, Phil Kennamer wasn't going to mess with Beebe Morton, who then tried to talk him out of murder.

"[Kennamer] said 'Gorrell is going to kidnap Virginia Wilcox. I am going to stop it. I am going to kill John Gorrell tonight.' And I said, 'With this knife?' And he said 'Yes.' And I asked him if he was really going to, and he said 'Yes.' I said 'Phil, do you think it is worth it?' And he said, 'Yes, I am terribly in love with Virginia Wilcox and I am going to protect her in every way I can.'"

Anderson then called two witnesses who quickly testified that they saw the defendant come into the drugstore between 10:30 and 10:45 that night, about the same time Snedden said Kennamer left the Owl Tavern, which was just a few doors down. However, what jurors didn't hear was that Sidney Born had told police in December that he and Kennamer left the drugstore at approximately 10:45. Since it was only one mile to the hospital, his testimony could have placed Phil at Gorrell's car while John was escorting his date back to the sign-in desk.

Shortly after eleven o'clock that morning, the city coroner, and Deputy Nathan Martin, were also rapidly questioned and dismissed. Although there was never any doubt, Anderson established cause of death, and that Phil Kennamer told Martin, "I shot Gorrell."

But there was one prosecution witness called to testify whom Moss did not want to rush. No, he was going drag this one out. He was going to make it hurt. This witness was special.

The State calls Sgt. Henry B. Maddux to the stand.

Moss's contempt for Sgt. Maddux stretched back before his claims of turning down a $25,000 bribe, as well as his contrived bravery to soldier on with his investigation despite an insinuation of bodily harm. He wanted to know about the photos Maddux took of a dead John Gorrell in the front seat of his Ford sedan. If he had custody of the negatives, which were police evidence, how did they get published in both of the Tulsa newspapers?

Maddux had crossed the ethical line when it came to damning his client in the press, and now it was time to get a little payback. But first, Gilmer had to take him back through the night Gorrell was killed.

"Approximately at what time, Mr. Maddux, did you see the body of John Gorrell Jr?" Dixie Gilmer began.

"About 12:30 on the morning of November 30, I believe," Maddux answered.

"I ask you if, at that time, you photographed either the automobile or the body inside of the automobile?"

"I did."

"Later, did you take a photograph of the head and face of John Gorrell at the mortuary?"

"I did."

It was a line of questioning designed to introduce two enlarged photographs of the dead victim. Moss ignored the death-scene photo, which he sorely wanted to talk about, but loudly objected to the head shot taken at the morgue, sometime after the murder. While the photographs were being examined by defense attorneys during their objection, Phil Kennamer noticeably leaned in and craned his neck to see the gory results. He was a little too obvious about it for reporters, and when he smirked and grinned at his handiwork, they took note of it.

Others observed the opposite reaction from the victim's parents. Doctor Gorrell buried his face in his hands as his wife ran from the courtroom in tears.

While the jurors studied the photographs carefully, Moss interrupted Gilmer to question Maddux on the minute details of photographing the victim in the car.

"When you took state's exhibit number six, did you open any of the car doors?" Moss began.

"Yes sir."

"What door?"

"Right door. Right front door," Maddux answered.

"Right front door," Moss repeated. "Where did you place the camera in order to take plaintiff's exhibit number six?" The answer to Moss's questions was obvious just by looking at the photographs, so why bother asking them, some wondered. But Moss had his reasons. He wanted his detailed questions burned into the memories of the jurors when it came time to confront Maddux later.

"In front of the right front door. Right door to Mr. Gorrell's right side," Maddux answered.

What made the photo most interesting to observers in the room is what it didn't show. "Kennamer has contended that he engaged in a violent death-struggle with Gorrell before he killed him," Walter Biscup wrote for *Tulsa World* readers. "The photograph showed there had been no struggle, that Gorrell's body was upright, and that his clothes were in no way disarranged."

Resuming his questions, the young prosecutor then led Maddux to note there was a small bump with a dark discoloration below Gorrell's right eye in the photograph. When Kennamer surrendered, he had no bruises or marks that would indicate Gorrell had fought back.

Gilmer then qualified for the court that the witness was a criminologist, and Maddux explained to the jurors that meant "the scientific detection of crime," and one of his duties for the police department was to "preserve physical evidence." But when Gilmer attempted to elicit from the police sergeant his opinion regarding which bullet wound came first, and the distance from which it came, Moss successfully objected.

"If he's testifying as an expert, I want to show he's not one," Moss demanded. "The only way you could tell that answer, to how far away the shots were fired, would be by actual demonstration."

After convening from the lunch recess, Moss recalled Maddux to the stand for cross-examination. "Immediately after court adjourned you refused to talk to Mr. Charles Coakley, one of the defense attorneys, about the facts you knew in this case and had not testified to, didn't you?"

"I told Mr. Coakley I didn't think it was my place to tell him anything at the time," Maddux answered. He'd been avoiding the defense attorneys ever since Kennamer was jailed.

"What did Mr. Coakley ask you?"

"He asked me the condition of the gun, if I had the gun in my possession. I told him I thought the proper place for that question was on the witness stand."

"Isn't it true that Mr. Coakley went to Mr. Anderson to get a court order to talk to you, and Mr. Anderson objected?"

Anderson loudly objected on the grounds that the question called for a hearsay response. Always eager to provoke the county attorney, Moss responded with a salty remark that was not printed.

"Just a minute, just a minute," Anderson snapped back. "I want to reiterate my objections to these remarks of defending counsel!"

Judge Hurst once more admonished Moss, who knew he was getting under Anderson's skin and thoroughly enjoyed it.

"How long have you been on the Tulsa Police force?" Moss asked, as he refocused his attention on his favorite defense witness.

"A year ago last January."

"Do you have the gun in your possession with which Gorrell was killed?"

But Gilmer objected and said the gun would be produced as soon as they had a chance.

"You've had plenty of chance," Moss replied angrily, which led to another squabble breaking out.

"Another sally from Gilmer brought a comeback from Moss, and once more Anderson jumped to his feet. He and Moss shouted back and forth, bringing sharp raps from the court," Phillips wrote.

"Mr. Gilmer's remark was first and improper. So was Mr. Moss's. Both of you keep quiet," Judge Hurst admonished. He had become a babysitter to a bunch of oversized children with law degrees.

Moss then took Maddux through a long dialogue on bullets, ballistics, the murder weapon, and the process of fingerprint identification—where he struck oil.

"So, you assert that because of the fact where you found the gun, and the tests you made to reveal fingerprints on any part of it, that some person had not only intentionally but successfully rubbed and obliterated the fingerprints on it?" Moss inquired.

"I don't know whether intentionally or by accident, but they were removed," Maddux replied.

Moss then got him to admit he had not dusted the butt of the gun, trigger, or leather holster for fingerprints. "It would be possible to get them off but I didn't do it," Maddux confessed.

"How many photographs did you make that night of the Gorrell body?" Moss casually inquired, getting back to the setup he was building.

"Just one."

"One single photograph and one single negative?"

"Yes sir."

"Now then, whatever reproduction of the photograph you made that found themselves in the papers of Tulsa were made from state's exhibit number six?"

"They came from the same negative," Maddux admitted.

"Did you make any other prints from the same negative and turn them over to the newspapers, from which they produced a likeness of state's exhibit number six?" Moss asked.

The color drained out of his face. He didn't like where this was going. "I made three or four prints and I suppose that the newspapers got them."

"Do you remember seeing the photographs in the Tulsa papers?"

"I believe I saw one of them."

Moss, who'd been leaning against the railing farthest from the witness, sauntered closer as he continued his questions. He was moving in for the kill. Maddux looked over at Gilmer for support, but there was nothing he could do.

"That photograph that you saw in the newspapers came from the state's exhibit number six. Nobody else took a photograph that night?"

Maddux shifted in his seat. "I don't believe they did."

"You don't know of anyone else?"

"I don't."

Moss turned to face the sixty-two newspaper employees in the room. "Do you know which industrious newspaper reporter it was who obtained it?"

"I would like to know!" Maddux thundered.

"Sorry I asked you. Was the reproduction in both papers?"

"I only saw one."

"Which one?" Moss asked with his hands out wide, palms up.

"I don't remember."

"Mr. Maddux, first in the development of the film, and from one in the newspaper, you became familiar with the details of the photographs, state's exhibit number six?"

"Yes sir."

"Was this picture in the newspapers made from the same negative?" Moss already asked that question, but he wanted to back the car up and run over Maddux again.

"I imagine it was the same," Maddux answered calmly. He wanted to appear nonchalant in order to downplay the beating he was taking.

"As far as you know, it was?"

"Yes sir."

And again. "As far as you know there is no difference between the exhibit number six and the newspapers?"

"Yes sir," replied the criminologist who had said earlier that it was his job to "preserve evidence."

The king of courtroom sarcasm rolled over the top of Maddux one last time. "And you came to the conclusion that one or both of the newspaper boys got hold of the photographs?"

"Yes sir."

The state rests.

Chapter Nineteen

THE STATE'S CASE WAS A mere skeleton of what many hoped it would be. Only fourteen of the fifty-seven witnesses subpoenaed had testified, while the rest were held in reserve for the rebuttal. Although few people felt it was weak, there was the general impression that it could have been stronger—with or without the Edna Harman fiasco. When reporters later pushed Anderson for an explanation, it put him on the defensive.

"We have made out a murder case against Kennamer. We didn't take long to do it and we perhaps didn't make it as dramatic as many [had] expected. We didn't need to. It was just a prosaic case. We didn't need to show a motive because it wasn't necessary. We proved that Kennamer killed Gorrell and that he had previously threatened his life," Anderson declared. "We also proved that the love Phil Kennamer claimed for Virginia Wilcox was 'dead' by his admission in a letter to her," he added, referring to the letter given to Snedden but never mailed.

Disappointment was felt in Kansas City, Oklahoma City, Chicago, and New York City newsrooms when editors learned that half their chance to get a hot story of scandal-plagued Tulsa youth had evaporated. Their hopes shifted to the defense.

With two hours left to go in Thursday's court session, Moss's opening statement was a fifty-five minute overview of his case, which gave a detailed picture of a tempestuous boy who was almost a genius but was driven to insanity by the rejection of the woman he loved and his need to protect her from the likes of John Gorrell. Walter Biscup noted that during the long, impassioned speech, eighty percent of it built the foundation for the insanity angle. It was the biography of a ne'er-do-well, as his defense attorney specified in detail all of his client's shortcomings and failures in life. As Moss carried on, Phil Kennamer's ego took a beating. His body language betrayed his humiliation when he slouched low in his chair, leaning forward, eyes on the floor, as if he were trying to crawl under the table and hide.

Moss recounted for the jury how the boy had dropped out of high school, military school, boarding school, Catholic school, and a private school in San Angelo, Texas, where he abandoned his mother. That was the time he was later found on a fishing boat, trying to sail to Rio de Janeiro to join a revolution. When he was brought back to Oklahoma, Kennamer held onto this ambition and often spoke of joining revolutions in Mexico, China, and Cuba, where his superior intelligence over nonwhite races would garner him a leadership position. He imagined himself an expert at military tactics because he'd once read a book on the subject that he borrowed from the local library.

When his parents realized their boy could not be kept in school, his father used his influence to get him job after job, none of which Phil kept for very long. "His father would pay his wages through his employers without Phil knowing," Moss informed the jurors. He burned through jobs as a gas station attendant, cub reporter at two newspapers, a driver for an oil company, and president of a semi-fictional advertising agency. He was working as an insurance salesman for a reputable company when he killed John Gorrell.

"Never has Phil been able, mentally, to content himself in a single character of employment for two months."

Moss's speech then chartered a course through the psychology of his client's "mental weaknesses" before moving on to how the "tragedy" was all John Gorrell's fault, and Phil Kennamer was Virginia Wilcox's righteous savior.

"Now then, gentlemen of the jury, you are wondering if this plan to kidnap Virginia was conceived by John Gorrell, or Phil

Kennamer," Moss said. "Upon that issue we will satisfy you beyond any question. That is one of the links of the state's case which the state proposed to put forward by Mrs. Harman."

J. Berry King nearly came out of his chair as if he wanted to object. After the threats of mistrial and trouble they had gone through to get her name out of the trial, the lead defense attorney had just slipped it back in when it suited his purposes.

By now, the pitch in Moss's voice was rising, and his hands gestured defiantly as he built up to a proclamation he wanted these jurors to take with them to their deathbeds. "Every statement that comes from a reputable or a reliable person upon the subject of this kidnapping places Phil Kennamer— uncompromisingly, courageously, single-handed and alone—in the position where he proposed [to take] a human life rather than let it take place.

"TRUTHFUL WITNESS," Moss shouted, "shall come into your presence and assert the fact to be—Phil would dare any danger—defy any hazard—take any chance—and go to any length, foolish and foolhardy as he was—Phil Kennamer always opposed—with all that he possessed—the carrying out of this plot against Miss Virginia Wilcox."

WHEN THE KENNAMER JURORS RETURNED to the rented house that evening, they found the one daily newspaper they were allowed had gigantic blocks cut out of it. Besides the Kennamer trial coverage, Judge Hurst ordered the Hauptmann death-penalty story also be removed. His trial may have been over, but the baby killer would remain above-the-fold news for weeks. Although national attention had shifted more to Phil Kennamer, he still played second fiddle to Bruno Hauptmann.

But it didn't seem that way in Pawnee, Oklahoma, where sixty-two newspaper reporters, photographers, stenographers, telex operators, and a radio station crew, representing more than a dozen news organizations, appropriated the entire courthouse. It was their job to get the story out, which they couldn't do without advanced technology.

"No one seems to notice the faint ticking of the telegraph instruments in the courtroom," *Tribune* feature reporter Ruth Sheldon wrote. But they weren't the old-style, Morse-code-sending units; these were teletypewriters, capable of transmitting sixty words a minute over a special cable installed and leased just for the trial. "There are eight of these sending keys, all of them the 'noiseless' type. They are not noiseless, but what sound does come from them is of such character that one would scarcely realize they are transmitting thousands of words."

Every day, photographers would lie in wait on the second floor, where they would ambush key witnesses going up or coming down from the third floor. When the flashbulbs popped, it would send an eerie light that seemed to penetrate every floor of the courthouse. The photographers scanned each new arrival and snapped photographs, not knowing if the role they played that day would be tomorrow's front-page news. Twenty-year-old Betty Watson found this out one morning when she came to the courthouse with her mother. She had been subpoenaed by the defense but was dropped from consideration at the last minute under mysterious circumstances, which sent reporters digging to learn more. Despite the fact that she would not take the stand, newspapers ran her photograph anyway because "she was strikingly attractive." Her photo became a substitute for the scandalous stories promised but never delivered.

She wasn't the only attractive individual involved in the trial. *New York Evening Journal* cub reporter Dorothy Kilgallen, [1]

---

[1] She quickly became just as famous as her father as a book author, columnist, celebrity reporter, game-show panelist, Broadway musical producer, and crime reporter covering some of the biggest trials of her time. She later got entangled in the Kennedy assassination, with a purported interview of Jack Ruby. She was also a harsh government critic. Her sudden

daughter of famed reporter James Kilgallen, had just arrived in Pawnee from Flemington. In another Ruth Sheldon feature story, the young woman proclaimed Phil Kennamer "more cute" than Bruno Hauptmann. "He is quite colorful. Seems to be a pretty nice fellow, young, good-looking," Kilgallen said. But she may have been attracted to his bad-boy image. "He looks to me like he's the kind who would get real drunk, drive a car real fast and do all those things."

The lawyers also fascinated her, especially Flint Moss. "That Moss—he's so colorful!" the twenty-one-year-old exclaimed. "I got a big kick out of the way he leaned against the rail with his feet crossed next to the jury and the way he played his smile on the jury. In Flemington, that wouldn't be allowed for five seconds."

Flemington also didn't have a dozen lawyers in the courtroom, bickering like children. So far, J. Berry King had kept his professional demeanor. But most of them, at one time or another, verbally attacked each other with caustic remarks, whispered insults, insinuations of incompetence and criminally liable behavior. Although Anderson couldn't seem to contain his bitterness, Flint Moss remained "the smoothest man in the courtroom," as Harmon Phillips wrote. He moved through the crowded corridors with cheerful greetings that were individualized to each recipient. His nickname for Deputy Nate Tucker was too racy to be repeated, but it always made Tucker smile. State hospital psychiatrist Floyd Adams was always acknowledged with a "there goes Doc Adams!" Moss could backslap and shake hands like a man running for office, and nearly everyone in Pawnee loved him.

---

death in 1965 led conspiracy theorists to claim she was murdered to silence her. Her father outlived her and died in 1982 at the age of ninety-three.

Friday, February 15, 1935

A COLD FEBRUARY MORNING DID little to curb the enthusiasm that Friday as spectators and newsmen eagerly anticipated all the sensations that would come from defense witnesses. Famed reporter Copeland Burg, working for the William Randolph Hearst–founded International News Service, caught up with the defendant as he was getting a haircut at a barbershop across from the courthouse. Under the watchful eyes of Sheriff Burkdoll, Kennamer laughed and joked with three of his pals who'd be coming to his aid as defense witnesses later that day.

"Just wait until I get on the stand," Kennamer teased Robert Thomas, Allen Mayo, and Claude Wright. "I'll tell the world something they never heard about you guys before and believe me I know a lot about each of you!"

When the laughter died down, Kennamer added, "But don't worry. Never mind. Everyone says *I'M CRAZY.*" It was a shot at his defense attorney's strategy, which he resented, but in that rare moment, he had what he'd always relished: an audience fixated on his every word. He was the center of attention. As witty as his jokes were, there was always a thread of self-pity woven into each one of them.

"Say, this guy Jack Snedden is sure my pal," he continued. "First he steals my girl. And I wrote Virginia a letter last August and gave it to Jack to mail and he just keeps it until now and then turns it over to the prosecution."

"Are you sore at Jack, Phil?" Claude Wright asked him.

"No, not sore. He is just a nut—like me—but he can go around and make trouble—my pal Jack."

This brought another round of laughter, and Burg noted the barber couldn't keep the shaving lather out of Phil's mouth as the boy jabbered on.

"I wish I had my school books with me and you could help me with my studies," Wright offered.

"No, no," Phil countered, "I'm *crazy now* and couldn't help you a bit." As Phil and everyone else chuckled, it nearly caused the barber to nick him with the straight razor. But his ego couldn't help itself, and he had to call out one of his friends as a liar.

"Say Tommie, you had a nerve saying I told you to come along and I would show you Gorrell's body. You know I didn't say that," Phil said in a dark tone.

Robert Thomas answered him with a nervous grin. He didn't know what to say to someone whose version of that night was different from all the other witnesses. Arguing with Phil Kennamer was pointless.

"Never before has there been a defendant like Phil Kennamer," Burg relayed to a national audience in his article.

JUST AS FLINT MOSS WAS set to call his first witness, he was interrupted by an unlikely source. Cartoon-faced J. Berry King, with his round cheeks, big nose, pointy chin, and coffee-cup-handle-shaped ears, had something to say. It was the first time he had had anything to say, and it caught Moss off guard.

"Your Honor, I am always inclined to be tolerant of any opening statement, entertaining and enlightening as the defense's was, but as counsel for the state I understood Mrs. Harman's former statement was not to come into the case," King said as he turned to face Moss. "I request the defendant to withdraw her name from the record."

"I refuse," Moss pouted.

"Then I ask the court to strike it from the record."

It was stricken. King one, Moss zero.

The first day of the defense's case unraveled slowly but would end with what Moss anticipated would be powerful and emotion-laden testimony for the twelve jurors, who were beginning to impress him as the no-nonsense type. With his first three witnesses called and dismissed in thirty minutes, the defense attorney introduced into evidence twelve Spartan

School of Aeronautics flying reports as specimens of John Gorrell's handwriting. Moss then called Judge Franklin Kennamer to identify a letter his son had written, after admitting that he himself, Moss, had not read the letter. Next, he formally introduced the actual extortion note, which Judge Kennamer declared was not in his son's handwriting.

When Gilmer passed on cross-examination, King jumped to his feet and shouted to Moss, "Do you mean you are offering evidence you haven't even read?" he asked, referring to the letter the defendant had written. Again, King was able to catch Moss off guard.

"Don't be surprised at anything I do," he answered quietly.

King two, Moss zero.

But Moss was too experienced to let anything in the courtroom affect him, and he moved on to Wichita, Kansas, handwriting expert Jesse Sherman, a veteran of more than 750 trials. While Moss reviewed Sherman's qualifications, the extortion note was handed over to the prosecution, where Dr. Gorrell had his first opportunity to inspect it himself. It was not as he had hoped. It was his son's handwriting after all.

"If the defendant is seeking to prove that Gorrell wrote the extortion note," Gilmer interrupted Moss, "we will admit it."

Stunned, Moss replied, "You admit that the handwriting on the envelope and two pages of the letter *is* that of Gorrell's?"

"Yes."

The prosecution was prepared for this but still maintained that Kennamer was the author of the note, even if he didn't actually write it. Privately, they believed Gorrell wrote it to get Kennamer off his back, or he was intimidated. According to the defendant himself, the note was written in his hotel room the morning of November 21, while the two were alone.

Admitting the note was written by John Gorrell deflated Sherman's testimony and whatever impact it may have had on the jury. Instead of fighting it, going along with it was the state's best strategy to reshape what it actually meant. If Kennamer plotted all this to portray himself as a hero, the extortion note would be the key to his entire story. Kennamer couldn't force Gorrell to kidnap Virginia if he didn't want to, but he could pressure him to write an extortion note. Once he had documented evidence in the victim's handwriting, Kennamer could do exactly what he did: build a story around it that portrayed Gorrell as the evil bad guy and himself as Virginia's brave defender.

Gorrell wasn't alive to tell what happened that morning when he wrote the extortion note, but the statements from nearly every prosecution and defense witness firmly established that Phil Kennamer was a prolific liar. The boy couldn't even keep his story straight between his two interviews with the *World* and *Tribune*.

All of this had made Flint Moss's job incredibly difficult. When Kennamer surrendered, he'd told reporters this was a simple case of self-defense. That argument was quickly shredded by multiple witnesses who said it was premeditated, forcing Moss to push an insanity defense as eighty percent of his opening statement. This put Kennamer in the awkward position of claiming to the jury that *it was self-defense when I did it, but I was also insane at the time and didn't know right from wrong.*

The only evidence of self-defense in the case was Kennamer's own account of what happened. To support that claim, the high-school dropout would have to tell the jury himself. Moss had to go along with it because Phil had dug that hole deep. Kennamer was all by himself on that one, but the best strategy for Moss was to simply overwhelm the jury with stories from family and friends, as well as expert witnesses, that supported his agenda.

The balance of the defense witnesses that Friday were designed to turn the courtroom into a sympathy festival—for Phil Kennamer, the prodigal son; Phil Kennamer, the abnormal child; Phil Kennamer, the love-sick dreamer. Moss firmly believed this was his best hope for an acquittal. If the jury found his client not guilty by reason of insanity, the court would be forced to let him go free. After all, the trial was not an insanity hearing, the outcome of which could put Kennamer in a state mental hospital.

Longtime Kennamer pal Claude Wright was not supposed to be an important witness that day, but his two hours of testimony fed the jury outrageous stories from the life of the defendant. He was the fourth witness called and one of three friends whose recollections would provide anecdotal evidence to support defense psychiatrists' claims that Kennamer was insane at the time of the "unfortunate tragedy." While Wright's testimony uncovered irrational and immature behavior, it was actually seen by many as just the sort of childish deeds and daydreaming that could come from any boy with an active imagination, but not necessarily one who was insane.

But that didn't mean there weren't peculiar stories to be told. Wright's most shocking account was the time Phil jumped out of a second-story window with a noose around his neck when he was just five years old.

"Phil was attempting to explain to the kindergarten teacher how to tie a knot in the rope and he tied a curtain-string around his neck in a hangman's knot and jumped out the window. He landed in a sand pile and wasn't hurt," Wright said.

While spectators gasped when they heard this, Phil found the memory of it amusing, and smiled to himself as he kept his face covered by his left hand.

"What happened to the rope when Phil jumped out the window?" Moss inquired.

"Everything went out with it."

"Was it heavy enough to hold Phil's weight?"

"No."

"Did it break?"

"No."

"So, the curtain fell down and Phil landed in the sand pile?"

"Yes," Wright answered. "The teacher was scared to death."

Besides his stories of Kennamer's daredevil escapades, his obsessive love for Virginia Wilcox, his numerous suicide threats, along with his quitting school or every job he ever had, wrecking cars, and drinking excessively—not to mention the tall tales he told—reporters focused in on Kennamer's self-confidence in his own intelligence.

"He thought he was smarter than the Mexicans," Wright recounted to questions about Kennamer's desire to join far-off revolutions. "'I could take them over and run them,' he said."

In a story he told Wright, Kennamer's ambition to be a leader was nearly realized when Harlem vice gangs proposed he should rule over their entire operation.

"On his last trip to New York City, he came back and told me that he was walking around and ran across two Negro gangsters in an argument. They were gamblers and bootleggers and had been cutting prices on each other and were trying to get organized and he got their confidence so that they told him he could handle their business. They arranged a second meeting and were going to get all the members together under Phil," Wright explained. However, his time as a Harlem crime boss was unexpectedly cut short.

"About that time his mother wanted him to come home and he left," Wright recounted, which caused many in the gallery to laugh out loud.

During cross-examination, Gilmer got Wright to admit that in spite of Kennamer's wild boyhood antics, there was nothing about them to indicate he didn't know right from wrong.

"In your opinion, Phil is an awful liar, isn't he?" Gilmer prodded.

"Yes sir."

"What I want to know is did he tell these wild lies about gangsters and things in front of his parents and your parents, the same as he tells them in front of you young fellows?"

"He is somewhat changed in front of his parents," Wright said.

"In front of his parents or your parents he doesn't give all that color to his yarns?"

"He has told my father some of his yarns."

"Would that, in your opinion, indicate that he knew right from wrong?" Gilmer carefully asked.

"Yes sir."

The witness accounts which would make headlines across the United States came after the lunch recess when Homer and Virginia Wilcox were called up, followed by the emotional testimony of Kennamer's father and sister Juanita. Taking his seat in the witness chair, Homer Junior looked around nervously and bit his upper lip. The courtroom was packed tight; all of the eighteen benches were filled, and young boys cutting class from the local school for Indians were standing along the walls. Just behind the door, Junior's mother waited, occasionally sneaking a peek into the crowded courtroom.

"Now . . . " Moss began as he leaned against the rail. Anderson had hidden his yardstick, and the defense attorney was forced to make do without it. ". . . tell the jury just what Phil told you about the plot to kidnap your sister on the part of Gorrell."

"He told me that Gorrell was in this gang in Kansas City and that he had told him last summer of the plan to kidnap my sister and he would prevent it at any cost."

"Homer, did he tell you what he would do if necessary to prevent it?"

"He said, if necessary, he'd kill Gorrell."

"Did you tell your father or mother about it?"

"No," Junior said flatly. "I took no stock in it at the time and I didn't want to worry them."

When the object of Phil Kennamer's unrequited love entered the courtroom, the excited whispers of five hundred people watching her created a loud buzz that followed her all the way to the witness chair. When she sat down, the clamor dramatically stopped. Until that exact moment, she was the unheard-from heroine in a tragic drama that left one boy dead, because another boy refused to go to police with the extortion letter and needed to be a hero.

Virginia Wilcox was fashionably attired in a blue dress punctuated with an enormous silver-fox-fur collar that cascaded down to her elbows. A dainty, blue-felt hat was pinned to her brown, wavy hair and was tilted down over her right ear. Her pleasant face, with its pale skin and coffee-colored eyes, typecast her as a tender-hearted young lady who knew better than to get mixed up with a boy like Phil Kennamer.

As the nineteen-year-old answered Moss's questions about his client's overwhelming displays of attention shown to her the last three years, she spoke in a clear, sweet voice. The expression she wore for twenty-two minutes was one of intense seriousness combined with repressed emotion, and it was painfully obvious she didn't want to talk about any of this. Phil's grand plan to be more to her than he was had boiled down to this one moment, and Virginia Wilcox never looked at Phil Kennamer once. Not that he would have noticed. He couldn't bring himself to face her either, and he sat with his head bowed, his hands covering his face completely.

None of it had worked out the way he'd thought it would.

After Virginia was dismissed, the accounts of Phil's suicidal tendencies by his father and sister caused many of the women in the gallery to shed tears for the defendant. The cold, steely reserve of Judge Kennamer was broken several times as he testified to his son's erratic, abnormal behavior. As he had done to his own friends, Kennamer harvested attention from his father with dark talk of suicide.

"The gray-haired jurist was unable to continue and began weeping. He removed his gold-rimmed spectacles and dried his eyes with a handkerchief," Walter Biscup wrote. "The judge's display of emotion did not appear to affect the prisoner, who maintained his customary position of leaning his head against his right hand propped on the counsel table by his elbow."

Kennamer's father was smart enough to tailor his one hour and fifty minutes of testimony with statements that reinforced an insanity defense. Just as he had done when his son had run away from home, or quit school, or quit his jobs, or crashed his car, his father was there to rescue him. Despite his reputation as a stern judge, he was now in the ironic position of having to mitigate his son's guilt as a boy who didn't know right from wrong. As biased as he was, Judge Kennamer did pass along one insightful revelation.

"He had a very emotional disposition," Judge Kennamer declared at one point. "He either felt very high or very low."

"Either in an extraordinarily happy mood or very despondent?" Moss offered.

"That expresses it."

Chapter Twenty

BIPOLAR DISORDER, WITH ITS EXTREME highs and lows, wasn't the only mental health issue Phil Kennamer was afflicted with. According to one of the country's leading psychiatrists, the boy had bigger problems. When *The Human Mind* author Dr. Karl Menninger took the stand, he was twenty minutes late. Normally, that would have been a problem for Judge Hurst, but not that day; Monday the 18th of February came with a sense of déjà vu. Over the weekend, state and national newspapers trumpeted multiple stories saying that Phil Kennamer would testify. This spawned another hysterical mob hell-bent on getting a coveted seat in the courtroom. If Menninger could have been there when the doors opened at 8:00 a.m., he would have recognized the Pawnee County Courthouse for what it became—a madhouse. *World* reporter Walter Biscup depicted the events of that morning for readers.

> Hysteria of the mob made its appearance at the trial of Phil Kennamer here for the first time today when a crowd consisting of all the people the courtroom would hold and a surplus of more than a hundred others raced through the doors and stormed up [three] flights of steps when the courthouse opened at 8 o'clock.

> It was a riot in miniature. They stampeded through the corridors, surged up the stairways four abreast, women and men alike. On the top floor all broke into a run for the last few yards of the race and those in the lead flung themselves elated into the seats of their choice.

Men and women shoved and elbowed alike. Women were knocked down on the stairs, clothes were disarranged, belongings were lost and forgotten in the scramble. There were shouts, laughter, squeals and some curses.

Three minutes after the doors were opened every available spectator's seat in the courtroom was occupied. A hundred more people took standing room at the rear and along walls. At the double doors just beside the jury box at least 50 more were wedged into a compact formation, with nothing to restrain them except the obvious fact that there was no more room inside. The corridor door at the back of Judge Hurst's bench was impassable.

Even the booming voice of Sheriff Charlie Burkdoll could not stem the rush. And deputies made no effort to check the dash of sensation-hungry hundreds until the courtroom was filled and comparative quiet was restored.

Those who could not get in were ejected from the [third] floor of the courthouse and a deputy stood guard at the second-floor landing, permitting none above that point who were not directly connected with the case. All morning long another 100 people stood patiently on the second-floor landing, hoping to be first in line after lunch.

Even after it was announced that the courtroom was full and [no more] would be admitted, additional chairs were carried in by latecomers who blithely explained that this attorney for the defense and that attorney for the prosecution "told me it would be all right."

As a result, by the time court convened, not a spare chair was to be found. Reporters, robbed of theirs by spectators who carried them casually from the press room, searched the courthouse from top to bottom without finding a single spare.

Influence was at a premium and there was much bitterness and some weeping among disappointed women who were turned away, only to see others turn the magic trick and squeeze chairs into spaces where there did not appear to be room for the furniture.

Furthermore, press tables became strangely filled with new faces. Many who probably never saw inside a newspaper plant protested emphatically they were reporters and obviously belied the fact by making prominent display of pencil and paper. As a result, Judge Hurst ordered the bailiff to exclude anyone occupying the seat of a bona fide reporter.

Phil Kennamer had a pretty good idea what Menninger was going to say, and he was still upset over the insanity claim. It could not coexist with his ego. It discounted his heroics. It discounted the intelligence he had used to outsmart Gorrell.

Everyone could clearly see *something* was wrong with Phil Kennamer—everyone except Phil Kennamer. There had to be a reason why he couldn't stay in school or hold a job, why he thought he was smarter than everyone else, why he was a liar and manipulated people, why he had absolutely no fear, why he drank like a fish and had crashed four cars, and why he enjoyed the attention that came with being a murder defendant without the shame of being branded a criminal.

They were about to discover the answer, which came in three words. In direct response to a forty-three-minute question by Moss in which he reviewed the entire case, Dr. Menninger declared Kennamer was "irrational" at the time of the unfortunate tragedy.

"Was he able to distinguish the difference between right and wrong?" Moss inquired.

"I don't think he could distinguish between right and wrong," the forty-one-year-old said. He was the youngest psychiatrist to testify during the trial and represented a new school of thinking that was more empathetic to criminals.

"Will you tell us why?"

"I think he was unable to distinguish right from wrong because he was incapable of accepting ordinary standards and substituted his own. His own egotism was so great that he had his own moral code, which to him seemed a better one than the one society accepts."

"Does the sort of insanity or mental illness which you have concluded the defendant has, is that a well-known kind of insanity—does it have a name?"

"In most books, it is known as psychopathic personality disorder," Dr. Menninger answered. In his medical opinion, which would endure throughout his life, psychopaths were not responsible for their crimes and should be treated instead of imprisoned.

"This type of insanity has been known for years as 'moral insanity' and by other descriptions, which have now passed out of use," Dr. Menninger explained. "Only in recent years has the name been changed to psychopathic personality disorder."

There it was. Three words that explained why Phil Kennamer was the way he was.

Oklahoma City psychiatrist Dr. Eugen Werner's time in the witness chair was far shorter than his colleague's. He would only affirm that Kennamer did not understand or appreciate the consequences of killing John Gorrell.

"You have heard the questions I have asked and propounded to Dr. Menninger?" Moss asked him.

"I have."

"Do you agree with Dr. Menninger?"

"I do."

Menninger and Werner's testimony may have been brief, but it explained more in three words than all the other witnesses combined—if anyone actually understood what psychopathic personality disorder meant, which most did not. But six hundred people didn't storm the courthouse and break a door off its hinges, again, to listen to why Phil Kennamer's brain was broken. Their interests were more prurient.

They wanted to hear from the defendant himself.

After the lunch recess, the nineteen-year-old told an incredible story that had witnesses doing things they never did, and saying words they never said. He took on a dozen of them at once with absolutely no fear of how their accounts differed from his own. Randal Morton was a liar. Jack Snedden was a liar. Robert Thomas was a liar. Alice Gorrell was a liar. In his world, everyone else was lying, but he was telling the truth— this time. He didn't even seem bothered by the fact that the story he told on the stand contradicted his own accounts previously given during his newspaper interviews.

"The prisoner, who undoubtedly suffers from ego-mania, appeared the calmest person in the room as he slowly enunciated the story which he hopes will bring him freedom," wrote Walter Biscup, who had gotten to know Kennamer well by now. "He was deliberate in every answer and it was this attitude of mental certainty, more than anything else, which convinced the lay audience that the youth was wholly sane."

When he first sat down, he fixed his gaze directly at Virginia Wilcox, who was seated with his family on their reserved bench in the front row. Her presence with the Kennamers was a bit of a mystery, and there was speculation that Flint Moss had something to do with it. This young, attractive girl from a wealthy family did not acquire that front-row seat by fighting through a mob of people. On Friday, she couldn't bring herself to look at him. Now, she caught him staring at her and returned his gaze with a cold, blank expression that was noted in several newspapers.

Flint Moss was sitting this one out, and he had turned over the direct examination to his co-counsel, seventy-eight-year-old Charles Stuart. Stuart was a short, heavyset man with a head and face marked by red telangiectasia blemishes and brown spots from years of hunting and fishing.

Phil began his story by calmly informing the jury that he'd met Gorrell during the latter part of August—before the meeting with Ted Bath and two weeks before Gorrell headed off to dental school. Besides the extortion note, the single greatest piece of evidence in his favor was his own claim that Gorrell had first discussed the kidnapping with Cochrane and Pat Burgess before Kennamer ever met him.

"I met John Gorrell the latter part of August or the first part of September 1934."

"State the circumstances."

"I was working for the Frates Company, an insurance company, and somewhere between 10:00 and 11:00 in the morning, Preston Cochrane called me and asked me to come to his room and when I got there, Cochrane told me to pay particular attention to the man he wanted me to meet, and that man was John Gorrell," Kennamer said.

"That was the latter part of August?"

"Yes sir."

"Did you hear that there was a scheme on the part of Gorrell to kidnap Miss Virginia Wilcox, or her brother Homer Wilcox?" Stuart asked.

"Yes sir."

"When, shortly after your last meeting with Gorrell, who told you of the plot?"

"I saw them separately. I saw Preston Cochrane first before my meeting with Gorrell. He told me of the plan to kidnap Virginia Wilcox, and later I saw Pat Burgess who told the same story."

"When was that?"

"The middle of September," Kennamer answered. "I was working in the insurance office. Gorrell called and asked me to meet him [at the Brown Derby Café] and asked me when I got there to come outside and meet [Ted Bath]."

"What was said?"

"He told me his plan," Kennamer said.

"Now, without going into detail, tell the jury if at that time or if you ever agreed to the plan to kidnap Virginia Wilcox."

"I—DID—NOT."

Kennamer's testimony of when Gorrell told him of the plan to kidnap Virginia contradicted his December 12 interview with the press, when he claimed Gorrell had not spoken of the plan to him until he went to Kansas City in November:

> After my investigation, I went to Kansas City about the middle of November and found Gorrell. We talked a bit and then I remarked how I heard something was coming against the Wilcox family. When Gorrell discovered I was interested, he said he did not know that I would be interested in anything like this.

He then told the jury of how he arrived in Kansas City on the evening of November 20. After checking into the Phillips Hotel, by his own admission, Kennamer bought the hunting knife from a department store, and then stationery and rubber gloves from a Walgreens, which Gorrell would use to write an extortion note.

During his Kansas City story, Kennamer, from the witness chair, once again portrayed his victim as the well-armed crime boss of a gang looking to graduate from petty robberies to kidnapping. In spite of Gorrell's determination to go through with it, Kennamer was able to talk him out of it, and into an extortion plot. After a night of drinking, Gorrell spent the night in Kennamer's hotel room. Excited by the prospect of making twenty thousand dollars, Gorrell woke up early, put the rubber gloves on without any suggestion from him, and immediately started writing the note—all while he was still asleep.

"Did he compose that note by himself without any suggestion from you?" Stuart asked.

"Yes sir."

"He completed it by himself?" Stuart asked one more time.

"Yes."

"Now, Phil, you got that extortion note, what was your purpose in getting this note and appearing to be in with John Gorrell in this scheme?"

"My purpose was to forestall Gorrell. I figured if he knew the note was in my possession, he would make no effort to go through with the scheme," Kennamer replied. He then claimed he only showed the note to four or five people, not the ten who reported to police he was shoving it in their faces to read.

"What did you tell them you were going to do with it?"

"I was going to see Gorrell when he returned and tell him the note was in my possession and I would turn it over to the authorities," Kennamer smugly declared.

It sounded good, but it wasn't what he'd told Floyd Huff who told Chief Higgins back on December 1: "He said he was undecided just what he would do with it. He was very positive in saying he did not intend to turn it over to police."

"Now, we come to the night of the *tragedy*," Stuart began. Like Moss, he was not using the words *killed* or *murdered*. "When did you get into communication with him?"

"About a quarter to six or seven Thanksgiving night," Kennamer said. "Gorrell called me."

"Did Gorrell arrange a meeting place with you that night?"

"Yes sir. A drug store directly across the street from St. John's Hospital."

"He told you he would meet you there at what time?" Stuart probed.

"7:30."

"I arrived there a little before 7:30 and two girls were there in the store. One of them, I think was Eunice Word, who testified here. They got up and asked the clerk if he knew John Gorrell. He said that he did. They asked him to tell Gorrell that they had to return to the hospital and for him to pick them up there. Possibly five minutes after they left, Gorrell came to the door, and I got up and met him at the door and told him that the girls had gone back to the hospital.

"We stepped outside and he said, 'How is this thing coming along?' and I said, 'You are busy now and I will see you tomorrow.'

"He said, 'I will be through early tonight,' and I said I wanted to get home early.

"He said, 'I'll have these girls in at eleven o'clock,' and I said, 'If you are through at eleven, I will meet you then.' I don't know whether he returned to his car or went across to the hospital."

His explanation was incredible. "These girls" established Gorrell as having a date with two women that night. But if the second girl was supposed to be Hazel Williams, Charlie Bard's date, she wasn't a nurse, and she didn't even work at the hospital. And although Phil telephoned four times that day looking for John, and once the day before, he portrayed himself to the jury as indifferent to when the two would meet up.

"Now, after he left to fulfill his mission with this girl at the hospital, what did you do?"

"I called a cab and went to the Owl Tavern," Kennamer answered. After a long discussion about the knife, who took the knife, how he got it back, and how it was taken again, he created completely new dialogue for Morton and Snedden.

"'What are you going to do?'" Morton asked him.

"I said, 'I am going to have a showdown with Gorrell.'"

"He said, 'You are going to kill him, aren't you?' and I said, 'No.'

"He said, 'I think you are,' and I said, 'No, you are wrong, I wouldn't get into anything like that.'

"He said, 'If there is any trouble I am going to take a hand in it.' I said, 'No, in the first place there will not be any trouble and the best way to start trouble would be for you and Snedden to go along.'"

Kennamer then declared that the only reason he had the knife was for self-defense. "I thought that if Gorrell anticipated that I was not going through with this, he would have someone else with him and they would beat me up or something."

After he finished his story about the knife, Kennamer explained to the jury how he then walked a few doors down to the Quaker Drug Store where he found Sidney Born at eleven o'clock that night eating a sandwich and drinking a Coca-Cola. He needed Sidney to give him a ride, but his friend tried to hand over his keys so Phil could take his car.

"No, you come on and take me," Kennamer said he told Born.

"What time did you leave to go to the hospital?" Stuart asked.

"Seven minutes after eleven o'clock," Kennamer answered.

"Did you see his car?"

"Yes."

"Did Sidney say anything about who was in it?" Stuart led.

"Yes, I told him what I was doing when he parked. Sidney said, 'He's there alright.' He said, 'Be careful,' and drove away."

"You got in the car with Gorrell?" Stuart asked.

"Yes sir."

"I will ask you whether or not, when you first got in there, you saw any gun on Gorrell?"

"No sir."

"Do you know that he had one?"

"No sir."

After driving slowly toward Forest Hills, a sparsely populated area at the time, where there were only two houses near the triangular median, Kennamer said he told Gorrell, "I never had any intention of mailing the letter. I told him that if ever at any time he considered going through with a proposition of that nature in regard to the Wilcox family, or another of my friends, that I would turn the letter over to the authorities."

Gorrell responded by pulling the gun out and screaming: "'By God, you will never do anything with that letter!' I couldn't say whether it was in the pocket or between the seat and the door. It was on the left side. He reached over to the left-hand side with his right hand and secured the pistol and brought it over with an upward and downward movement."

"When he made the downward movement, where was the gun pointing?"

"The pistol was directly in my face," Kennamer replied.

The courtroom grew quiet as Kennamer told this part of the story. The jurors watched intently as he mimicked with his hands how Gorrell tried to shoot him in the face. It looked awkward on many different levels. First, if Gorrell was steering the car with his left hand, going underneath his left arm with his right hand to retrieve the gun appeared to be the longest, most cumbersome way of going about it. Second, if Kennamer was sitting less than two feet away, it would have been problematic for Gorrell to extend his right arm out in order to level the gun at Kennamer's head. If Gorrell had done so, the barrel would go past Kennamer's head and would be hitting the passenger's side window because of how small the front seat was in Gorrell's Ford.

"What did he do then?"

"He pulled the trigger."

"Did the gun go off?" Stuart asked.

"No sir."

"It snapped?"

"Yes sir. There was a brief struggle. I secured the pistol in my hand. With my left hand I was pushing him in the face. He still had a hand on the gun. I was attempting to and did turn the pistol toward him and away from my face, and there was one explosion. I presume I pulled the trigger, though I couldn't swear to that. There was another explosion simultaneously with the car striking the curb."

This is the explanation that had a problem. If he was pushing John in the face with his left hand when the gun fired, how did the bullet miss his own hand? If it happened the way he described, it was a miracle that the bullet didn't plow through his left forearm or hand.

After the "tragedy," Kennamer said he wiped the pistol clean and walked back to the Owl Tavern, where he told Robert Thomas what he had done.

"I called him over and told him I was in an awful jam," Kennamer said. "He said, 'What?' and I said, 'I have just killed John Gorrell.' And he said, 'In a wreck?' and I said, 'No, I shot him.'

"He laughed and said, 'Why?' and I said, 'I had to do it.' And he said, 'Take me out and show me the body,' and he was laughing, and I said, 'For God's sake, don't laugh, this is serious!'"

Stuart then guided him back to the woman all of this was for with questions meant to play to the jury's softer side. "Now, Phil, I am compelled to ask you a personal and very delicate question. When did you first meet Virginia Wilcox?"

"Sometime in October 1931."

"And was that her first date with you?"

"Yes sir."

"Did you actually fall sincerely in love with that girl?"

Everyone in the courtroom was staring at him. They wanted to hear him say it. This was the romantic angle to the story that helped pushed it into the national spotlight.

"Yes sir," Kennamer whispered.

"Do you love her now?"

Kennamer nodded, and his voice cracked when he mumbled, "Yes."

"And from the time you got this extortion note until the time of this tragedy, were you constantly thinking of your meeting with Gorrell and how you could prevent this tragedy?" Stuart asked.

"Yes sir."

"And was that your purpose in your mind from the time you reached Tulsa with that extortion letter until the night of the killing?"

"Yes sir."

He was doing it all for the woman he loved. It was a sentimental story of a brave knight going into battle, unarmed and disadvantaged, to save the beautiful princess from the dark and powerful antagonist. It was a clichéd plot that never grew old and should have ended with "and they all lived happily ever after."

In Kennamer's mind, that's how it was supposed to end. But since it didn't, the fairy tale of the knight and the princess was the version his defense attorneys needed to sell to the jury to get an acquittal.

Chapter Twenty-One

INSTEAD OF POUNDING KENNAMER TO DUST, King's cross-examination was weak. It began strongly but then waned into a conversation with the special prosecutor probing him with questions in which King didn't already know the answers. Even so, he was able to get Kennamer on the record with statements he knew would be contradicted later by rebuttal witnesses.

"Do you know right from wrong?" he began.

"I think so," Kennamer replied.

"Have you always known right from wrong?"

"I think so."

"If you have made any wrong statements in your testimony, if you have made statements that are not true, that contradict with statements of other witnesses who have testified, do you still think those statements were true?" King grilled.

"No. I would think they were wrong."

King tried again. "You do not understand me. If your answers have been contrary to the answers of other witnesses, you still think you were right in making your answers?"

"Yes sir. I know I was right," Kennamer countered.

The boy's answer was as expected—egotistical—and it confirmed what Dr. Menninger had told the jury earlier that day.

King wanted the jury to hear it again. "You are certain?"

"Yes sir."

"This is not the first statement you have made as to the facts in this case, is it?"

"No sir."

"As a matter of fact, you have made several?"

"Yes sir."

King then confronted him with an Oklahoma City newspaper story in which he said one of the objectives for his trip to Kansas City was to convince Gorrell to write the extortion note. Since there was never any evidence or supporting testimony that Gorrell was ever going to kidnap anyone, King wisely used Kennamer's own words against him.

"'I knew Gorrell would demur in writing this note and one object of my trip to Kansas City was to persuade him,'" King quoted Kennamer from the article.

"Yes sir."

"You knew, then, Gorrell would demur?"

Kennamer shifted uncomfortably in his seat. His answer was barely audible. "Yes sir."

"You would use your power of persuasion to have Gorrell write that note?" King pressed.

"There should be more to that article, Mister King. Some qualification." But there wasn't. And after Moss pushed King to read the entire article to get the right context, Kennamer was still forced to acknowledge that he'd persuaded Gorrell to write the extortion note.

"Couldn't you have induced him to write the note without gloves?"

"I don't think so," Kennamer replied.

"But you did prevail on him to write it?"

Kennamer paused before conceding with a "Yes."

King was able to score another point with the jury when he brought up the name of Hanley "Cadillac" Booth. The defense knew Anderson was going to call him as a rebuttal witness.

"Did you have any conversation with this man last July in his Oklahoma City apartment in which the kidnapping of Miss Wilcox was discussed?"

"I did not."

"To be exact, did you not, at that time, notify this man, Mr. Booth, that you were interested in getting into some 'bigger money' and asked him if he was interested in extortion or kidnapping some of the wealthy oil people in Oklahoma and in which conversation you went on to tell him about the Wilcox girl?"

He felt the sting of Virginia's gaze. "No, I—DID—NOT!" Kennamer shouted. It was exactly what King wanted him to say. When "Cadillac" took the stand tomorrow, his testimony would cast doubt on Phil's response.

Toward the end of his cross-examination, King questioned him about what happened in Gorrell's car, where he put Kennamer on the defensive.

"You knew John's car?"

"Yes."

"When Sidney delivered you there, you saw Gorrell's car at the curb, the engine running and either the right-hand or left-hand door was open?"

"I am almost certain neither door was open."

"You entered the car before John returned?"

"No."

"Isn't it a fact, that you got the gun out of the left-hand pocket and had it in your possession when he returned?"

"No, Mr. King, that is *NOT* the truth."

"Tell us what happened then," King offered with a wave of his hand.

"I got in the car from the right side. I am almost certain the door was closed. Gorrell was seated at the wheel. I think the first thing he said was, 'I've been waiting twenty minutes.' I told him I was sorry I had been delayed. The next conversation was of a trivial nature."

King grunted. "Any sign of nervousness on the part of either of you?"

"I couldn't say as to myself. Gorrell seemed morose, restrained and not as cordial as usual," Kennamer said.

"Who suggested the route to take on leaving the hospital?"

"No one made a suggestion."

"John Gorrell sought the scene of his own death?"

"He was at least driving in that direction," Kennamer said in an exasperated tone. His annoyance with the special prosecutor was becoming more noticeable. He then repeated the conversation he and Gorrell had had before the actual killing.

When he was done talking, King again consulted his Oklahoma City newspaper and asked Kennamer if he had not said this: *'Did you ever hear of the double-cross?' I asked Gorrell. I told him he was getting the double-cross now.*

"It would be impossible for me to say it is accurate, however, it is almost entirely correct so far as the conversation I had with Gorrell."

"Was that portion 'double-cross' used?"

"I think the expression was used," Kennamer replied.

"And you did give him the 'double cross' when you fired two shots into his head, written with his own blood in the letter 'K,' which the blood formed on his cheek, your characteristic signature?"

"I DID NOT!"

"Phil, after John had been killed, what did you do with the gun?"

"I either put it on the floor or seat."

"Were you so excited you don't recall?"

"Yes."

He could sense Kennamer was getting frustrated, and King wanted to keep provoking him. "Then, why did you wipe the blood off the handle?"

"I know I didn't wipe the blood off because there wasn't any there," Kennamer replied in a flat tone.

"Did you wipe off the fingerprints?"

"I have a recollection of wiping the gun across my coat."

"You were certain the gun had been snapped once or twice before it was fired?"

"I know it was snapped once but my memories, thereafter, are incoherent."

"How long was it before the two shots were fired?"

"One to two seconds." That was exactly the answer King wanted. While Moss had blocked Maddux from testifying that the wounds indicated the second shot was fired more than a minute later, the prosecution found a new expert—one whom Moss couldn't get dismissed.

"Do you recall the posture of the body?"

"I couldn't describe it, but my impression is his head was forward when I left."

"How did you get back to the drug store?"

"I walked all the way, two miles." This was disappointing to those hoping he would name his accomplice. For some reason, many people thought his two-mile walk in bad weather was improbable.

As King wrapped up his interrogation, he scored one final point against the nineteen-year-old.

"Did you deliver the note to anyone before you surrendered?"

"Yes, to Father Stephen Lanen, instructor at Cascia Hall."

"What was your reason?"

"Because I had no wish to be apprehended or killed with the note in my possession," Kennamer acknowledged.

King saw his opportunity, and went for the jugular. "Yet . . . you killed John Gorrell over it?"

"In a sense."

"You thought one death over the note was enough?"

"Yes."

King was finished with him. He had done well enough, but missed the opportunity to push Kennamer further with doubts about the struggle over the gun. How did John get that bruise near his right eye? How did the first bullet miss his hand completely if he was pushing on John's face? At the very least, there would be the pitting and burns from the muzzle blast on his hand. And during his story, Kennamer said he found Sidney Born in the drugstore drinking a coke at 11:00. But in December, he told police and reporters he entered the drugstore at 10:30.

Although he had missed these points, King did set Kennamer up to fail when the rebuttal witnesses came forward.

On redirect, Stuart felt the need to undo some of the damage.

"Who is Booth?"

"He is a bootlegger in Oklahoma City," Kennamer answered.

"At times you did business with him?"

"I was only there twice."

"This Father Lanen, he is a Catholic priest, and had been your teacher?"

"Yes."

"You had confidence in him and that's why you turned this note over to him?"

"Yes sir."

Stuart turned to consult with Moss and Coakley, and then Moss stood up and barked, "Your Honor, the defense rests."

There would be no testimony from Preston Cochrane or Pat Burgess. They were not going to back up Kennamer's claim that John Gorrell *first* told them about his Wilcox kidnapping scheme *before* they ever introduced him to the judge's son. The jury would just have to take the word of Phil Kennamer that the idea originated with Gorrell. And there would be no testimony from the beautiful Betty Watson. An unconfirmed rumor hinted in the newspapers that Kennamer had professed his devotion to her as well. That was the supposed reason the defense declined to call her. Phil, apparently, was dizzy for her, too.

Tuesday, February 19, 1935

FOR HIS REBUTTAL, ANDERSON AIMED to prove two facts to the jury on the last day of the trial: Phil Kennamer was not insane, and in fact, he was the original architect of any crime aimed at Virginia Wilcox.

The base-run hitters for Anderson's rebuttal were three psychiatrists, who did agree with Menninger's medical diagnosis, but not his legal opinion. Yes, Phil was a psychopath, they all said, but he wasn't insane, and he knew right from wrong. The most intriguing testimony came from "ol' Doc Adams," whose definition of psychopathic personality disorder seemed to fit the life of Phil Kennamer perfectly.

"A psychopathic person is an individual of unstable emotion, usually showing from early childhood. The symptoms are restlessness and they are uncontrollable, and as children are unable to be properly trained and are unresponsive to guidance of the parents. In school, there are certain types that are brilliant and other types that do not do so well and are on the border line of being feeble-minded," Adams testified.

As he spoke, Harmon Phillips looked over at the defendant to get his reaction. He looked bored as he sat with his right arm on the table and his chin cupped in his hand. All that day he stole long, furtive glances at Virginia, who never returned his stare.

"As they advance in school and age they are hard to control and cause parents and school authorities trouble," Dr. Adams continued. "They are hard to keep in school and as they leave school, they are restless and stubborn, go from one job to another, chasing a rainbow, staying with work only a few months, losing interest usually. Quite a number of them become alcoholics, drug addicts, and sex perverts. A lot of them do not come in contact with the law."

Although their medical experts may have been heavy hitters, they were not Anderson's homerun hitters. His Babe Ruth, Lou

Gehrig, and Jimmy Fox were an ex-bootlegger, a former confidant of Kennamer's, and a blood expert.

Bail bondsman Hanley "Cadillac" Booth was forced to testify by subpoena. He didn't want to tell his story but Anderson needed Cadillac to refute Kennamer's claim that Gorrell was the one who had hatched the kidnapping plot.

"Do you know Phil Kennamer?" King began.

"Yes," Cadillac said as he pointed at him. "I first met him in July 1934, at my home with Jeff Griffin and Billy Harper, Oklahoma City newspapermen."

"Did you see him again after that?"

"I saw Phil about two weeks later, in August."

"What was the purpose of his visit to your home at that time?"

"Phil and a friend came to my home to purchase some whiskey, which was my business at the time. I sold them some."

King framed his next question as slowly and clearly as he could. "Did Phil Kennamer, at that time and in that conversation, discuss with you extortion, kidnapping, or robbery of some of the wealthy oil people in Tulsa, in which conversation he went on to tell you about the Wilcox girl?"

"Yes sir."

King wanted him to say that again, so he repeated his question. "When Phil was at your home was extortion, kidnapping or robbery mentioned by Phil?"

"Yes sir."

This was bad. Moss had to shut this down. "Did you think he was serious or not serious?" Moss interrupted.

"I couldn't tell," Booth said as he shrugged his shoulders. "I didn't pay any attention to him."

"Why didn't you pay any attention to him?"

"It didn't mean anything to me," Booth said flatly. It was true. He had told Kennamer he was in the bootlegging business, not the kidnapping business.

"How many times have you been convicted?" Moss inquired. He knew the answer, and wanted to discredit the witness as he had done with Huff.

"About one hundred times. I never was convicted, I always pleaded guilty. A hundred times in municipal court, two sentences to the county jail, one fine, one term served and fine paid in federal court."

It was a strong answer and it left Moss with no place to go.

The prosecution's Lou Gehrig was Kennamer pal Otto Kramer, and when he took the stand, he knocked it out of the park. The twenty-one-year-old accountant began by explaining that for the last three years, he was a close friend of Phil Kennamer, who often discussed with him his infatuation with Virginia Wilcox.

"Have you ever had any conversation with Kennamer when the name of Virginia Wilcox was injected?" Gilmer queried.

"Yes. Several."

"Was the substance of these conversations about the same?"

In spite of Moss's best efforts to object the witness out of the chair, he was blocked by Gilmer, and Kramer was able to make his point.

"They amounted to pretty much the same, very little variation," Kramer answered. "He stated he was very fond of Miss Wilcox at one time, and she didn't care for his attentions, and he felt very bitterly toward her and her family and said he was going to get even, if it took his last day."

Those in the front who could see her turned to look at Virginia. A strange, knowing smile broke across her face, and she looked down at her shoes to hide it. It was as if Kramer's statement confirmed something she had already known or suspected.

With enlarged photographs of Gorrell's head wound, Dr. Cecil Knoblock "proved the surprise witness of the trial by adding the final punch to the state's attack on Kennamer's claim that he and Gorrell engaged in a struggle before he killed him," Biscup reported to *World* readers.

Over the loud objections from the defense, Knoblock declared the first .22-caliber bullet struck Gorrell in the right forehead and the second one came lower, and closer to his ear.

"Can you say what interval of time elapsed if any between the two shots?" asked Gilmer.

"I can't explain the chemical examination in a few words. The nature of the abrasion affects the blood clotting. Taking all things into consideration, the fact that the blood of the second wound has flowed over the face, as well as the first, I think it is fair to say the first blood would coagulate in a minute and a half. The blood from the first wound flowed down and of necessity was clotted before the second wound was inflicted."

"What is the minimum amount of time that you think elapsed between the firing of the two shots?" Gilmer asked.

"There can be no denying that there was an interval because there was a crossing of the two paths of blood. Considering the facts that cause blood to coagulate, there would have to be at least a minute."

Moss did his best, but despite sparring back and forth with Knoblock, he was unable to shake his testimony. For Anderson, it was as good a time as any to rest his rebuttal, and when Moss followed him, the trial of Phil Kennamer was over.

Chapter Twenty-Two

THE KATZ DEPARTMENT STORE decided to take another chance with their going-out-of-business sale. After everyone calmed down, the crackerjack promoter from the big city returned with an important modification to the old banner:

YOU ARE LOSER

if You Don't Attend Katz Department Store Quit Business Sale!

With a fifty-foot sign blazoned across their storefront, it got people's attention. Locals and out-of-towners wandered in just to see what they were offering.

Over at the Midway Barbershop, the barbers were more than pleased with all the out-of-towners who needed a shave and a haircut. Judge Kennamer was there every morning at 7:30, and his son was there every other day. Facial hair was no longer in fashion, and it was a great time to be a barber.

Things weren't going as well for Charlie Graham who ran the Graham Hotel, where the defense team was lodged. He was just hoping to break even on his restaurant business. With all the added mouths to feed, he'd had to bring in extra help, which ate into his profits.

But there was one group of Pawnee residents unconcerned with the Kennamer trial. Every morning on the north side of the courthouse square, families crushed by the depression formed a line outside the offices of the Federal Emergency

Relief Agency. "None of them so much as glance at the courthouse, but wait patiently for admission," Ruth Sheldon wrote. Outside of the defendant's egocentric world, there was another one with problems of its own.

And the world of one Tulsa family was shattered on a cold Thanksgiving night. The pieces remained scattered like rubble during Christmas, and then New Year's Day, with all of its hopes and promises. For ten days in February 1935, John and Alice Gorrell endured explicit death photographs, an egocentric killer, smooth-talking defense attorneys denouncing their son, and some jackass doctor from Wichita who excused a psychopath as someone not legally responsible. Doctors like Menninger studied schizophrenics, psychopaths, sexual deviants, and folks who were truly psychotic. It was the pastors who focused on grief and sorrow, and all their answers pointed to a heavenly world. But John and Alice still had to live through this one, rebuild their lives, and endure for the sake of their remaining son, Ben, and their daughter, Edith Ann.

Throughout the trial, the Gorrells kept mostly to themselves. True to their nature, they were quiet and never answered questions or volunteered their opinions. They barely spoke at all, and the out-of-town correspondents quickly learned what the Tulsa writers already knew: to respect their privacy. But that kind of silent endurance comes with a price, and John made a payment on that debt one afternoon when he collapsed on the floor of his hotel room with a nervous breakdown, immediately after the closing arguments ended. Through a choked throat, clogged with despair, he pushed out the words, "My son . . . my son . . . " Alice Gorrell rested on top of her husband, stroking his thin hair without bothering to wipe her away her own tears.

For the Associated Press reporter who spied on this fragile moment through a cracked door, it felt wrong to be there, and he left as quickly as he could. "Incoherent and apparently semi-conscious, the doctor mumbled of his dead son and sobbed.

'When the other children came home for the holidays, my son was not among them."'

It was a moment too private to be witnessed by any outsider.

The closing arguments in the Phil Kennamer trial set new records in Oklahoma legal history, with seven attorneys who spoke for nearly eight hours over two days. With no objections to hold them back, they fixed bayonets and charged. They attacked each other's witnesses, and they attacked each other's evidence, and when they were done with that, they attacked each other with pumped-up indignation for all the legal atrocities the other side had committed. They hurled clever one-liners and sarcastic remarks that reporters ate up and regurgitated for their readers. For the twelve grim-jawed, stone-faced jurors who gave nothing away in their expressions, it went on and on and on until it became a two-day endurance challenge of verbal diarrhea.

When it was all over with, there was a notable difference between the two sides. The prosecution's arguments were outlined and proactive. They were pragmatic but long—winded—summaries that reviewed their best evidence and introduced provocative new ideas. The defense, on the other hand, was reactive. While eloquent, they were also emotional and disjointed. Always following behind a prosecuting attorney, one defense counselor or another was unwittingly drawn into a debate with the previous speaker.

Veteran Tom Wallace opened for the state with a concise analysis of their case that emphasized three main points: Kennamer told others he would kill John Gorrell; Gorrell was shot to death by Kennamer; Kennamer admitted killing him. Wallace then closed by calling for a life sentence or a hefty term for manslaughter.

Those anticipating an eloquent plea from Moss were not disappointed, but his argument was scattered, with conclusions that were far-reaching. After launching into a self-imposed warning about the unfairness of criticizing the victim, Moss eventually got around to criticizing the victim. To get there, he took a roundabout course by knocking off the state's witnesses as the low sort of people John Gorrell consorted with. First, it was Floyd Huff who was "lower than a human can sink" for being an ex-con. Then it was Ted Bath's turn; he was demoted to the dregs of humanity because he worked in the oil fields.

"Do you know what kinds of fellows are connected with pipeline work?" Moss asked rhetorically. This apparently meant the criminal kind, because John's mere association with him revealed he was up to no good.

Moss then unwittingly criticized Gorrell for not speaking up when his own client proposed to Bath that he seduce Virginia Wilcox to get naked pictures of her. "Not a word, gentlemen, from Gorrell. NOT—A—WORD—OF PROTEST," he said before whispering, "not a syllable."

Even though he had protested when Barbara Boyle's name was mentioned, Gorrell didn't do the same for Virginia and somehow, in Moss's mind, that made Gorrell a bad person, but not his client, who had proposed the scheme in the first place. He repeated this hypocritical error when he attacked Gorrell for not speaking out when his own client suggested armed robbery after Bath turned down the blackmail scheme.

"Then, when they talked about holding up the pig stand, who told Kennamer it was dangerous, someone might get killed? It was Ted Bath, not John Gorrell."

As he neared the end of a ninety-minute speech, Moss continued his attack on the victim for writing the extortion note and not exposing it later to the police. Kidnappers were the "most vicious sort of criminal," but don't judge him for saying that because, after all, Moss "didn't mean to be offensive to anyone." However, Gorrell was a "potential snatcher," and it was Phil's "Christian duty" to stop that kidnapper.

"I want the day to dawn in America," Moss thundered like a Baptist preacher, "when by the consecrated effort of the government—KIDNAPPERS CANNOT EXIST!

"If I see right, every human who followed this trial— everybody who is acquainted at all with its details—knows that when Phil Kennamer is freed of this crime—WE—have taken a step forward in stopping forever and ever—kidnapping in this state."

When King spoke after the lunch recess, he showed the capacity crowd why it was great for the prosecution to have a charismatic politician on their side. His crafty remarks were the most quoted by wire reporters and appeared in newspapers nationally. They also earned him the wrath of defense attorneys. He began with a folksy, down-to-earth appeal to the small-town jury, in which he praised them for their honesty and intelligence, adding, "It comes from the depths of my heart."

Getting down to business, he criticized Moss's long history of using the insanity defense. "Flint Moss carries in his vest pocket the plea of insanity and when he is hired, it is understood that THAT is to be part of the defense—if they will stand for it. THAT—is his stock and trade—an insanity plea."

From that foundation, King adroitly blasted away at numerous defense arguments and hypothesized new arguments of his own: that despite telling Snedden he would kill Gorrell in Kansas City, Kennamer waited until he got back to Tulsa so he would be in the protective sphere of his father's judicial district; that Kennamer forced Gorrell to write the note at the point of a knife; that Gorrell couldn't have known the Wilcox address unless Kennamer had given it to him; and that it couldn't have been John's idea because Kennamer first told Cadillac and then brought up the idea again to Ted Bath in Gorrell's presence two days before he left to go to dental school. And then there was his friend Otto Kramer, who gave them all the motive when he said Kennamer felt bitter toward the Wilcox family and wanted to get even with Virginia.

"I think he fell in love both with her charming personality and her father's millions. I think he was a mule-headed, precocious, stubborn youngster who just couldn't see how Miss Wilcox could resist his attentions—his, the attentions of the son of a federal judge—and it piqued his pride."

King then criticized Phil's strategy for enlisting a younger boy like Homer Junior, whom he could easily influence, with the hope that he would tell Virginia or her father, and the family would then welcome him as a hero.

"I wonder if it has occurred to you why, if he is all that he is pictured to be, why did he not go to his own devoted father and tell him of the kidnapping plot?" King asked rhetorically. "Now we find him back home with the note. Why didn't he take it to his father? Show it to some official? Why didn't he say John had written the note he had in his possession to some person of authority? That is all he needed to do."

In asking for a guilty verdict, King demanded that the jury "do what his father, Federal Judge Franklin E. Kennamer, failed to do—check him in his career of crime."

John McCollum blew right into a hyperbolic denunciation of King, the unfairness of the prosecution, and the attempted assassination of Judge Kennamer's career, before ending with a plea that his client be murdered instead of sent to prison—or something like that. No one could really understand what he meant.

"This trial has been conducted in such a way that it has driven me to conclude that the prosecution has endeavored to destroy fairness. I am going to make the statement now, and you will remember it, that they are trying to use this lawsuit for the purpose of destroying Judge Kennamer," McCollum said with sincere outrage.

The Pawnee defense attorney then put all the blame on J. Berry King and declared that the sole reason he was brought into the case was to do the dirty work of a political assassin. McCollum then wandered far off-point with a long defense of

Judge Kennamer that had little to do with the innocence of his client until he was near the end, when he said the prosecution had not provided the jury with a motive. Nor had they proved, in his mind, that Phil had entered the Gorrell car before John did, which led him to conclude that Phil had somehow been framed for murder by John Gorrell, who carried the gun that killed him.

"Was Phil framed? [By] the other boy? Yes. He proved that. They did. He drove around on that evening with this gun in evidence," McCollum cried out as he held up the Herrington and Richardson revolver. "This gun was taken from his person and put in the pocket of the car. That was just a few minutes before he was to meet Phil. Just as handy a place as you can put a gun in unless you sit there and hold it in your hand."

It was a statement that left the prosecution scratching their heads. *John Gorrell framed Phil Kennamer for murder by leaving the gun out in order to get himself killed?* Or, was he saying the prosecution was framing his client with the theory that Kennamer found the gun before Gorrell returned to his car?

It was hard to comprehend what McCollum meant about anything, or the logic in his conclusions, and it didn't improve as he wound down his speech. In reviewing how the medical experts recommended Phil Kennamer be treated for his psychopathic personality, McCollum made another confusing statement to the jury. "I would rather have a man commit murder than ask me to send a helpless, mentally deficient boy to the state penitentiary. That is an awful thing to think about. Send this boy to the penitentiary among hard, heartless characters because you have no other place to send him? There is ample law in Oklahoma to take care of him."

It was another head scratcher. So, John McCollum would rather murder a man, his own client perhaps, than send the helpless, mentally challenged Phil Kennamer to the penitentiary? If he was asking for his client to be found not guilty by reason of insanity, it was a curious way of going about it.

Prentiss Rowe was less prone to overblown hyperbole. Fighting off a flu bug that had ravaged Pawnee, the 240-pound assistant county attorney commanded attention without ever having to raise his voice. Since his work on the jury selection, Rowe had taken a backseat during most of the trial. When given a chance to speak to that jury one last time, his immediate approach was to return to the topic that seemed to dominate the closing arguments, Judge Kennamer. Like all the others, he was overly philosophical on the role of juries and the legal system. Like all the others, he took the scenic route to get to any of the few relevant points the entire case boiled down to. When he did get there, he was surprisingly eloquent, more so than any of the other attorneys.

And where the others were anxious to fill the air with words, Rowe gambled on silence. In order to illustrate Dr. Knoblock's testimony that Kennamer fired the second shot at least one minute after the first one, Rowe held up his watch and stood in silence for sixty seconds.

"The jurors gazed fixedly on the watch," Biscup wrote. "The lawyer dropped his arm and shouted, 'Does that look like self-defense?'"

Rowe also had the foresight to defend John Gorrell's reputation and to call into question Kennamer's contention that his victim was a criminal at heart. "It is my deduction that Gorrell would not go on down the line in this career of crime. It is hardly true that a young man who is willing to spend three nights a week working, in order that he may educate himself and fit himself for the future, is likely to turn criminal on a moment's notice."

Thursday, February 21, 1935

THE FOLLOWING MORNING, CHARLES STUART argued that is exactly what John Gorrell was: a cold-blooded criminal. Repeating much of what Moss had already said, Stuart again and again drove home the few good arguments the defense had. And just like Moss, he didn't want to speak ill of the dead, but of course, "my judgment and my duty compel me," Stuart said, before launching into his attack on Gorrell's character.

"Burgess and Cochrane told Kennamer that this man was preparing a scheme to kidnap his girl. What did Kennamer do? He made up his mind to go to Kansas City," Stuart said.

"What for? To get the very evidence which he says he did get so he could stop him. What Gorrell wanted was the easy money—he didn't care one iota about the girl. He wrote the letter," Stuart insisted as he waved the letter in their faces. "Gentlemen of the jury, here is the letter. It is a pity that a young man of that age, that Gorrell, having all the surroundings of a Christian home—blessed with education—blessed with all the good things of the earth—SHOULD WRITE THAT LETTER!

"IT—is one of the most cold-blooded—exact—brief—severe letters of extortion—that I have ever read."

In Stuart's determination, Phil Kennamer showed "inexhaustible patience, inexhaustible forbearance," by thwarting Gorrell's devious plot. Then, he took the heroism of Phil Kennamer to a level even Phil Kennamer had never imagined.

"They have chased this boy to the sacred temple of justice and you must see to it that no prejudiced testimony shall enter this case by the poison-spewing of his enemies," Stuart declared as he paused and turned toward the prosecution. "I love a brave man and I hate a coward. I believe that you are brave men, and like brave and true men you will tell this court that this boy is not guilty."

After Stuart took his seat at 10:45 that morning, there was only one attorney left for the jury to endure. As everyone in the courtroom cast their gaze toward Holly Anderson, the defense was visibly surprised when his protégé William Gilmer stood up. They had been led to believe Anderson would do the closing, and they had even invoked his name into their own arguments.

This was Gilmer's big opportunity. His performance during the trial had been acclaimed in the newspapers, and he had matched wits with Moss well enough that it impressed everyone, including Moss. But it was more than that. When the young lawyer stood up and began his address to the jury, with a nervous voice that wavered a bit before he found his confidence, it was a symbolic gesture that the torch had been passed from Anderson. In the next election, Gilmer would be named the new county attorney.

Walter Biscup took note that it was a strong contrast between the final two speakers. ". . . one by a veteran defense attorney who is seventy-eight years old and has practiced law fifty-six years, the other by a thirty-three-year-old prosecutor with ten years' experience."

True to his nature, true to his youthful energy, Gilmer unleashed his wrath on Kennamer and did what no one else had done up to that time: he pounded the boy into dust. Gilmer's forty-five-minute summation "was the most vitriolic presented by an attorney in this lawsuit, it was agreed," Biscup wrote.

Harmon Phillips saw that fire in the young attorney as well. "Gilmer proved the sparkplug of the arguments, pacing back and forth and nervously wiping his hand with his kerchief. His voice rose to a shout repeatedly as he literally pounded home his point on the jury-box rail."

The young prosecutor didn't waste time with a preamble. He didn't wax philosophical on the role of the legal system in general, or juries in particular. And he did not unwittingly bore those twelve tired men for the selfish pleasure of hearing the sound of his own voice. With notes in hand, he rapid-fired his points, which always hit their target.

"I'm handicapped in this," he began with a nod toward his much older counterpart. "I won't attempt to match the wisdom of Judge Stuart. That would be ridiculous for me to even try. I can't answer his argument because I saw nothing of an argument in his case."

Stuart grinned when he heard this. In spite of the boy's jab at him, mutual respect had developed between them during the trial.

"I want you to believe me when I say the state has tried to be fair in this case. I want to be fair to Phil Kennamer and his father," Gilmer continued. "But I want to be fair to the parents of that dead boy too!

"When Phil Kennamer at the age of five was talking about a hangman's noose, John Gorrell was in kindergarten.

"When Phil Kennamer was running away from school, John Gorrell was going right ahead.

"The only thing Phil Kennamer ever finished in his life was the murder.

"I ask you to deliberate in your own cool, sober way, and you go back and see whether the arrogant, supercilious, pampered son of a federal judge has a right to put himself in the place of the law, court, and jury on that Thanksgiving night and pass judgment on John Gorrell—convict John Gorrell—and to put himself in the place of almighty God and say to him, 'you must die.'

"He hasn't the right to do that and you know it!" Gilmer boomed.

A few minutes later, the young prosecutor circled back to the same theme. "You have the picture of a good, industrious boy and that of a pampered wastrel. KILLER—KIDNAPPER—KENNAMER—there he sits!" he said, with his finger pointing at Phil Kennamer. "You know it and I know it, and I think Flint Moss and C. B. Stuart know it too."

As Gilmer neared the end of his summation, one of the shortest of all, he walked back to the prosecution table, picked up the enlarged death photographs and returned to hand them to the jury foreman.

"When you start figuring out this self-defense plea, look at these photographs. I want you to remember these photographs of John Gorrell when you go to your jury room.

"Who was the probable aggressor of the argument in the car that night? Phil Kennamer.

"Who on Thanksgiving night called the Gorrell home three or four times during the day? Phil Kennamer.

"Who sought him out? Phil Kennamer.

"Who started talking of killings and kidnappings? Phil Kennamer. That's the first word of testimony you heard, that Kennamer was going to kill. He told Cadillac Booth of easy money and kidnappings. He shows all the way through he has criminal tendencies and was abnormal.

"He started the whole thing. We all know he did. At every stage Kennamer was in it.

"The defense says they got out there and stopped [while the two were in Gorrell's car]. The scuffle starts and he was pushing him in the face," Gilmer said as he demonstrated on Anderson in front of the jury box. It was a demonstration planned well in advance. "[If Kennamer] was pushing him in the face, why wasn't the blood smeared?"

Why wasn't the blood smeared? Uh-oh.

It was the single best point raised over nearly eight hours of closing statements. If the struggle for the gun truly happened the way Phil Kennamer said it did, and the bullet missed his left hand, which was pushing on John Gorrell's face, why wasn't the blood smeared as a result of his hand being there? With his hand there, the blood from John's wound would have been obstructed and followed a different course. It was a great point but one that came too late. When Kennamer was on the stand, King could have nailed him on these issues with a reenactment. How did two bullets miss his hand or wrist? Why didn't he have muzzle-flash burns on his hand? Why wasn't the blood smeared?

As he neared the end of his fiery debate, Gilmer asked for something that surprised everyone—and most of all, Phil Kennamer.

"Now let me tell you this—as surely as you send that boy to the penitentiary, the reaction on the part of the father, and I wouldn't blame him, the natural thing for him to do then is for that father to try and get him of that penitentiary and start to get him out the first day he goes in.

"We are going to ask you for the extreme penalty, gentleman," Gilmer said with pause. "We are going to ask you to send this boy to the electric chair with the same calmness and coolness in your judgment that he showed John Gorrell on that Thanksgiving night. Send him down there and rub him out the way he did that poor boy in his car. Give him the extreme penalty. That is what we ask you to do."

JURY DELIBERATIONS LASTED ABOUT as long as the closing arguments. When Gilmer finished five minutes before noon, the jury took a forty-five-minute lunch before deliberating. On the fourth floor of the courthouse, they were locked into one of four rooms, where they debated Phil Kennamer's guilt for five hours. At 5:30 p.m., they were allowed to leave for dinner at a secluded location and then took a long walk to clear their minds in the cold February air.

With the jury in seclusion, Kennamer was taken back to his cell. Judge Hurst retired to his farm to inspect his pecan trees. Surprisingly, nearly all of the defense team left Pawnee, and only John McCollum remained. Holly Anderson lounged in the tiny press room and chatted with reporters nearly the entire time. All the other prosecutors disappeared except Dixie Gilmer, who went back to the hotel to rest.

With nothing to do but wait, those who had to be there found ways to occupy their time, and in doing so, discounted the dignity of the courtroom. It was as if they were all schoolchildren again, but the teachers were gone and they were locked in the schoolhouse. Inside Judge Hurst's chambers, four reporters cleared off his desk and began playing cards. Another reporter fell asleep on a gallery bench. As a gag, his colleagues woke him up by setting off a camera flash in his face. One reporter's wife, who accompanied him to watch the nationally followed trial, sat at the judge's bench and toyed with his gavel. When five hundred spectators cleared out, they left behind a jumble of newspapers, paper cups, pop bottles, bottle caps, peanut shells, and lunch sacks. The smoking rule, strictly enforced for ten days, was ignored. The trial was over, after all. Cigarette stubs started appearing here and there for the first time, and the smell of tobacco smoke permeated the courtroom.

Judge Kennamer paced the corridor for nearly an hour before settling down to chat with some friends of his as he puffed on a cigar.

Doctor Gorrell also paced and puffed on a cigar for thirty minutes, and then retired to the Graham Hotel, where eighty-five days' worth of pain and sorrow fought their way out of his chest cavity to a nervous breakdown. Several hours later, John and Alice sat together and wrote out a statement to the press on hotel stationery.

> Mrs. Gorrell and I should now like to be relieved of the pitiless publicity that has of necessity pursued us since the tragedy that deprived us of our boy.

> We have done what we could to co-operate with the proper authorities in the presentation of the case to the courts.

We find no fault with the trial in its several stages and shall accept the verdict of the court and jury as parents should who have no other refuge in periods of grief as great as ours has been. Our only emotion toward Judge and Mrs. Kennamer is one of the deepest sympathy.

Whatever the result, we trust no Tulsa father or mother shall ever be called upon to sustain the sacrifice we have made.

Perhaps the result may bring an awakening. John would want us to be brave under such circumstances. We shall strive to be so in memory of him.

For our sake, please let the press and public conclude that with the final expression of the courts, the tragedy shall remain sealed within our hearts.

John and Alice Gorrell meant every word of what they wrote. According to their grandson, John Robert, they never spoke of the case publicly, and barely mentioned it within the family. If they spoke of John Jr., it was to recall more pleasant memories and his achievements, not his death.

At 8:55 p.m., the jury foreman rapped on the door to let the bailiff know they had reached a verdict. Fifteen minutes later, the pale-faced prisoner was brought in, and he sat between his father and John McCollum, the only defense attorney present. When Dixie Gilmer walked in with Anderson, Kennamer's hate-filled glare followed the young prosecutor all the way to his chair. His "rub him out" with the electric-chair comment had rubbed Phil the wrong way. His scowl was so intense Biscup declared it was Phil's strongest show of emotion during the entire trial.

Surprisingly, the courtroom filled up with spectators who only had twenty minutes to get there from the time Judge Hurst was notified to when he was handed the verdict. The Gorrells were among them and soon, it would all be over with.

The verdict, with Kennamer's fate written on it, was passed to Judge Hurst, who read it before handing it to Court Clerk Nora Harshbarger: ". . . We find the defendant guilty of manslaughter in the first degree and being unable to agree upon the punishment leave the penalty to be assessed by the court."

Judge Hurst thanked the jury and scheduled sentencing for two o'clock Saturday. He secretly dreaded having to determine the sentence, and wanted two days to consider his decision.

As he sat there, wearing the same blue-checked suit he'd worn the night he killed John, Phil Kennamer took the news quietly, his face blank. His left arm slowly slipped to the back of his father's chair then up to his shoulder to comfort the man he would need now more than ever before.

Chapter Twenty-Three

Saturday, February 23, 1935

JUDGE HURST WAS RUNNING LATE. It was another nerve-wracking waiting game for everyone—except the defendant, who maintained his usual look of boredom. Although Flint Moss was rested with more sleep than he'd gotten in two weeks, his anxiousness was aimed at the motion for a new trial he'd filed with County Clerk Nora Harshbarger at 1:45 that afternoon. It was now ten minutes after two, and it was possible that the judge was giving serious consideration to the fourteen reasons why his client should receive a new trial. Moss called the verdict "terrible" and declared that it went against all the evidence presented. He was dressed in a black-and-white-checked suit, which he claimed he wore "only when I am mentally low."

When Judge Hurst did finally appear, he patiently listened to Moss and McCollum argue for a new trial based on faults they found with both him and the prosecution. In typical fashion for the two, their exaggerated indignation was disproportionate to the fourteen errors they called into question.

"I don't believe there is a reversible error in this lawsuit," Judge Hurst announced after allowing them to go on for ninety minutes. "If I thought there was, I would not wait for your motion. I would grant a new trial asked on my own motion. I think the defendant has had as fair a trial as could be had."

After asking for sentence recommendations which ranged from four to ninety-nine years, the minimum and maximum allowed, Judge Hurst bellowed, "The defendant stand up!"

Kennamer took a step forward and, with some military bearing in his stance, he showed, at least physically, he was ready to accept his punishment. The spectators in attendance surpassed any other day during the eleven-day trial, but this time, it was nearly all residents from Pawnee County. The well-dressed, high-society types from Tulsa and Oklahoma City, who always seemed to get the front two bench-rows, were gone. Virginia Wilcox, who had sat with the Kennamer family the last few days, was gone. Judge Franklin Kennamer, who was reportedly too ashamed to be there as his son was sentenced to prison, paced back and forth in the tiny press room, smoking a cigar. Alice Gorrell had finally had enough and stayed home, but her husband occupied his usual seat alongside Anderson, Wallace, and Gilmer.

For most of the trial, reporters ignored the words of Judge Hurst and instead focused their attention on the lawyers—Moss, Gilmer, and King in particular. But now they regarded his statement carefully and printed every word the jurist said.

"The court has tried to be fair throughout this trial. The court has tried to give you every right. As good a jury as could possibly be found tried this case.

"They rejected your pleas of insanity and self-defense. They held that you did not kill Gorrell with a premeditated design. I think it was because you went unarmed and killed him with his own gun. The evidence would have justified the jury in finding premeditation.

"Your act brought heartache to two families, both of them innocent. Throughout the trial, I have observed that while your father was broken-hearted, you have not shown very much concern, and I have been shocked at that. I can't understand how a boy who has inflicted this misery upon his family could feel as you have seemed to feel.

"It is my duty to assess the punishment that I think society has a right to demand and no more. I ought not to give you one minute more by reason of your father or one minute less. But society has to be paid. A serious offense has been committed. It would be dangerous to society to turn you out too soon.

"You shall receive the punishment that society has the right to demand. It is therefore the judgment of the court that you serve twenty-five years in McAlester prison."

During his rebuke, Phil stood motionless. His eyes dropped down only when he heard of the pain he caused his father. When the judge declared he was given a fair trial, he swallowed hard and nodded his head. It was a silent confirmation he would soon proclaim his disagreement with.

In light of all the Gorrells had just endured, it was an ironic twist that the state law allowed those convicted of manslaughter to be released on bond, pending appeal of their case. Kennamer was given ten days to come up with the $25,000 bail—$1,000 for each year of his sentence. With four months to prepare his appellate brief, and the typical schedule for the state Criminal Court of Appeals, Kennamer could live as a free man for one year. If the appeals court ruled against him and he served his time wisely, lenient state laws governing the parole process could allow him to get out of prison after serving one-half to three-fifths of his sentence.

John Gorrell's killer could go free after serving just twelve years.

In spite of this, Dr. Gorrell put on a brave face to reporters. "I am satisfied with the verdict and sentence. The judgment of the court is my judgment, as I said before the verdict came in."

It was not an easy decision for the jury, foreman Jacob Clark later told reporters. At no time did they consider the first-degree-murder charge, or the insanity claims. While two jurors held out for acquittal until the last hour, their final decision had come through on the twelfth vote.

Back at the sheriff's office, reporters caught up with Phil, who was ready with a statement in which he demanded to be quoted verbatim. Although he attempted to sound magnanimous, he only proved to everyone who read it that he was a true egotist who needed to get in the last word.

"So far as the closing statement of Judge Thurman Hurst is concerned, it was fair," Kennamer said after lighting up a cigarette. "He made every effort to conduct the trial in a fair, rigidly impartial manner. That that end was not achieved was no fault of Judge Hurst. I feel, though, that it was not a trial in the ordinary sense of the word, but more approached the semblance of a Roman holiday.

"The clamor set in the press at the outset was of such a nature it was impossible to find twelve men whose minds were free of bias. I think the jury was representative of an intelligent and honest citizenship, but in their subconscious minds had been poured such a stream of virus it was impossible for them to be fair and impartial.

"For Messieurs King, Anderson, Gilmer, and Wallace, I have only the deepest contempt. Those gentlemen engaged in every low practice known to the courts—from intimidation of witnesses to the introduction of extraneous matters which were intended only to prejudice the minds of the jurors.

"In its final analysis, the issues were not drawn between the state and the defendant, but between the corrupt representatives of a certain vicious element and this defendant's family. The aim was not to destroy me but to destroy my father's honor. In that, I thank God, they have failed miserably before the eyes of the world.

"What the ultimate result will be as far as I am concerned I do not know, but I feel that whatever comes, strengthened by the knowledge that I acted honorably and from necessity, I cannot fear the future."

After he made those remarks, an inmate in the county jail revealed to reporters the limitations of Phil Kennamer's honor. On the day before his sentencing, Phil offered to bet ten dollars to one dollar that no prisoner in the jail could correctly guess how many years he would receive. Clifford Owens bet he would get twenty-five years. Shortly before he was escorted to the courtroom that afternoon, Kennamer canceled the bet.

"I was afraid he'd be right," he said later.

In spite of his denunciation of the press, the day after his verdict, Kennamer sent a jail trustee out to buy a copy of every newspaper about himself that could be found. "His appetite for journalistic reports upon himself has never diminished," the *World* reported. "He read them with the same lack of emotion that characterized his conduct throughout the trial."

On the day after his sentencing, he sent the trustee out again to buy more newspapers to indulge "his appetite" for reading about himself. And there was plenty to read. Hundreds of large and small daily newspaper throughout the Midwest ran it as their top story with wide headlines below the masthead. In New York, newspapers like the *Brooklyn Daily Eagle*, the *New York Times*, and the *Long Island Daily Press* shared the verdict or sentence with their readers from the front page. The same could not be said of West Coast newspapers, where the outcome was often buried inside. But where Kennamer's story was not front-page news, nearly every paper in the country that subscribed to a wire service did run a small announcement, or a photo with a short caption, that described his fate.

In Tulsa, the news of his sentence was met with general approval. An editorial in the *Tulsa World* proclaimed the outcome "legally and morally just" and that it "coincided with the public interest." After Flint Moss had attacked both the *World* and *Tribune* in his change-of-venue motion, the editorial pages of those newspapers avoided publishing any opinion of the case during the trial. It was a wise move on their part to avoid being condemned by defense counsel, who would have used anything they wrote against them in either their motion for a new trial or an appeal. But now that it was over, the *World's* editorial page had something to say.

> There is remarkably little public dissent from the conviction or the sentence.

The entire case and the revelations it entailed left scars upon the community which only time can heal. Under such mixed and complicated circumstances, some writers and professional observers overreached themselves. A large collection of "outside" writers appeared, people who were looking for special features and who harped with fervor upon certain odd items. There was overplay of emotions; there was phantasy; there was speculation unjustified by facts. That scribes did go beyond their proper professional duties and strained too much for effect is certain.

It has been too freely asserted here and elsewhere that the killing of Gorrell showed a rotten condition of affairs in social and youthful circles. This wholesale condemnation is very unfair. Because a few bad, untoward, dangerous actions and pursuits came into conjunction and resulted in a bitter tragedy, it is not fair to conclude that all Tulsa or any relatively large number of people were involved.

A profound lesson in law and order has been learned. Jurors will convict for crimes [even though] sensationalism may seemingly obscure the deadly facts. It is reassuring to see the law coolly and judiciously applied. It is fine to see public officials and jurors stand up to their duties and opportunities and to see their actions approved by the responsible citizenship.

But in the background there was one authority figure whose actions were not met with approval. Instead of looking for "outside" observers who "strained too much for effect," the *World* should have looked closer to home. If anyone was hell-bent on planting the seeds of hysteria, it was Sergeant Maddux, who was up to his old tricks of trying to impress a superior with a sensational new claim. On the day the verdict was announced, Lt. Earl Gardner told the press that "he had been advised by Maddux that Gorrell was killed by bullets from two different guns." The chief of detectives added that this might mean two persons were involved in the slaying.

Detective George Reif, the secondary on the case, backed up Lt. Gardner's claim of what the criminologist had said, telling the press, "Maddux tried to bring this out on the stand in Pawnee." However, he was unable to do so after defense attorneys admitted the two bullets were fired from Gorrell's gun.

If Maddux had done so, it could have led to a mistrial. When reporters questioned him about it, the police sergeant was visibly surprised. Caught off guard, he refused to comment at that time, and the *Tribune* noted it was just one of several occasions that Maddux "refused to verify statements attributed to him."

It was precisely because of stories like that, and many of them traced back to Maddux, that talk of a grand jury investigation into the entire Kennamer-Gorrell case would soon be back on the front pages of Tulsa newspapers. It had been suggested in December, after Born's suicide, by low-level city employee and self-styled public crusader, Arthur Sweeney.

"I believe that all of the evidence in the case covering both the slayings and the activities of the young people should be aired. I am convinced that there is much being held back," Sweeney said in December. At that time, Judge Hurst requested he postpone his petition for a grand jury investigation until after the trial.

Sweeney only needed one hundred signatures and, if successful, it would be only the fifth time in Tulsa history a grand jury was convened. To everyone's surprise, Sweeney's renewed efforts were met with quiet approval by Gilmer and Anderson, who thought it necessary to force Sergeant Maddux and Commissioner Oscar Hoop to answer for some of the statements they had made.

Even though Kennamer had the opportunity stay out of prison during his appeal, his father didn't have $25,000 to post his bond—just yet. To save him from embarrassment, Charles Stuart announced to the press two days after sentencing that he had advised the judge to keep his son in prison during the appeal.

"We think it wise not to release the boy from prison," Stuart professed to reporters. "That was my advice to his father and he has agreed to follow it. We think the boy is better off in prison while the case is being appealed. If he were released, this conviction would be hanging over him while he was out. As it is now, we believe the conviction will be reversed and Phil will walk away from McAlester penitentiary in a few months a free man."

In truth, there was nothing wise about it. Even after all that Phil had put them through, Judge Kennamer had indulged his youngest son his entire life, and he wasn't about to stop now. He just needed more time to solicit wealthy, influential friends to pledge property to secure the bond. Phil took the news well and expected as much when reporters asked him about getting out on bail. But there was another, more important question reporters wanted to ask him.

"Have you read of the statement attributed to Sgt. Maddux to the effect that two guns fired the two shots into Gorrell?"

"Yes, I read it," Kennamer said with a frown. "It's a damnable falsehood! It's just another of his efforts to attempt to drag in someone else in this matter. Now that they have me, they will try and get someone else involved—one of my friends. There's absolutely nothing to it."

Kennamer may have told a lot of lies, but he was certainly telling the truth now. When the knight needs to slay the dragon to win the heart of the princess and the confidence of the wealthy king, there can't be two knights in that story. There could only be one, and that was him.

"Personally, I don't believe in ballistic science," he went on. "And anyway, I don't think Maddux is a ballistics expert or ever could be!"

March 4, 1935

SINCE HE WAS GIVEN TEN DAYS to come up with $25,000, Kennamer was obligated to wait out those days in the Pawnee Jail. As he left the jail for the last time, he gave photographers his customary glare. It was the same scowl he'd given them for more than two weeks. They were only doing their jobs and, as much as he disliked them, they were thoroughly tired of him.

But they still had one more photograph that their editors were demanding: a picture of him as he entered the state prison. To get it, they had to follow in their cars behind Sheriff Burkdoll, who was accompanied by "Pawnee Bill," who toured the world with his "Pawnee Bill's Historic Wild West Show" that he'd founded in 1888. As the three climbed the one hundred steps to the outer door of the administration building, Kennamer indulged the photographers with a cheerful smile to show how brave he was.

It was just for show. When he got inside, he lost the cool air of indifference he had perfected during his trial. Inside the deputy warden's office, he looked around with apprehension. He was relieved to learn that his head of curly hair would not be shaved. In a time when men and boys always wore hats outside, Kennamer's vanity kept him from covering up his crowning glory.

Inside, he was given a rule book and told to familiarize himself with it. From then on, he was prisoner 31-420. As the photographers turned to leave, he gave them one last Phil Kennamer quote.

"I'll make a good prisoner and don't intend to break any of the rules," he declared with bravado. "If all the walls should fall down, I wouldn't try to escape. I'm going to do my time the right way."

With celebrity criminal Phil Kennamer, the son of a federal judge, tucked away in prison, prosecutors could now turn their attention to two more people who needed to atone for their sins: Edna Mae Harman and Sergeant Henry Bailess Maddux.

Part Four: The Politics of Justice

It is doubtful if any more official, legal, social, or political pressure has ever been used in this country to circumvent justice. There has not been a month since the night of the shooting that powerful friends have not been active, at many times under coercion, in the intercessions for young Kennamer. These consistent efforts were directed toward anyone who in any way might be helpful.

— *Tulsa Daily World* Editorial

Chapter Twenty-Four

THE COURT ACTION AGAINST EDNA Harman went from a trial to a hearing in ten minutes. Two days after she was arrested for contempt of court, her husband posted bond, and her trial was set for March 11 in Pawnee. When court opened that Monday morning, her lawyer was given the opportunity to plead his client not guilty. William Chase then told the court he intended to prove that Mrs. Harman was not a professional witness, and that she was in genuine fear for her life if she testified. But to Judge Hurst, none of that mattered. He was there. He saw her outburst. She violated the subpoena requiring her to testify, disrupted the proceedings, and nearly caused a mistrial with her behavior.

When Chase was finished, Judge Hurst released a formal finding of fact which established Edna Harman's guilt. Trial over. The proceedings then became a hearing to determine her punishment, which could include one year in jail and a fine of $1,000.

The story of when Edna Harman first approached the Kennamers, and then the Gorrells, plotted to benefit financially, who she did it with, and how she planned to do it, was one of the most confusing aspects of the entire case. No single newspaper reporter was able to outline her entire saga from beginning to end with enough clarity for it to be entirely understood. Like most unstable individuals who are backed into a corner from a controversy of their own making, Edna Harman sought to free herself from the forces closing in on her by playing the victim to garner sympathy, and obfuscating the truth in order to create confusion.

She first inserted herself into Tulsa's most sensational murder case in late December when she telephoned the

Kennamer home with a claim that she knew some "valuable information" concerning Phil. But when his sister visited with Edna at the apartment building she managed on South Quaker Avenue in Tulsa, Opal Kennamer discovered what Harmon Phillips would later learn—that something wasn't quite right with Mrs. Harman.

"[She] told me she was certain my brother was insane and contemplated suicide when she saw him one day in the apartment," Opal told the Pawnee courtroom. She quickly realized the mother of three had nothing that would contribute to Phil's defense and left. But just because she was done with Edna Harman, that didn't mean Edna Harman was done with the Kennamers.

In early January, Judge Kennamer received an anonymous letter through the mail, requesting a loan of $2,500 in exchange for a vague promise of something that would benefit his son. It was typed on stationery that bore the watermark "Executive Bond," and communicated a hyper-emotional message that betrayed the sender as a cuckoo bird desperate for money.

> Dear Sir: I and no one else know facts concerning your son, others involved, and still others in danger of becoming involved.

> The good I can do for Phil and everyone connected is inconceivable, if you will only have confidence in me and lend financial aid that is imperative to the welfare of us all.

> Coming directly to the point, twenty five hundred dollars is needed. I am corresponding with you because your son is implicated and as a last resort.

> Your helping me will in no way involve you, cause anyone the slightest harm nor will it impede justice. Quite the contrary, justice will then be possible.

> It is necessary, for the success of my efforts that my identity remain unknown until this case is concluded at

which time I will make myself known to you and repay the money. Believe me, you would be amply repaid if you never heard from me again. If I could only explain now—but I dare not.

The fate of more than one now rests on your decision. Your decision as to my truth and sincerity. I realize you have only this letter on which to base your decision and that you could so easily have me apprehended, although it would profit no one and only bring greater and final disaster.

Again, I beg, please have faith in me. Help me to help all. If you will trust me, make a package as small as possible of packets of fives, tens and twenties to total twenty five hundred dollars. When package is ready and to inform me so and that you will help, place this ad in the *Tulsa World's* "Lets Swap" column:

Electric train for bicycle 9-8763.

I will then get in touch with you to name the time and place to receive the loan. Act immediately as valuable time has already been lost, because of my reluctance to ask you for help.

If this ad does not appear within 48 hours I shall consider your answer, no. But I again beg you to trust me and co-operate.

(Signed) U.R. Good

Judge Kennamer dismissed the letter's sender as just another crackpot. Ever since his son was arrested, he had received numerous anonymous letters from individuals seeking something, promising something, or from cons and ex-cons who enjoyed the pain he was going through by having a son in jail accused of murder.

When the "Let's Swap" ad did not appear, the sender grew more frustrated but wasn't willing to give up. A short time later,

James Barnett, described in newspapers as "a negro voodoo doctor," walked into Judge Kennamer's office in the federal building and laid an envelope on his desk. The anonymous letter, which was later published in the newspapers, encouraged Judge Kennamer to go to 405½ Latimer Place to seek out a man who had been able to alter the outcome of another well-known Tulsa murder trial a few years before. In a conspiratorial tone, the letter promised that if he did, his son might benefit, but only with a payment of $1,200.

Judge Kennamer then asked Barnett if the sender intended to tamper with the jury, and that all he wanted was a fair trial for his son. Barnett, who was given two dollars to deliver the message, replied he didn't know the contents of the letter. The judge then grew irate and ordered him out of the office. Fearing he was in trouble, Barnett, who was more involved then he let on, quickly gave up the name of the letter's author as well as her address; it turned out to be Edna Harman. The second letter was linked to the first by a similar typeface, an "Executive Bond" watermark on the stationery, and Barnett—who said Edna had discussed both letters with him and two other people.

The next day, Opal and an unidentified man went to the Latimer address, which turned out to be Barnett's home. Although Jim was not there at the time, they met a woman who told them a "voodoo doctor" had gone to see Judge Kennamer about fixing the case with the jury the day before. Several hours afterward, a woman came around to ask Jim what the judge had to say. She was later identified as Edna Harman.

Opal then went from Barnett's home to see Edna, who told her that her brother and another boy had rented an apartment from her. However, the description she had of Phil did not match, and the Kennamers, once again, concluded Mrs. Harman could be of no help. Instead of turning over her two letters to police, they wrote her off as one of the many attention seekers who were trying to insert themselves into a nationally known case.

Although she had struck out with the defense, Edna Harman next saw an opportunity with the Gorrells. Just after the venue change was announced, she approached Dr. Gorrell with the same story Tom Wallace had told the jury: that she had rented an apartment to Kennamer and another boy, spied on them as Kennamer was writing a letter—supposedly *the* letter—and overheard him remark, "That fellow has got yellow. He has backed out. I am going to Kansas City and I am going to put the skids under him."

Gorrell then took this information to Holly Anderson, who sent his investigator, Jack Bonham, to interview Mrs. Harman, who told him the same story. But as the doctor would later testify, before Edna could come to Pawnee to testify, there was just one little thing she needed first—one hundred dollars. [1]

"Before Mrs. Harman would consent to come to Pawnee to testify, [Dr. Gorrell] was to guarantee payment of her expenses up to $100," the *Tribune* reported. "She told him she could not afford to come to Pawnee on the regular witness fee basis of $1 a day and mileage."

Her request was politely turned down, and she was handed a subpoena to testify.

When Moss learned Mrs. Harman would testify, he recalled her name from the time she had approached him some years before with an offer to sell her testimony to benefit his client who was facing a murder trial. Besides knowing of the Kennamers' experience with her, he started asking around and learned from half a dozen defense attorneys from Tulsa to Oklahoma City that over the last twelve years, she had approached them with similar offers and, in two known cases, she had actually testified.

The hearing in Pawnee presented a unique opportunity for the Kennamer defense and prosecution to work together against a common foe. Given the nature of the hearing, the

---

[1] The 2014 equivalent of $1,700, when adjusted for inflation.

defense was allowed to put on their case first. From the stand, Edna, her three children, and her husband all told of how they had received threatening phone calls, observed strange men lurking near their apartment, and were threatened by defense team investigators, whose shoulder-holstered weapons were displayed a little too obviously for Edna's comfort. Mrs. Harman's strategy was to deny everything, point by point, and to burst into tears at appropriate moments during her testimony. And just like Phil Kennamer, everyone else—Opal Kennamer, Flint Moss, his two investigators, Dr. Gorrell, Dixie Gilmer, Tom Wallace, and star witness Jim Barnett—was lying, but she was telling the truth.

The hearing lasted two days and, by the end of it, the witness statements and circumstantial evidence against her were too overwhelming for Judge Hurst, who branded her a "professional witness."

"I am convinced this defendant attempted to obtain money from Judge Kennamer as well as the other side in the trial. A mere fine is not sufficient punishment in this case," Judge Hurst declared as he sentenced Edna Harman to thirty days in jail and a fine of $250.[2] Normally, that would have been the end of it, but this was Edna Mae Harman, and Edna Mae Harman was too proud to have her reputation sullied with a jail term for contempt of court. Her lawyer boldly announced they would appeal the judge's decision. This action required Judge Hurst to vacate her current bond and set an appeal bond for $1,000. Like the last time, she was forced to sit it out in jail for a few days while her family came up with the money.

Seven months later, on October 22, William Chase argued his client's case before the criminal court of appeals. Their decision on the matter came in March 1936, one year after her original conviction. It was a long time to wait for a judgment that was boiled down to two sentences:

---

[2] The 2014 equivalent of $4,300, when adjusted for inflation.

"Orderly trials and proceedings in court are not to be obstructed and nullified by [the] whims or temperamental outbursts of a witness. We are satisfied the punishment assessed is not excessive but on the contrary, is reasonable and humane."

Normally, that would have been the end of it, but this was Edna Mae Harman, and Edna Mae Harman, to her credit, was a fighter. Instead of being carted off to jail, her lawyer requested, and received, several thirty- and sixty-day extensions for the start of her jail sentence. By September, the patience of Judge Hurst, Carl McGee, and Holly Anderson had reached its limit. On Friday, September 18, 1936, both Anderson and Hurst made it clear to reporters that unless Mrs. Harman surrendered the following day, a warrant for her arrest would be issued. When asked about serving her time, Edna told reporters that she "did not intend to stay over there that long." She avoided arrest and waited another two days before beginning her sentence on September 21.

But instead of paying the fine, her husband, Orlan, would not or could not come up with the $250. Instead of serving thirty days, she had to suffer the indignity of paying off that fine at the rate of one dollar for every day in jail. She requested and was denied release in November, but by January 1937, a pardon-and-parole attorney pleaded on her behalf. Hurst, who by then was a state supreme court judge, gave his recommendation for her release. On January 21, 1937, after serving 123 days of a thirty-day sentence, Edna Harman was paroled from the Pawnee County Jail by Governor Ernest Marland.

WHEN PHIL KENNAMER WENT TO prison, the hysteria did not go with him. It was forced to linger behind in Tulsa and was amplified when Maddux's two-gun theory was leaked to the press. The drama from his attention-seeking remark would play out for the next five weeks. It also reinforced the public's demand that a grand jury be called to reinvestigate the entire case from top to bottom, including the bribery allegations, the obscene photographs, and Sidney Born's death, which led to an investigation that many believed was bungled from the beginning. The common denominator in all those could be traced back to one man, who was just now sensing the storm clouds gathering around him. After waiting for more than twenty-four hours, Maddux denied saying that two different bullets and guns were used to kill Gorrell.

"I never made such a statement. It is not true," Maddux declared Saturday night after Kennamer was sentenced. "As far as I know, the two bullets were fired from the same gun."

But it came too late, and the damage was already done. With Anderson on an out-of-state vacation, Gilmer was forced to reopen the entire investigation, and he called for all the evidence to be brought to him. He had grown impatient with the entire case, which was being kept alive by wild gossip and the latest controversy over the bullets. This spawned new tensions between the county attorney's office and the city's detective bureau, with Commissioner Hoop thrown into the middle of it.

Of the two .22-caliber bullets removed from victim, only one of them was capable of being compared to test bullets fired from the same gun. Although it matched, the shell casings left some doubt. The primer marks may have been the same, but the secondary markings from one shell casing to the other were different. When Gilmer sent the fatal bullets and the gun to the state crime bureau to be tested, the difference in the secondary marks to the shell casings was enough to stump the examiner, who issued a purposefully confusing statement.

"No identification. Bullets with test bullets are each other. Fatal shell identical with test shell," his telegram read.

The state examiner's muddled statement raised enough doubt with Gilmer that he called for the pistols of two key witnesses in the case whose names featured heavily in local rumors—Homer Wilcox Jr. and Jack Snedden. Both of their weapons were sent, along with Gorrell's gun, to the Bureau of Investigation in Washington, DC. After several false starts and communication with J. Edgar Hoover himself, the examiner there concluded that the fatal bullets and shells all came from Gorrell's gun—five weeks after Sgt. Maddux started the rumor.

The entire two-gun saga was a false controversy that never would have happened if common sense had prevailed. The morning after the murder, Charles Bard told investigators that Gorrell had asked for more bullets, and then showed him the three bullets he had in the nine-shot cylinder. Two empty shell casings and one live round were later found in his weapon, and two bullets were retrieved from his head. If he was shot with two different .22-caliber pistols by two different killers, there should have only been one empty shell casing in the revolver.

For the two-gun theory to be believed, the killer or killers would have had to remove one unfired bullet from the chamber of Gorrell's gun and replace it with the fired shell from the second gun.

A side-effect of the two-gun drama was the suspicion by Gilmer that the police department was withholding evidence, preferring to bring it out during the grand jury. When he called for more information about the purported bribe offer, both Maddux and Hoop were slow in giving it to him. During an interview with the *World* that was published on March 10, the assistant county attorney lost his temper.

"If [Commissioner] Hoop has information and will not give it to the county attorney's office, we think he is deliberately obstructing justice," Gilmer snapped.

It was an audacious statement, and interdepartmental gossip against Sgt. Maddux was building. He had finally gone too far, and he wasn't the only one who could sense a backlash was coming—Hoop saw it too. He had unwittingly hitched his wagon to Maddux when he made the bribery claim. Now, he couldn't distance himself fast enough from the criminologist who had a target on his back.

"All I know about [the bribe] is what Sergeant Maddux told me three months ago," Hoop told the *World* in the same article.

"Insofar as my own personal knowledge of the bribe offer is concerned, all I know is what Maddux told me."

To save himself, Sgt. Maddux released a prepared statement, before the federal ballistics examiner's report was released, in which he tried to explain the rumors and proclamations attributed to him regarding the bullets, the bribe offer, the obscene photographs, rumors that Homer Junior was involved, and perceived slights on his part against the character of Flint Moss or Judge Kennamer, whom he now praised as "ethical" men he held in high regard. It was a verbose document fraught with denials, self-justifications, claims of integrity, and the confidence that he had the full support of Oscar Hoop and Chief Carr. It did not address, however, the widely held belief that he had ended the Born investigation too soon.

But Tulsa County wasn't content to let Sgt. Maddux have the last word on anything; that was the job of the most ambitious grand-jury investigation yet called in the city's history. Only eighteen of the prosecution's fifty-seven witnesses testified during Kennamer's trial, which, to everyone's dismay, only established the boy's guilt in the slaying of John Gorrell Jr. The trial did nothing to stamp out, once and for all, the persistent rumors regarding Kennamer's unknown accomplice, as well as who murdered Sidney Born, and who offered Sgt. Maddux the $25,000 bribe. Those criminals were still out there, and they needed to be brought to justice. The public also wanted to know who was behind the local vice gangs, which had corrupted the youth of well-to-do families with gambling, liquor, and Mexican weed that, when combined together, probably led to those blackmail photographs that Sgt. Maddux said were in a bank vault.

The grand jury would put an end to the mystery. The grand jury would stamp out, once and for all, those persistent rumors. The grand jury would shine the light of truth and justice on the guilty, who would then be indicted and held accountable by the grace of God and all that is holy.

When the twelve jurors were selected, Judge Hurst impressed upon them the seriousness of their duties as well as the wide-ranging mandate which also called upon them to explore public corruption and to inspect the jail facilities with regard to prisoners being held without due process. He pointed out to them that the hearing, which would be held in a jury deliberation room on the third floor of the courthouse, was off-limits to the public. The press was barred from photographing or talking to any of the witnesses after they had testified, and no transcript would be made. While the proceedings were under the supervision of Anderson and Assistant State Attorney General Owen Watts, it was the jury's job to question witnesses and then make their recommendation.

"Regardless of who may present matters to you, you should investigate them if there seems to be a basis," Judge Hurst told the twelve men. "You are an independent body, you are not a grand jury of the court, county, nor the petitioners, and it [is] your duty to act independently."

The grand jury began calling witnesses on April 9, and over the next twelve business days, 165 people offered up what they knew and answered questions. Reporters for both the *Tribune* and the *World* took up positions in the corridor and, although they were careful not to ask questions or take photographs, they were able to correctly surmise some of the elements under consideration by identifying the people who sat outside waiting to be called. The death of Sidney Born was obviously explored by calling in those who found him, the doctor who attended him, high-ranking police officials, and a squad of detectives familiar with the case. They also called in, several times, Dr. Sidney Born Sr., who had hired two private investigators to find his son's killers. During the trial, he had made the announcement that two young local men would soon be arrested for his son's murder. Although it never happened, there was speculation that it could happen at any moment. The jury even subpoenaed Phil Kennamer to seek information regarding Born's death but were disappointed when he "left behind him a maze of theories, uncorroborated allegations and personal opinions," the *World* reported.

Besides calling Sgt. Maddux, the jury listened long and hard to Oscar Hoop, who testified on several different occasions. He turned over to them the affidavit Maddux had given him regarding the alleged bribe offer. The jurors also heard from nearly all of Maddux's superiors, and most of the other detectives, who told the grand jury everything they knew about the case and their colleague, Sgt. Maddux.

On April 19, the eighth day of the proceedings, the grand jury requested a meeting with all four of the city's commissioners. When it was over, Oscar Hoop spoke with Chief Carr in his office before the two of them demanded that Sgt. Maddux meet with them at once. What happened next became front-page news throughout the state that weekend.

"When I walked into Chief Carr's office Friday morning, Chief Carr and Commissioner Hoop were seated. Hoop immediately told me that I was going to be indicted by the grand jury for concealing evidence from the grand jury," Maddux told a *Tulsa World* reporter. "Commissioner Hoop said that my testimony before the grand jury was not the same as his in regard to the bribe offers and that the members of the grand jury had told him that unless I left the department, I would be indicted. He gave me thirty minutes to resign or be fired."

Maddux then said he told Hoop and Chief Carr that he didn't want to embarrass the department, but he explained that he was broke and wanted time to look for a new job. He asked for and received permission to date his resignation for May 15.

"I brought the resignation back into Chief Carr's office," Maddux continued, but Commissioner Hoop was not there. He returned in about ten minutes, and read my resignation. He took his pencil out and marked the date [May 15] out, substituted April 19, and had me approve the change by initialing it."

When asked it about it that same day, Hoop first tried to deny it, and then later confirmed it when he told an Associated Press reporter, "Maddux is through. He's out."

Unknown to Maddux, when he spoke to Hoop about the bribe offer in December and in several meetings afterward, the commissioner had taken notes of what the criminologist had said. Those notes revealed that Maddux's claims about the bribe changed each time he told it. Testimony from his fellow officers and superiors also likely confirmed the revelations brought out by Hoop.

When the jury concluded their investigation the following Wednesday, their report eviscerated Sgt. Maddux, whom they blamed for a good portion of the false rumors that had plagued Tulsa for the last five months. They also found no evidence regarding Gorrell's murder that was not brought out during the trial, and concluded that there was no evidence that Born was murdered, but only because Maddux had failed in his duties.

> At the outset, let us say that the vast amount of purported evidence turned in has been voluminous and the major portion founded upon rumor.

> Our investigation has failed to disclose any material matter which was not brought out in the trial of this case. We have accepted the report of the ballistics expert of the department of justice on the proposition that both bullets found in John Gorrell's head were fired from the same gun.

> We have been unable to ascertain the existence at any time of any nude, compromising or obscene pictures involving any people connected with this case or any citizens of Tulsa, and we are of the opinion that no such pictures exist.

> We found no evidence of a $25,000 bribe having been offered to any member of the police department.

We have also made what we deem a very thorough, complete, and exhaustive investigation into the death of Sidney Born Jr. At the present time, the grand jury is unable to determine whether or not Sidney Born Jr. committed suicide or was murdered.

We feel that as a result of the Kennamer-Gorrell case and the Born case, that this community has suffered irreparable damage and injury. These cases were highly publicized and due to the prominence of the parties involved, many and various rumors were started and an untold amount of gossip engaged in. We feel that these matters have been enlarged upon, distorted, and exaggerated, and our investigation has further disclosed that these rumors were without foundation.

In this connection, we have spent many hours trying to ascertain the source from which these rumors emanated. We have reached the conclusion that former police Sergeant Maddux was in large measure responsible for a great portion of the inaccurate and unfavorable publicity. We are also of the opinion that Sergeant Maddux failed to make a complete examination into the death of Sidney Born Jr. Also, that he was solely responsible for the unfounded statements and rumor that the bullets found in the head of John Gorrell were fired from different guns.

This grand jury was considering filing of an accusation and ouster against Maddux, but prior to the [completion]of action along this line, the grand jury received information that he had resigned, which meets with the hearty approval of the grand jury.

The *Tulsa Tribune* was among the many who were happy to see Sgt. Maddux go, and they reminded readers that in addition to his many other transgressions, he had tried to play them for fools when he told them about the Wrightsman note.

During the noon hour [on December 3, 1934] Maddux sent word to [a *Tribune* reporter] that he had in his possession a $10,000 extortion note which had been mailed and delivered in Tulsa. He would not admit that it was the letter to Wrightsman he had exhibited, and the announcement was given wide publicity both in Tulsa and elsewhere.

'You'd give your right arm to see this letter,' Maddux said to the *Tribune* reporter, exhibiting an envelope on which was printed the name and address of C. J. Wrightsman, Tulsa oil man. Maddux declined to discuss its contents.

[Later] that afternoon Maddux told reporters the note he had shown and his announcement referred to the same instrument, but late in the day he said for the first time that the note was three years old.

In a long editorial, the *Tulsa World* gave high praise to the grand jury, and commended them on their findings, which the paper confidently declared would silence, once and for all, the persistent rumors that had plagued the city for five months.

The grand jury found out that, beyond all question, too many people had talked too much, and that the big talkers, when time for a showdown came, didn't really know anything. This flood of rumors was the real cause of the convening of the grand jury; its careful work should settle all the talk and make the rumor mongers subside.

Every opportunity has been given these gossips to tell what they know, if anything, and they have failed to make good. The grand jury report should be a standing rebuke to all such people, and it should remain as a caution to all to quit making unfounded assertions or dangerous surmises.

Just prior to the release of the grand jury's report, Maddux was planning to fight his forced resignation in district court. He changed his mind after reading the strong statement that came out against him.

Under normal circumstances, that would have been the end of Henry Bailess Maddux, but Henry Bailess Maddux had one more dirty trick up his sleeve that Tulsans would learn about one year later.

Chapter Twenty-Five

THERE WAS NO WAY IN HELL Phil Kennamer was ever going to serve twenty-five years in prison. This was the era of long sentences by law-and-order judges but also of early paroles courtesy of lenient state laws, pardon-and-parole boards eager to please, clemency by outbound governors, and a lucrative system of "parole brokers." According to Oklahoma state law at the time, Kennamer could be out of prison in less than twelve years with good behavior. However, the definition of good behavior itself was incredibly loose. As long as he didn't kill anybody, at the most, he would only have to serve fifteen years. But serving twelve or fifteen years was only necessary if his release could not be successfully achieved through back channels.

And there was no way in hell Judge Franklin Kennamer was going to let his son rot in prison while his legal team fought for an appeal. When Charles Stuart told the press, "We think the boy is better off in prison while the case is being appealed," that's not what he really meant. What he really meant was that Judge Kennamer needed more time to schmooze six of his prosperous friends throughout Oklahoma to pledge property worth $104,000 to secure the $25,000 appeal bond. When the judge and a new attorney, Eben Taylor, appeared in Judge Hurst's chambers on May 21, they came with the deeds and an excuse: Phil was sick with influenza. It was the second time in five months he had gotten sick with the flu.

When reporters peppered him with questions as he was released from prison, the boy was in high spirits. Although he had been in the prison hospital for nearly a week, he was obviously feeling better when he launched into a tirade against Tulsa reporters in general, and Lee Krupnick in particular.

"If that photographer is here to take a picture of me, he'll get his camera broken." Phil then told reporters about his seventy-eight days in prison, which included his work in the twine factory, and a journalism course he started but never finished because it took too much time away from reading books.

"The officials at the prison have been very kind to me," Phil added. "I have learned a number of things since coming to prison, some good, some bad. I didn't mind working in the twine plant but if I come back, I hope they'll put me on the road selling twine instead of in [the] factory."

If the prison officials were nice to him, it may have been because his father was friends with the warden. It was a friendship that would later prove beneficial.

Kennamer stayed in Tulsa that night at his parent's home but left the next day for his father's farm near Chelsea, Oklahoma, where he remained for the majority of the time during his appeal. Occasionally, he would make forays into Tulsa, which included a brief visit with his new enemy, Jack Snedden.

Three weeks after his release, his defense team filed their brief with the Oklahoma criminal court of appeals. In it, they outlined nineteen legal atrocities committed by the prosecution and allowed by the court. When Moss argued for his client on October 1, he launched into a scathing attack of Gilmer, Anderson, and his nemesis, J. Berry King, and fired off words and phrases like "unfair," and "deprived of constitutional rights," and "taking advantage of a minor," and "vicious, pernicious, and vile," as well as "prejudicial, inflammatory remarks."

He was also not shy about blaming Judge Hurst, who, because of the media, "was swept off his feet," and had imposed an excessive sentence. They also blamed him for not declaring a mistrial during the Edna Harman fiasco, even though Anderson himself had called for one, which Moss had rejected.

1936

Although Gilmer asked the judges for a mandate to send Kennamer back to prison by Thanksgiving, their decision didn't come until March 13, when they rejected Kennamer's appeal with the declaration that he had had a fair trial with an unbiased jury and that the sentence was not excessive. Jumping on the bandwagon of the court's decision, Governor Ernest Marland brazenly declared, "There will be no clemency for the youth during my administration."

Instead of going back to prison, Phil remained free while his lawyers followed standard procedure and prepared their response to the appellate court's decision. The law allowed them to petition for a rehearing that would open the door for a do-over of their appeal—but it was a long shot.

As the defense team regrouped, Judge Kennamer took the rare step of brazenly announcing to the press that a private investigator had uncovered new, documentary evidence.

"We have some really new evidence," Judge Kennamer told the press in Oklahoma City. He and his son were there to present it to the governor, and to ask for a new investigation into the entire case. "It will make you sit up and take notice when it is divulged. The attorneys will present it when the time comes."

That time would come on April 11, when the defense launched a two-pronged attack to petition Judge Hurst for a new trial, and a motion for the criminal court of appeals to rehear their arguments, based on the new evidence.

On the face of it, the new, documentary evidence provided by a private investigator was intriguing. But just as Moss and Stuart laid a trap for the prosecution in Edna Harman, it was the prosecution's turn to set a trap for the defense. After it was over, and the dirty tricks were laid bare, Flint Moss would recuse himself from the defense team—permanently.

In the petition for a second hearing before the appeals court, the defense attached four affidavits. The first one declared that one of the jurors, before the trial, had stated his opinion that Phil Kennamer was guilty, "and therefore was a prejudiced juror."

The second and third affidavits asserted that Jack Snedden had lied on the stand when he said he'd asked Kennamer at the Owl Tavern on the night of the murder if he was going out to kill John Gorrell, and Phil had answered "Yes." That affidavit was made by a Pawnee jailer who said he had overheard a conversation between Kennamer and Snedden in the courthouse restroom during a trial recess.

"Kennamer asked Snedden why he did not tell the truth when he testified," the second affidavit declared. "Snedden said 'I can't because I'd get in trouble and I'm afraid to.'"

The third affidavit was from Owl Tavern proprietor Jack Arnold, who professed that Snedden was highly intoxicated Thanksgiving night, and that he came in the next day with a hangover and remarked that he couldn't remember anything about the night before.

But it was the fourth affidavit that Judge Kennamer was counting on to free his son. It was made by a twenty-one-year-old man from Illinois who declared he was a friend of Gorrell's during the single semester the two attended Knox College in Galesburg, Illinois, during the fall 1933 semester. It was accompanied by two letters, allegedly written by Gorrell, but signed "Jeff" and "Steve," which portrayed the sender as an outlandish, over-the-top, "criminal mastermind," the defense stated. In one of the letters, dated September 1934, "Gorrell" attempted to draw Wright into his criminal enterprise.[1]

---

[1] This was the first and last mention that Gorrell attended Knox College, and it had never before been brought up by his father on the witness stand,

A group of local boys has started to organize for the new administration coming in soon [Sheriff-elect Garland Marrs]. We have the slot machine racket for Tulsa lined up pretty well. We have the sheriff where he will play ball with us and seeing that Oklahoma is a dry state, we have sent for a man to get the liquor concession under control. I wonder if you might be able to come down and get in on the ground floor.

. . . To make things easier on all concerned, we have the federal judge's son well in the gang so there is might little danger anywhere.

. . . I am going to K.C. and handle the K.C. end of the business with the [gang members], etc. As far as your end is concerned, I'll have to write you from K.C. on Sunday.

In his affidavit that was taken in the boy's hometown of Canton, Illinois, Wright further stated that Gorrell had proposed to rob three safes on campus and kill the night watchman if necessary; to fly drugs and aliens from Mexico into the United States; and in 1933, to kidnap a high-society girl from Tulsa, fly her across the border into Mexico, and hold her for $50,000 ransom. To top it all off, Wright's affidavit conveniently declared that Gorrell "indicated [that] if anything went wrong, Phil Kennamer was to be the fall guy." From looking at her picture in a crime magazine, Wright identified Virginia as the intended kidnap victim, and claimed that she and John had been writing each other since 1933.

To pile on more inflammatory accusations, the defense motion also claimed the prosecution bought and paid for testimony because Dr. Gorrell *did* pay Edna Harman the one hundred dollars. He was lying, they asserted, when he said he

---

who said his son had attended the University of Tulsa and Oklahoma A&M before attending dental school. There was also no statement, either confirming or denying, that he wrote this letter to Wright.

didn't pay her, (even though she was forced to take the stand by subpoena, which would nullify any reason Dr. Gorrell would have for paying her the money she requested).

When the affidavits and letters were made public, the backlash came hard and fast. Garland Marrs denied ever knowing John Gorrell in his lifetime. John Gorrell and Virginia Wilcox never knew each other, and it was stated at trial that Phil Kennamer had to supply Gorrell with the Wilcox address. In 1933, John Gorrell didn't have a pilot's license, and he couldn't fly anywhere or rent an airplane.

When Jack Snedden heard about the libelous claims made by the defense, he sent a telegram from Princeton University, where he was attending school, to Dixie Gilmer, who released it to the press.

> I have just learned that part of the evidence upon which Kennamer seeks a new trial is based on the premise that my testimony was untrue and that I was intoxicated when Kennamer was disarmed and that I was afraid to tell the truth.

> Those allegations are, of course, maliciously false. Last summer, Phil approached me and requested that I change my testimony. Because of my refusal, my family and I have been subjected to indignities.

Gilmer and Dr. Gorrell had been waiting for this moment since December 1935. When the press came to them looking for a response, they detonated their own bomb: the private investigator working for the Kennamers was Henry Bailess Maddux. As it turns out, Maddux had approached Judge Kennamer in the fall of 1935 with information about Wright that he had gathered during his investigation. The disgraced, former detective then worked out a secret deal with the judge to get "documentary evidence" that Gorrell was a big-time criminal mastermind who was ready to frame his son. As part of their agreement, the judge agreed to pay Maddux $250 and gave him assurances that he would use his influence get him a job with the Federal Bureau of Investigation.[2]

Anticipating all of this to come out sooner or later, Gilmer was quick with his statement, which may have been prepared in advance.

"At the instigation of Judge Kennamer and some of his attorneys, Maddux went to Canton, Illinois, and represented himself there to the prosecuting attorney as a deputy sheriff from Tulsa County and acting on behalf of the prosecution in this case. As a result of this fraud, these affidavits were secured," Gilmer's statement began.

However, when Maddux handed over the letters and affidavits to Judge Kennamer, the judge reneged on their agreement and, instead of paying him the $250, the ex-police sergeant only got fifty bucks. Feeling betrayed, Maddux outlined what had occurred, in a letter to Dr. Gorrell dated December 24, 1935, and offered to sell him the evidence he had gathered from Wright. He ended his letter with a postscript that stated: "I got $50 and a lot of promises."

Doctor Gorrell refused to pay for Maddux's "evidence," and together with Gilmer, the two went to Canton, Illinois, to question Wright, who not only recanted his sworn affidavits, but shifted all the blame to Maddux.

"We obtained a sworn statement from Wright," Gilmer's declaration continued, "who said as a result of fraud, misinformation, and duress, Maddux obtained his affidavit and that the inferences to be drawn from his affidavit were erroneous. Wright told us that it was never his intention to defame young Gorrell's character. He told us that Maddux dictated his, Wright's, statement, and it was 'largely a creature of Maddux's imagination.'"

---

[2] The agency changed its name from Bureau of Investigation to the Federal Bureau of Investigation in 1935.

In addition to exposing Maddux, Gilmer castigated Judge Kennamer as being "'guilty of misconduct' in moves planned to gain further reprieve for his son," the *World* reported.

A few days later, the criminal court of appeals denied Moss's motion for a rehearing of his client's appeal. They also granted a request from the assistant state attorney general when they issued a writ of prohibition forbidding Judge Thurman Hurst from ever granting Phil Kennamer a new trial. This obliterated any chance he had of gaining his freedom through the courts. There would be no new investigation. There would be no new trial based on documentary evidence that would "make you sit up and take notice." The high court's decision was the legal equivalent of saying: *Go away and never come back.* The judges even went so far as to remark that since the boy had violated no federal laws, he couldn't appeal his case to the United States Supreme Court.

On April 21, a disgusted Kennamer surrendered to the warden and expressed his opinion of the court's decision. "Whatever influence swayed the court in their findings it was not in the high principles of law secured to us under the constitution." He ended by telling reporters the high court had no respect for government.

"Thank God it's over," Dr. Gorrell told the *Tribune* when told of Kennamer's return to prison. "At least, I hope it's over. I hope we can begin to forget about this case. It has been an awful strain on my wife."

But it would never be over. The Kennamers were never going to go away. They were never going to stop. They were right and everyone else was wrong. It would just keep going— on and on and on—until one of them was dead.

Chapter Twenty-Six

1936

WITH THE STATE COURTS NOW off-limits, Judge Kennamer chose to pursue his son's freedom through backdoor channels to both the governor's office, and to the pardon-and-parole board. When the fifty-seven-year-old gathered the support of affluent friends to secure bail, he subconsciously signaled the strategy he would use to get his boy out of prison. Instead of going at Governor Marland directly and publicly, the Kennamer family lobbied influential contacts to take the lead and swamp the governor's office with private conversations, phone calls, and letters advocating for clemency. All of this was done quietly, behind the scenes, and away from the prying eyes of the press.

But by October of that year, rumors were getting back to the Gorrell family that something was going on. Their son's killer was only eight combined months into his sentence and already, the pro-Kennamer allies were campaigning for his release. On October 12, eyebrows were raised when the *Tulsa Tribune* revealed that Phil, his father, and a new attorney had held a secret meeting, outside of prison, in the home of an assistant deputy warden. This prompted the Gorrells to meet with Governor Marland to ask if a formal petition for clemency had been filed, and if the prison was giving Phil special treatment. They were assured that no application had been filed, and that Kennamer was being treated the same as any other prisoner. But the state's leading politician then made a statement that was indicative of things to come. "The only thing that will change my mind (about clemency) is the production of newfound evidence," he told reporters outside his capitol-building office.

As would soon become clear to the entire state of Oklahoma, when Governor Ernest Marland prematurely announced in March, "There will be no clemency for the youth during my administration," that wasn't what he meant. What he really meant was: *I'm wishy-washy, and despite what the Pawnee jury voted, and the findings of the grand jury, and the ruling by the criminal court of appeals—my actions regarding Phil Kennamer can easily be influenced.*

1937

This much was proved when he announced six months later, in April 1937, that he "[had] been urged by close personal friends to consider the Kennamer case and grant clemency," an Oklahoma City newspaper reported.

"I think in fairness, I should look into this," Governor Marland continued. "I will look into it myself, in the next year."

This unprovoked announcement was met with suspicion from the Gorrells and Dixie Gilmer, the new county attorney. As governor-elect in December 1934, Marland had visited Tulsa after the murder and had spoken with authorities. When pervasive gossip raised doubts about everything, he had assigned his own investigator to look into the murder, but his findings matched those of the grand jury—that there was no more to the case than what was already said in the courtroom or from the grand jury. Now, in spite of everything else, Marland allowed himself to be prejudiced by the persuasiveness of others who convinced him Phil Kennamer had been treated unfairly.

By July, sixteen influential citizens with ties to Judge Kennamer—including a state district judge and the governor of Alabama—had personally written Governor Marland requesting parole for Phil Kennamer. Another petitioner, a local attorney from Tulsa, tried to argue that Phil Kennamer was persecuted because he *is* the son of a federal judge, and that he did not actually murder John Gorrell; someone else did, and Phil was "taking the rap" because he thought his father's position would set him free.

His letter, like many of the others, incorporated histrionic language that overstated far-fetched claims of important new evidence, based on what boiled down to as—gossip. A few weeks later, two other attorneys used this same approach to assert that "a majority of Tulsa citizens believe Phil Kennamer has been punished sufficiently for the slaying of John Gorrell."

That statement was soon discredited. With the Kennamer camp clearly one step ahead, Dixie Gilmer, the new county attorney, and Dr. Gorrell were forced to play catch-up. During the entire month of June 1937, they circulated a petition demanding that Phil Kennamer be kept in prison. "It is a travesty of justice that we should be required to take such a preventative measure," Gilmer told the Associated Press.

By July 4, they had gathered 5,455 names, with 3,783 of them coming from Tulsans.

But when Governor Marland placed the sixteen pro-Kennamer letters in one pan of a balancing scale, and the petition with 5,455 names in the other pan, the appeals for parole weighed heavier—according to his scale of justice. This was proved a few days later when he took the unusual step of informing Fred Cunningham, lead attorney for the state pardon-and-parole board, that he was taking "personal charge" of any possible clemency action for Phil Kennamer, and that it was still under consideration.

Based on popular opinion alone, Governor Marland could have closed the Phil Kennamer file for the remaining two years of his term. Instead, his remarks and actions indicated he was leaving the possibility of parole open and was merely biding his time until the public outlook was more favorable. The case, Cunningham later told the Associated Press, was ". . . in a state of suspended animation."

True to his nature, Phil had his own plans to get out of his prison sentence. Along with 3,600 other convicts, prisoner 31-420 woke every morning at six o'clock and put on the regulation uniform of blue denim trousers, a blue-and-white-striped shirt, and a blue denim coal-miner's cap. After a quick breakfast, all able-bodied men were required to be at their work stations by seven thirty. His first prison job had him starting off at the bottom, working as a spool tender in the prison's twine factory. When he returned to prison following his failed appeal, he continued to work various positions in the twine factory until he was promoted to a low-level job in the prison library.

In mid-October 1937, the young man who was once insulted by his defense attorneys' claims that he was mentally ill personally requested a sanity hearing with prison doctors. The irony was not lost on Tulsa newspapers.

"It (the insanity defense) was rejected by the youth himself who on the witness stand, insisted that he was sane," the *Tribune* reminded its readers.

1938

After that effort failed, his next scheme was revealed during a January 22, 1938, self-arranged interview with the press in which he promised to leave the country and never return. The story conveniently coincided with the regular monthly meeting of the parole board, as well as intimations from Governor Marland that he would act on the case before he left office in twelve months.

"If I were released, and it were possible under the terms of my release, I would leave the country permanently and go to South America to work for a company with which I have been promised employment," Kennamer announced. "All I want to do is get away from here [and become] a man without a country."

The job was real and his statements calculated. What Kennamer was offering, with his father's support, was a conditional parole that would, hopefully, meet with the approval of those who were against him. A month earlier, Governor Marland had revealed that he was under intense pressure to grant clemency. This latest attempt, the Kennamers hoped, would put him over the top.

But when his case was never brought up during the monthly clemency meeting, Phil's next bid for freedom came two weeks later when he demanded that the new Pawnee County attorney charge a prosecution witness with perjury. Although the papers didn't mention his name at first, it was another attempt to shift blame elsewhere and get revenge against the young man who had testified to Phil's premeditation of murder—the young man who had stood between him and Virginia Wilcox, and the same young man who had married her in October of 1936—Jack Snedden.

In his letter, Phil claimed that Marion Hamby, the Pawnee jailer, would support his accusation of perjury and declared, "[he] will be glad to sign the complaint as required by law." However, when County Attorney Horace Ballaine spoke with Hamby, the man said he "[did] remember something about it," but his "memory was hazy on exactly what happened."

After striking out three times in five months, Kennamer retreated back into his world and began writing a book about the injustice he was forced to endure. In August, the twenty-three-year-old got one of the best jobs in the entire institution as a clerk in the prison's treasury office. His work, overseeing the prisoners' private accounts, ended at four thirty in the afternoon. Instead of attending the educational courses that were available to most prisoners, Kennamer returned to the cell he shared with James Arthur Camp, twenty-eight, who was serving a twenty-five-year term for armed robbery. There, he would indulge in his favorite pastimes of reading, working on his book, or writing letters.

While Phil lived a comfortable life in a six-by-sixteen-foot cell, the Gorrells were forced to endure yet another tragedy. On a return trip from Los Angeles, daughter Edith Ann suffered serious injuries after she lost control of the car she was driving on wet pavement near Grants, New Mexico, on September 1. The sedan rolled several times, breaking her back and shoulder, and nearly pulled her scalp off. Her brother, Ben, nineteen, suffered only minor cuts and bruises. After Edith was stabilized in an Albuquerque hospital, the two were flown back to Tulsa. Despite several operations, she remained paralyzed from the waist down.

The Kennamers were suffering too; after a long fight with cystic fibrosis, devoted mother Lillie Kennamer, was dying. It was an unfortunate situation that created an opportunity for Phil, when her doctor advised Judge Kennamer that she wouldn't survive another winter in Oklahoma. To extend her life, he recommended she be moved to Arizona, where the warm, dry climate would ease her frequent coughing spasms. But there was just one problem—she refused to leave without Phil. Friends who visited with her said she was emaciated, bedridden, and all she wanted to talk about was her youngest son.

With the help of a high-ranking state politician, Judge Kennamer requested and received a clemency hearing with the parole board, who would be asked to consider a ninety-day compassionate parole for Phil to accompany his mother to Arizona. During the time period, medical furloughs were occasionally granted and, historically, a significant number of them morphed into a permanent parole.

The hearing was held on October 31 in the famed "blue room" inside the state capitol building with a packed crowd of several hundred people, most of them pro-Kennamer-family supporters. The merits of the Gorrell-Kennamer case were off-limits. Board members were only interested in the health of Phil's mother and the parameters of parole, if granted.

As they had done so many times before, John and Alice Gorrell were again forced to be the watchdogs of justice for their son's killer. In their corner was the indefatigable Dixie Gilmer, who was placed in the awkward position of lobbying against the dying wish of a long-suffering woman, who, by all accounts, was a lovely person.

When called to testify, Judge Kennamer gave a detailed description of his wife's recent decline. The medical opinion of her doctor was read into the record and reported on by the *Tribune*. "In his opinion, Mrs. Kennamer's condition had been aggravated by worry over her son, and added the companionship of her son would prolong her life 'which at any rate, would not be of long duration.'"

After several dozen more people testified, most of them in favor of temporary parole, the five-member board retreated into a private room and returned fifty minutes later with a favorable recommendation to the governor. The public hearing by the board, the capitol correspondent for the *Tulsa World* intimated, was merely for show.

"It was obvious from the moment board members entered the (private) room that the only question for decision would be the length of time consumed in writing the recommendation to be made to the governor," Edward Burks wrote.

But instead of giving Phil the customary ninety days his father had requested, the parole board generously doubled it to six months, which shocked supporters and detractors alike, and smacked of favoritism. For Governor Marland—a man who was married to his dead wife's niece-turned-adopted-daughter but later had her adoption annulled when she was twenty-eight so they could get married—it was a win-win. His administration was finally able to give the Kennamer camp the victory they had always wanted, and it would also shift the possibility of granting permanent parole to the new governor, who would take office on January 9, 1939.

Dixie Gilmer and the Gorrell family had finally been beaten. Alice Gorrell, who had lost twenty-five pounds since her daughter's accident, and who was once again being forced to fight for justice for her murdered son, made a rare public statement to the press: ". . . I only wish there were some way the pardon and parole board could send my boy back to me."

But nobody from the governor's office or the parole board wanted to listen to them anymore, and the time the Gorrells had left with their only daughter was slipping away. Edith Ann died of pneumonia on September 12, 1940, just twelve days before her twenty-fourth birthday.

1939

For the next five months, Phil Kennamer, now twenty-three, lived by the discipline required to meet his parole. In addition to attending to the needs of his dying mother, he was obligated to be employed, and after four weeks of searching, the former office clerk found work as a warehouse employee, unloading barrels of oil and supplies for one hundred dollars a month. This was a new Phil Kennamer, more reserved and mature. His combined thirty-two months in prison had tempered his arrogance—a little.

On March 5, Lillie Kennamer was transported back to Tulsa where she could spend her final days with her family. She died on Sunday, March 12, at the age of fifty-four.

The fate of Phil Kennamer was left to Governor Leon Phillips, who said he would review the entire case file and the appeals-court decision. He took his time and granted several two-week parole extensions while Phil kept working at his job in Arizona. But on May 29, Governor Phillips ordered him back to prison.

"The story of this case is a sordid one; a disobedient and willful boy, idleness and inattention to school, refusal to continue in any job, a carefree life, culminating in a frequent use of intoxicating liquors and finally in taking of human life without legal excuse," Phillips wrote.

He then agreed with experts who said Phil had his own moral code outside of the one prescribed by the people and laws of Oklahoma.

"We cannot [disregard] the verdicts and judgments of the juries and courts upon the insistence of friends, or to relieve the aching hearts of relatives because of the crime of some member of the family," Phillips continued. "I think justice requires that I . . . reject the plea for further clemency."

Governor Phillips, unlike his predecessor, had a backbone, and when he sent Phil back to prison, the strong language with which he ordered it sent a message to those in the Kennamer camp that he considered the matter closed for discussion. For the next two years, pleas for leniency were filed and disregarded.

1940-41

During that time, Judge Kennamer, now a widower, was preoccupied with personal problems. In May 1940, after fifteen years on the bench, he retired nine years early on a disability pension, citing fatigue and arthritis. One year later, he raised eyebrows when he filed for divorce from thirty-two-year-old Pauline Fox Kennamer. The two had gotten married on February 19, 1940, in a secret ceremony in Benton County, Arkansas, where the sixty-one-year-old gave his name as Elmore Kennamer, fifty-one, from Big Cabin, a village twelve miles east of Chelsea.

Pauline, an American Indian woman with two children, divorced her husband Clifton on July 31, 1939—four months after Lillie Kennamer died, and six months before she married the judge. Clifton was the former caretaker of the Kennamer farm, where Pauline was also employed as a cook and housekeeper. She left her new husband after one month of matrimony, and fled to Missouri for some unspecified reason. Judge Kennamer was granted a divorce on July 16, 1941, citing gross neglect, failure to prepare meals, clean the home, and care for her husband who was ill. His retirement had come just three months after his secret marriage, and some wondered if the two events were linked together, and how.

Although Governor Phillips was a stern man, Judge Kennamer was relentless in his quest to free his son through clemency. By 1941, his backdoor lobbying had reached the level of desperation, and it consequently blew up in his face when he tried to coerce the governor with a semi-controversial letter between a Phillips political appointee and a Tulsa banker pushing for a clemency hearing on behalf of the judge.

The Phillips appointee wrote a reply to the banker explaining that the governor was too preoccupied with another legal problem, as well as raising $2,500 for legal fees, to consider a drawn-out clemency hearing for Phil Kennamer. When Judge Kennamer read the letter, he interpreted it as subtle request for a $2,500 bribe. He then tried to leverage those letters into an underhanded threat that the governor grant a clemency hearing or else he would take the letters to the state senate, where they would be made public. When Governor Phillips was informed of what was going on, he released all the letters to the newspapers, and berated the former judge with language no one had dared use before.

"He (Judge Kennamer) is not going to come out here and get a public hearing," Phillips told the Associated Press. "He doesn't rank it. We've wasted too much time on this matter as it is. He can go back and sit down. He is not running my clemency policy or this state. If he has anything he wants to say, or any names to name, he can give it to the newspapers or put up a sign."

A few days later, Governor Phillips answered a reporter's question with a declaration that no clemency for Phil Kennamer would be considered for the remaining two years of his term. He was aware that in the state's thirty-four-year history, no other prisoner had received as much attention in the press, or from the pardon-and-parole board, or from powerful, influential people clamoring for his release, as Phil Kennamer. He was done with the matter.

1942

But the Kennamers weren't. After a failed bid to get the case to the United States Supreme Court, Phil tried his luck with Gov. Phillips again in 1942. With the nation in a two-front war, low-level prisoners were being granted clemency on the condition that they joined the armed forces. To fight for one's country as a patriotic citizen was a noble endeavor, and it presented ex-convicts with a perfect opportunity for redemption. In February, Phil took a chance with Governor Phillips, offering to join the military as a condition of his parole. Phillips, who had eleven months left in his term, kept his word, and rejected his offer.

But everything changed for Phil Kennamer on November 3, when Democrat Robert S. Kerr won the general election to become the twelfth governor of Oklahoma. He was one of the five members of the pardon-and-parole board that had granted Kennamer a six-month furlough to be with his dying mother.

1943

As soon as Kerr was sworn in, the Kennamer family wasted no time in wrangling a clemency hearing for Phil, which was scheduled for April 20. Like his previous inquest in the state-capitol building, this one was crowded and came with a foregone conclusion under very peculiar circumstances. Letters in favor of parole were read aloud with great animation and flourish, while the letters against parole were mentioned, but never read. Despite Dixie Gilmer's contention that Phil had never expressed remorse and had recently told him, "I'm not sorry and I will never be sorry," the board retreated to a private room where, in a matter of minutes, they voted unanimously to recommend parole on condition of joining the army.

Phil, who was allowed to attend this hearing, personally thanked the governor after the meeting adjourned. When the press caught up with him outside, he said he wanted to sign up to become a paratrooper. After serving six years, seven months, and sixteen days in prison, twenty-seven-year-old Phil Kennamer was a free man.

While taking a philosophical outlook toward his parole, an editorial from the *Tulsa World* blasted his father's relentless efforts to free his son.

"It is doubtful if any more official, legal, social or political pressure has ever been used in this country to circumvent justice. There has not been a month since the night of the shooting that powerful friends have not been active, at many times under coercion, in the intercessions for young Kennamer. These consistent efforts were directed toward anyone who in any way might be helpful."

His parole, fought and won by backdoor politics, discarded the justice the Gorrells had fought so desperately to keep. The *World*, disgusted with the hearing, and disgusted with the entire Kennamer saga, expressed their "sincere hope that it will never be necessary to refer to this case again."

As noble as that ambition was, they should have known better.

Chapter Twenty-Seven

0400 Hours, August 15, 1944
Somewhere off the coast of Southern France

THE CIGARETTE BUTTS IN PHIL KENNAMER'S ears did little to buffer the roaring sound of the C47's twin Pratt-Whitney engines. With his arms resting on his reserve parachute, he glanced now and then to the red and green lights adjacent to the opening where the exit door had been removed. Red was for "get ready," green was for "go," and after sitting in what was essentially a giant tube for almost four hours, he was ready to jump into enemy territory. For him, as for all the other men, the waiting to do something was much worse than actually doing it, and he just wanted to get it over with.

Ever since he'd joined the army one month after his parole, the last 449 days of his life had boiled down to this moment. First, there were sixteen weeks of basic training at Camp Mackall, North Carolina, and then three weeks of jump school at Fort Benning, and then back to Mackall. There, the famous Phil Kennamer became a small fish in a big pond. His position in the world was demonstrated by how low in the Army's hierarchy he was assigned. He was a member of a three-man machine-gun crew commanded by Corporal Lark Washburn, in a platoon from Charlie Battery of the 460th Parachute Field Artillery Battalion (PFAB), which, at the time of his training, was part of the 17th Airborne Division.

When they weren't marching, running, drilling, eating, or sleeping, Charlie Battery was training—always training. There was hand-to-hand combat training, judo training, bayonet training, training on the Springfield M1903, training on the M1

Garand, training on the M2 .50-cal, the Thompson submachine gun, the M3 submachine gun, the carbine, the Browning automatic rifle, the M1911, the M1 bazooka, the M9 bazooka, hand grenades, the rifle-propelled grenade, the field radio, the field telephone, gas mask with riot gas, no mask with riot gas, compass training, map training, contour map training, field first aid, and, last but not least, training on how to assemble, disassemble, load, aim, fire, clear, and clean the 75-mm pack howitzer.

And that was all before jump school, which included landing training, cable sliding in a harness, jumping out of a mock C47 with a four-foot fall, tower jumping in a parachute chair with a 250-foot fall, and then tower jumping with a real parachute. Then came the real jumps, five of them over five days, which amounted to: stand up, hook up static line, equipment check, shuffle toward door with seventy-five pounds of gear, brace on door with both hands, push with right leg, tuck in arms, pray the tail section doesn't hit you, wait for the chute to snap-jerk you like a rubber band, watch ground, hit ground, roll on ground, collapse chute, and remove harness.

To field-test that education, the 460th PFAB spent the month of February participating in combat training maneuvers in the Tennessee Mountains. By March, Kennamer's unit was deemed ready for combat. His battalion was reformed with the 517th Parachute Infantry Regiment and a company of airborne engineers, to form the 517th Parachute Regimental Combat Team. This outfit of roughly twenty-five hundred men was expected to do battle as a small division.

On May 31, 1944, two troop-transport ships carrying that small division landed in Naples, where they fell under the command of the 36th Infantry Division, which had been fighting in Italy for the last six months. On June 18, the unit received their baptism by fire on the Moscona Hills, north of Grosseto. For the next eight days, the 517 pushed the Germans back as they advanced up and down and up and down the hills of

Tuscany, while the sixteen 75-mm pack howitzers of the 460th provided artillery support. By the morning of June 26, the 517th PRCT, along with other units, had gained thirty-nine miles of enemy territory and were on the outskirts of Suvareto when they were relieved by the Japanese-American soldiers of the 442nd Regiment.

As paratroopers, they had been sent to Italy for one reason: "the big show," the invasion of France. The allied invasion of Normandy had already taken place, and the top brass were calling for an invasion of southern France from the Mediterranean. This was Operation Dragoon, the forgotten cousin to Operation Overlord—the Normandy invasion. The German 19th Army Group had more than two hundred thousand soldiers spread wide and thin throughout the south of France. The allies sought to open another French front that would push the Germans back and secure the ports of Marseilles and Toulon, where troop transports could deliver forty to fifty divisions of soldiers who were in America, waiting to fight in Europe. These ports had the facilities capable of handling such a large-scale disembarkation of men and equipment.

The amphibious assault would come ashore west of Cannes at the beaches of Fréjus, Saint-Tropez, and Cavalaire-sur-Mer, on the morning of August 15. Leading this attack would be nine thousand British and American paratroopers under the newly formed First Airborne Task Force. In the predawn hours, the paratroopers would land a few miles north of those beaches, secure their positions, and block German movement into the main assault area. The landing zones for the five-one-seven would be just south of the populous city of Draguignan, and were roughly shaped into a diamond marked by the villages of Trans-en-Provence at the top, Les Arcs to the west, La Motte to the east, and Le Muy at the bottom.

After the 517th PRCT was pulled off the line, it was moved to a staging area near Rome, where passes into the city were liberally granted. July 1944 was an exciting time for Phil, who wrote letters to his father about the Roman Coliseum, and the Sistine Chapel, with its famous ceiling painted by Michelangelo. On July 26, he celebrated his twenty-ninth birthday with his pals from Charlie Battery, which included his section leader, Corporal Lark Washburn, and Corporal Milton Rogers, who remembered him distinctly in his 2007 online memoirs.

"He had been paroled from the Oklahoma State Penitentiary, where he had been doing time for manslaughter. He was quite a revelation to us country kids who had never been anyplace or done anything," the Utah native wrote.

Often, Rogers was Kennamer's partner in games of Pitch against Washburn, who partnered with Private Owen Burnham. "I was on the losing side most of the time because my partner overbid his hand severely," Rogers wrote. "He couldn't let anybody else win the bid. We made fun of him and reviled him. He named us (Washburn, Rogers, and Burnham) 'those SOBs from Utah.' In army language that is almost a compliment."

But Rogers gave as good as he got, and he saddled Phil with the nickname "Buffalo Phil."

"I'd hung that name on him," Rogers continued in his memoirs. "He was bad out of shape when he got to our outfit and couldn't keep up on the runs. I said, 'Kennamer, you look like a buffalo at the end of a long stampede,' and the name stuck."

Another soldier from Charlie Battery, Merle McMorrow, agreed that Phil was in poor physical shape because of his age, but he persevered and was popular with the other soldiers. "Phil Kennamer slept in the bunk above me at Camp Mackall," McMorrow said in a 2015 interview. "At night, after lights out at ten, Phil would recite Shakespeare by heart until we fell asleep. He was a good friend and well-liked by everyone."

In early August, the entire First Airborne Task Force began their final preparations for Operation Dragoon. Charlie Battery, under the command of Captain Louis Vogel, would be attached to the 1st Battalion of the 517th Infantry Regiment. Together, they were in the ninth and last series of C47s that would drop paratroopers at approximately 0453 hours.

On August 10, the 460th PFAB was on lockdown, and "movement in and out of the bivouac area was banned, and no further contact with military or civilian personnel was allowed," a unit history report stated.

In his memoirs, Cpl. Rogers recalled a conversation he had with Phil on the night of August 14, just a few short hours before his battalion boarded the 180 C47s that would carry them to the drop zones.

"Phil . . . was three or four years older than I was, and partly due to our advanced years we had become pretty good buddies," Rogers wrote. "We couldn't sleep as well as those young kids without nerves, so we sat up and talked till time to load in the planes.

"We were out of about everything to talk about, and finally got to religion. He said he didn't believe in God, didn't believe in much of anything. (Prior to joining the army, Cpl. Rogers had been an LDS missionary.) I said, 'You mean you think that if you get shot tomorrow it's all over?' He said, 'Yep, that's what I think.'"

Several hours later, at a little past four in the morning on August 15, 1944, Phil Kennamer and fifteen other paratroopers were sitting impatiently inside the C47 as it neared the coast of France, taking them closer and closer to the enemy. There wasn't much to see in the darkness except when one of them whipped out a Zippo, cupped his hands around the delicate flame, and leaned in with the cigarette clenched in his mouth. Beneath Kennamer's jump boots was a small pile of smashed cigarette butts—evidence of how long he'd been sitting there. While some of the other men—boys really—tried to sleep through all that noise, he had stayed awake. And in staying awake there was nothing else he could do except sit, smoke, and wonder. Wonder about today. Wonder about the enemy.

Wonder about home. There was a lot to wonder about two thousand feet above the Mediterranean.

And then he saw it—the red light—and felt the movement of fifteen men rising, hooking up their static lines, and checking the chute and equipment of the man in front of them. Each of them sounded off: *Sixteen okay! Fifteen okay! Fourteen okay . . .*

The green light would come on three minutes after the red. Three minutes can be a long time. Waiting. Waiting. Wait for it. Wait for it.

Twenty seconds after the light flashed green, the cargo bay was empty.

Most of Charlie Battery landed north of Trans-en-Provence, near the road leading to Draguignan, the after-action report stated. Like most of the other task-force units, they had missed the landing zone by miles. They were supposed to land further south, near Le Muy, but this was not unexpected, and Captain Vogel managed to assemble two of the 75-mm pack howitzers, which had parachuted down in fourteen pieces, and three-quarters of his men, including Kennamer's platoon led by twenty-one-year-old Second Lieutenant Harry Moore from Wichita, Kansas. Vogel radioed 1st Battalion and received orders to proceed south to a predesignated assembly area. With patrols set up on the flanks, Charlie Battery moved out, keeping to the main road between Draguignan and Trans, because the guns had to be hand-towed. They were soon met by forty infantrymen from 1st Battalion under the command of Lt. Ralph Allison.

Three hundred yards from Trans, a German machine gun fired on the group, sending everyone dashing for cover. Kennamer and his platoon leader volunteered to take it out. After moving into position, Lt. Moore took a firing stance and pressed the trigger on his Thompson submachine gun.

After getting off a short burst, it jammed.

The German MG-42 swung toward their position and opened fire, killing the platoon leader instantly.

According to what a "commanding officer" later told another officer, after Lt. Moore was killed, Kennamer started shooting with his Thompson. With the range and position already calculated, the MG-42 opened fired again, hitting Phil in the chest. Although he went down, he got back up again, "four or five more times," and each time he did, the machine gun fired off another burst, eventually killing him.

The reports differ on how many times Kennamer was shot. The commanding officer's story was published in the *Tulsa Tribune* in January 1945, and quoted an unnamed officer who assisted in the burial. He reported Kennamer had been shot seven times, and that his commanding officer, presumably Captain Vogel, said "Phil got up 'four or five times' after being knocked down by enemy bullets."

However, his pal Cpl. Rogers wrote in his 2007 memoirs that he saw Phil's body later that morning and counted two or three fewer bullet wounds.

> We had another lieutenant from a battery, Lt. Roberts, and pretty soon he came with the information that Phil Kennamer and Lt. Moore had just been killed. I got down the line a ways and there they lay. Phil had a nice row of bleeding holes, maybe four or five, across his chest. It had been maybe seven or eight hours since we were talking about such matters; he then knew more about the hereafter than I did. . . . When Charley Nielson was mourning Phil, Lark [Washburn] said, "Well, it's probably for the best. He was always overbidding his hand."

A third account published in a 2001 book about the 517 PRCT described what happened on the road to Trans-en-Provence this way: "En route, shots sent everyone diving for cover. Lt. Harry Moore and PFC Phil Kennamer yelled they would deal with the problem. Five minutes later, when the firing ceased, the gun crews started forward. 'We found Moore and Kennamer face down in the road, both of them dead,'" reported a soldier who was there.

Soon after they were killed, the machine-gun nest was knocked out with point-blank fire from a howitzer, and encirclement by a squad of infantrymen led by Lt. Allison, Captain Vogel wrote in his after-action report. During the skirmish for Trans-en-Provence, Jacques Debray, a French paratrooper and guide for the American soldiers, was also killed during hand-to-hand combat with two German soldiers.

On a visit to Oklahoma for a legal matter during late November 1943, Kennamer had told *Tulsa World* Managing Editor Edward Burks about a premonition he had.

"Something just seems to tell me," Kennamer said to his dinner guest at the family home, "that I won't come back. I hope that if I die under the flag of my country, those who have condemned me will hold me differently in their memories."

His wish was granted. News of Phil Kennamer's death spread nationally when it was made public on September 27, one day after the army officially notified Judge Kennamer on his farm in Chelsea.

Governor Kerr declared that Kennamer's death on the battlefield justified the parole board's decision to grant his freedom. "He has joined the ranks of Oklahoma sons who have given their lives that we may be free," Kerr said in solemn tone to a *Tribune* reporter. "No man can do more."

Editorials from scattered newspapers throughout Oklahoma and Texas proclaimed that with his sacrifice came redemption.

"Such a sacrifice will purify any life and clear the record of any individual of any errors of his youth," declared the editor of the daily newspaper in Ardmore, Oklahoma.

"It isn't easy to atone for a crime," the *Denton Record-Chronicle* stated on September 30, "but Phil Kennamer ... has done as much as any man can do in atonement. Kennamer is no more a hero than thousands of other Americans who have laid down their lives in battle, but at least some of the black mark on his name should be erased by his sacrifice."

The *Daily Oklahoman* had more eloquent words with its praise for Oklahoma's fallen son. "No matter what Phil Kennamer ever did and no matter what mistakes he ever made, he died in a uniform for country's sake, and that settles all scores. Let us forget the errors of youth, however serious those errors may have been, and remember only that Phil risked his life and gave it freely out yonder in the battle and the storm."

This caliber of public absolution was exactly what Judge Kennamer wanted—before 1944. Although he finally got it, it came with a price he was never willing to pay. For on the morning of September 26, when he received that telegram from the War Department, Franklin Elmore Kennamer discovered what John and Alice Gorrell learned on the floor of a Pawnee hotel room:

That God has not invented pain like the pain of losing a child—and all the pain that came before could barely be remembered. In the years that remained, when they were lost in their quiet yearning for those lives they would never see, they were broken by the theft—of the way it was supposed to be.

Did You Enjoy This Book?

If you enjoyed this book, I would be grateful if you could post a review on Amazon and/or GoodReads.com. Your support really does make a difference. As an independent researcher and writer who is doing nearly all of this on his own (except for my editor), reviews and word of mouth are my only sources of marketing. By telling your friends and family on social media outlets, this true story can reach others who may find it just as fascinating as you did.

Epilogue

Holly Anderson: 1897-1974

After leaving office in January 1937, Holly Anderson worked in private practice for two years until he entered the state House of Representatives in January 1939. His first act was to introduce a bill requiring a three-day notice for obtaining a marriage license in order to prevent "gin marriages," in which couples from Texas crossed the border into southern Oklahoma to marry on a whim because they were drunk and horny. In 1942, after Anderson had already won the Democratic nomination for reelection, he resigned from public office to join the US Army Air Force with the rank of lieutenant, where he served as a technical training officer. After the war, he returned to private practice and died on May 3, 1974. He and his wife, Virginia, had two daughters.

William Dixie Gilmer: 1901-1954

William "Dixie" Gilmer served as the Tulsa County Attorney from 1937 to 1946, where he developed a statewide reputation as an aggressive prosecutor. With his popularity and name recognition firmly established, he entered the Democratic primary for governor, but lost to Roy Turner, who went on to win the 1946 election. In 1948, Gilmer beat Republican incumbent George B. Schwabe to represent the First District of Oklahoma in the US House of Representatives. His congressional career only lasted one term, and he spent most of that time in Walter Reed Hospital being treated for tuberculosis. Schwabe regained his seat in the 1950 election, and Gilmer returned to Oklahoma, where Governor Johnston Murray appointed him to serve as state commissioner of public safety. During his time with the Murray administration, he introduced several improvements, including the use of radar in state patrol vehicles. He died from his illness on June 9, 1954, two days after his fifty-third birthday. He and his wife, Ellen, had no children.

J. Berry King: 1888-1962

After the Phil Kennamer trial, J. Berry King entered private practice, but poor health forced him to retire by the 1950s. A World War One veteran, he was active in the American Legion as well as the VFW. He was known to be an avid newspaper reader and often wrote letters to various Oklahoma columnists and editors. In a 1959 letter to an Oklahoma City newspaper columnist, he described himself as "chairman of the bored." He died on November 24, 1962. His wife, Sadie, moved to Houston, Texas, and died there in 1984. They had no children.

Henry B. Maddux: 1898-1953

Following his public termination from the Tulsa Police Department, castigation by the grand jury, and procurement of a discredited witness statement for Judge Kennamer, which he then tried to sell to Dr. Gorrell, Maddux lived in Tucson, Arizona, and Roswell, New Mexico, where he owned and operated cemetery monument companies.

In 1947 he moved to Albuquerque, New Mexico, where he worked in the insurance business as a risk manager and sales director. He retired from the life insurance branch of the American National Insurance Company in 1952 and died of a heart attack on January 2, 1953.

Although his obituary says he was fifty-two when he died, military records available from Ancestry.com indicate he was born on December 30, 1898, and was actually fifty-four years old at the time of his death. His obituary also reveals that

Maddux was "…an internationally recognized rifle marksman. His awards include the International Wimbledon trophy as the best marksman in the world, a dozen other trophies, and fifty medals."

Captain Henry Maddux, of the Texas National Guard, *did* win the International Wimbledon marksman trophy in 1923. He also won second place in a 1922 national competition when he was a lieutenant. In spite of his actions during the Kennamer-Gorrell case, he served his country in the military during peacetime and in war, earned several promotions, and distinguished himself as a one of the best marksmen in the world during the 1920s.

Austin Flint Moss: 1880-1943

After Moss quit the defense team following Kennamer's failed appeal in April 1936, he continued in private practice, but a heart condition forced him to enter semi-retirement a few years later. In March 1943, he retired for good and moved with his wife, Marjorie, to Long Beach, California, where he died later that year, on December 16, at the age of sixty-three. He lived long enough to see his client paroled.

Hon. Charles Bingley Stuart: 1857-1936

Defense attorney Charles Stuart died on October 30, 1936, six months after the Oklahoma Criminal Court of Appeals rejected Kennamer's appeal and banned his case from the Pawnee County Court. As a former federal judge during territorial days, and one of Oklahoma's most famous litigators, Stuart inducted into the Oklahoma Hall of Fame on April 26, 1937. His death notice in the *Daily Oklahoman* was full of praise and declared him to be "the most feared and most respected man ever to practice law in Oklahoma."

Judge Franklin Elmore Kennamer: 1879-1960

After Philip died in 1944, Judge Kennamer lived a quiet existence on his farm near Chelsea, Oklahoma, until he died of heart trouble on May 1, 1960. He is buried in the Chelsea Cemetery near his daughter, Opal, who never married. His second wife, Pauline, used her ex-husband's last name until she died in 1955. She is also buried in the Chelsea Cemetery.

Edna Harman: 1891- or 1893-1958

As near as I can tell, Edna Harman managed to keep her name out of the newspapers until she died in San Diego, California, in 1958, at the age of sixty-five or sixty-seven. Different authoritative sources list her birth year as either 1891 or 1893. In spite of the controversy she created during the Kennamer trial, Edna Harman had a family who loved her dearly, and she was known to be an active member of her church in Tulsa.

Sidney Born Jr.: 1915-1934

No one was ever arrested in connection with the death of Sidney Born. Although the coroner declared he committed suicide, Born's life insurance company sided with the family and paid the $1,000 death benefit to his father.

Virginia Wilcox: 1916-2008

Following her October 1936 marriage to Jack Snedden, Virginia and Jack had two children: Jack Robin Snedden Jr. (1938-2003), and Beverly Virginia Snedden [Freese] (1939-2014). After serving in the merchant marine during World War Two, and then enjoying a successful business career, Jack Snedden died of pneumonia on November 12, 1946, three days short of his thirty-first birthday. Virginia later remarried, but she had no more children. Her grandson, and the son of Beverly, Jim Freese, is also working on a book about the Kennamer-Gorrell case. Virginia died in 2008 at the age of ninety-two.

Philip Kennamer: 1915-1944

In Trans-en-Provence, along the main road to Draguignan, near the intersection of Impasse Notre Dame and Place de 16 Aout 1944, beside a small chapel, there is a tiny city park where the locals have erected a war memorial to the three soldiers who died there during Operation Dragoon. The memorial is a rough-cut stone with an iron Patriarchal Cross, and an engraved marble slab that, when translated, reads: "In Memory of Debray Jacques, Harris T Moore, Phillip (sic) Kennamer, American parachutists who died facing the enemy on August 15, 1944, for the liberation of the village."

In 1947, Philip's sister, Opal, finished the book he started writing while he was in prison and titled it: *The Inside of the Kennamer Case*. On August 26, she confidently declared to *Tulsa Tribune* editors that the manuscript was on its way to the publisher. However, there is no record the book was ever published, and I could find no copy in existence.

Philip's body was buried in France until it was exhumed, returned to the United States, and interred at Memorial Park Cemetery in Tulsa on May 8, 1948, when funeral services were held. He is buried in the same cemetery where John Gorrell Jr. and Sidney Born Jr. were laid to rest.

Dr. John and Alice Gorrell, 1881-1961, and 1885-1959

John and Alice Gorrell died in 1961 and 1959, respectively. After losing John Jr. and Edith Ann, they raised their two remaining children Benjamin Franklin Gorrell and daughter Nancy Jane. Ben went on to become a well-respected eye, ear, nose, and throat doctor, like his father. Doctor Ben Gorrell and his wife, Mildred, had three children, John, Benjamin Jr., and Elizabeth Ann, who died in 1992. John is retired and lives in the country near Sand Springs where he is fixing up a twenty-five-foot Sea Ray Cruiser and builds birdhouses for the young patients of a children's cancer wing of a Tulsa hospital. Ben Jr. is a successful insurance executive in Tulsa. Nancy Jane married George Coe and they had three children together: Mary Ann, Janie, and Andi. Nancy Jane died in 1995.

Photos Available for Online Viewing

This book only contains 15 of the 60+ available images related to the story you are about to read. If you would like to view all of them, please visit the Deadly Hero Photo Gallery on my blog. HistoricalCrimeDetective.com.

Acknowledgments

IT IS DIFFICULT TO FIND words to adequately thank all the people who helped me with the research for this story. Without them, this book would be much less than what it has become.

It begins with the research department of the Tulsa Public Library, where the kindness of Nick Abrahamson, Jennifer Greb, Kathy Harger, Mary Moore, and Sheri Perkins was overwhelming. They were always professional, accommodating, and helpful. Sheri was particularly helpful with her multi-sourced answers to obscure research questions, and for introducing me to the oral history collection, where I found thirty-five-year-old interviews that added color and depth to a few of the book's characters.

I couldn't have written this book without visiting the Pawnee County Courthouse, where Judge Patrick Pickerill gave me a tour and let me explore, and Court Clerk Janet Dallas answered questions and provided historical perspective.

Dodie O'Bryan, from the Pawnee County Historical Society, was as cheerful as she was helpful, providing valuable information and answering questions.

I also want to express my sincere appreciation to Jean Loup-Gassend, author of *Operation Dragoon: Autopsy of a Battle: The Allied Liberation of the French Riviera August-September 1944,* who helped me understand Operation Dragoon, American paratroopers, and the First Airborne Task Force. His attention to detail is appreciated. We traded dozens of emails, and he was always informative and encouraging.

I also want to thank Operation Dragoon veteran, Merle McMorrow, 92, both for his help with my book and for his service to our country. During our email discussions, he patiently explained to me what it was like to be a paratrooper, to have served during World War II, and to have been friends with Private First Class Philip Kennamer. His book, *From Breckenridge to Bastogne: The Accounts of a World War II Paratrooper,* contains many amazing stories about his time in the service.

Deadly Hero would be a grammatical and style nightmare if it weren't for my editor, G. F. Boyer, who went far beyond her primary duties to provide me with helpful suggestions and encouragement. In twenty years of writing, she is the coolest editor I've ever had.

I wanted to save the Gorrell family for last. I met John Robert Gorrell, John Gorrell Jr.'s nephew, last summer while doing research for this book, and he was gracious enough to have me over to his wonderful home. I thank him for being helpful to me and for his encouragement to work on this story, even though it must be a difficult subject for his family.

From my heart, thank you, everyone.

Also by Jason Lucky Morrow:

The DC Dead Girls Club: A Vintage True Crime Story of Four Unsolved Murders in Washington D.C. ▪ Published 2014, 88 pages, $1.99 Kindle only on Amazon.com

Famous Crimes the World Forgot: Ten Vintage True Crime Stories Rescued from Obscurity, Volume I ▪ Published 2014, 288 pages, $3.95 Kindle, $10.67 paperback.   **Silver Medal Winner**: 2015 eLit Book Awards, True Crime Category.

---###---

Photos Available for Online Viewing

This book only contains **15** of the **60+** available images related to the story you are about to read. If you would like to view all of them, please visit the Deadly Hero Photo Gallery on my blog. **HistoricalCrimeDetective.com.**

Sources

DURING THE 1930S, EDITORS OF Tulsa's dailies had a unique style when it came to laying out the front pages of their newspapers. On many occasions, especially as the Gorrell-Kennamer story began to unfold, they would trumpet a two to six column headline in large type, and then beneath that singular headline, they would run two or three separate news stories related to the case, but each one covering different angles. Above each of these stories would be three to five sensationalistic teasers or sub-headlines that were meant to pull the reader in. Since I could not consider those teasers to be actual headlines, I was forced to use the main one, although it was for two or three different stories. Therefore, when you consider the headlines below, please keep in mind that many of those that began on "page 1," could represent more than one story.

TDO = *The Daily Oklahoman*, Oklahoma City, Oklahoma
MDNR = Miami Daily News Record, Miami, Oklahoma
TAEN = The Ada Evening News, Ada, Oklahoma
TDA = *The Daily Ardmoreite*, Ardmore, Oklahoma
TT = *Tulsa Tribune*, Afternoon Newspaper, Tulsa, Oklahoma
TDW = *Tulsa Daily World*, Morning Newspaper, Tulsa, Oklahoma

Part One

CHAPTERS 1-5

"Mystery Slaying Hinted in Death of John Gorrell," *TDW*, November 30, 1934, page 1.

"Murder Seen by Police in Death of Dental Student," *TT*, November 30, 1934, pages 1 and 16.

"Startling Mystery Unfolds in Inquiry of Gorrell Murder," *TDW*, December 1, 1934, pages 1 and 4.

"Phil Kennamer, Son of US Judge, Surrenders, Admits Shooting of Young Gorrell," *TT*, December 1, 1934, pages 1 and 4.

"Phillip Kennamer, 19, Son of Judge Kennamer, Confesses Slaying of John Gorrell Jr., Café Owner Held as Police Delve into Extortion Note," *TDW*, December 2, 1934, pages 1, 12, and 13.

"Kennamer, 'Crazy with Worry,' Delayed Making a Confession," *TDW*, December 2, 1934, pages 1 and 12.

"Funeral for Murder Victim Conducted from Tulsa Church," *TDW*, December 2, 1934, page 13.

"Youth's Confession That He Shot Student Starts Quiz into Wide Extortion Plot," *TT*, December 2, 1934, pages 1, 4, and 5.

"Youth Denies Any Accomplices in Gorrell Killing, *TT*, December 2, 1934, page 5.

"Faced by Gorrell Fiancée, Kennamer Maintains Poise, Self-Defense Claim Belied," *TDW*, December 3, 1934, pages 1 and 3.

"What Price Civilization?," Editorial, *TDW*, December 3, 1934.

"US into Probe as Kennamer is Arraigned and Returned to Jail," *TT*, December 3, 1934, pages 1 and 4.

"Kennamer Tells Friend of Slaying: Federal Jurist's Son Offered to Show Gorrell's Body to Substantiate Story," *TDW*, December 4, 1934, pages 1 and 8.

"U.S. into Probe as Kennamer is Arraigned and Returned to Jail," *TT*, December 4, 1934, pages 1 and 4.

"Boy Confident as He Waits in Jail," *TT*, December 4, 1934, page 4.

"Gorrell Shot by Surprise Officers Say after Study of Photograph," *TT*, December 4, 1934, page 4.

"Doris Rogers' Mother Denies Daughter Knew about Slaying," *TDW*, December 4, 1934, page 8.

"The Truth About Tulsa's Kennamer-Gorrell Case," Part One, by Chief of Detectives Thomas J. Higgins as told to C.F. Waers," *The Master Detective*, June 1935.

"The Truth About Tulsa's Kennamer-Gorrell Case," Part Two, by Chief of Detectives Thomas J. Higgins as told to C.F. Waers," *The Master Detective*, July 1935.

CHAPTERS 6-8

"Coolidge and Daugherty Agree on Kennamer as U.S. Judge; Long Wrangle over G.O.P. Pie Put to End," Associated Press, *TDO*, January 25, 1924, page 1.

"Who is Frank Kennamer? His Wife Knows," *TDO*, January 26, 1924, page 5.

"State is Prepared to Try Kennamer, Anderson Claims," *TDW*, December 5, 1934, pages 1 and 2.

"Wilcox Hints 'Master Mind' Lured Youths," *TDW*, December 5, 1934, page 1.

"Sheriff's Office Personnel Ready," *TDW*, December 5, 1934, page 1.

"Chronology of Salient Events in Kennamer-Gorrell Case," *TDW*, December 5, 1934, page 2.

"An Engrossing Case," Editorial, *TDW*, December 5, 1934.

"Girl Companions Account for Wilcox Boy's Time," *TT*, December 5, 1934, pages 1 and 4.

"Third Man in Gorrell Case in Missouri Jail," *TT*, December 5, 1934, pages 1 and 4.

"Maddux Forecasts Another Arrest in Gorrell Killing; Attorney-General in Case," *TDW*, December 6, 1934, pages 1 and 7.

"Fantastic Story in Magazine Parallels Threat on Gorrell," *TDW*, December 6, 1934, page 7.

"Kennamer Named as Bandit by Wagoner County Couple," *TT*, December 6, 1934, pages 1 and 8.

"Wilcox Extortion Note Not Written by Phil Kennamer," *TDW*, December 7, 1934, pages 1 and 12.

"Anderson 'Thrown' Curve in Kennamer Phone Till," *TDW*, December 7, 1934, page 1.

"Anderson Ends Death Quiz with New Motive Discovery," *TT*, December 7, 1934, pages 1 and 10.

"No Development in Gorrell Death," *TDW*, December 8, 1934, pages 1and 14.

"Young Friend of Kennamer Took His Knife," *TT*, December 8, 1934, pages 1 and 12.

"New Death Quiz Conference as Police Raid Sunset Bar," *TT*, December 9, 1934, pages 1 and 8.

"Kennamer's IQ is 120 but His Success Rate is Low," *TT*, December 21, 1934, page 2.

"The Truth About Tulsa's Kennamer-Gorrell Case," Part Three, by Chief of Detectives Thomas J. Higgins as told to C.F. Waers," *The Master Detective*, August 1935.

Part Two

CHAPTER 9

"Suicide Stills Murder Witness: Death of Sidney Born Jr. Brings Sharp Criticism of Officials in Charge of Kennamer's Custody," *TDW*, December 10, 1934, pages 1 and 2.

"Death of Born Brings Newshawks Back on Job," *TDW*, December 11, 1934, page 2.

"Figures in Kennamer Case take Steps for Own Safety," *TT*, December 12, 1934, pages 1 and 8.

"Reign of Terror in Slaying Wake," *TDW*, December 12, 1934, pages 1 and 8.

"Youth's Suicide Brings Series of Wild and Unfounded Rumors," *TDW*, December 10, 1934, page 2.

"Death of Thomas Only a Rumor," *TDW*, December 10, 1934, page 1.

"Pranksters Active," *TDW*, December 14, 1934, page 1.

"The Truth About Tulsa's Kennamer-Gorrell Case," Part Three, by Chief of Detectives Thomas J. Higgins as told to C.F. Waers," *The Master Detective*, August 1935.

"Police Call Born Death Suicide, File Charge for Wilcox Jr.," *TT*, December 11, 1934, pages 1 and 4.

"Inquiry into Death of Born May Take a 'Surprise Turn' Today, Authorities Indicate," *TDW*, December 11, 1934, pages 1 and 7.

"Scenes Connected with Tragic Death of Sidney Born in Travis Park," *TDW*, December 12, 1934, page 3.

"Small Area Covers Points in Tragic Deaths," *TDW*, December 12, 1934, pages 1.

"Kennamer's Attorney Names Author of Extortion Plot, John Gorrell Jr., Hatched Scheme," *TDW*, December 12, 1934, page 8.

"Quiet Prevails on Crime Front," *TDW*, December 13, 1934, page 1 and 3.

"Thomas Freed of Liquor Charge in Kennamer's Court Last March," *TDW*, December 13, 1934, page 10.

"Price Advances New Murder Theory that Moss Explodes," *TT*, December 13, 1934, pages 1 and 10.

"New Murder Charges May Be Filed in Gorrell Slaying; Sheriff Seeks New Witness," *TDW*, December 14, 1934, pages 1 and 11.

"Kennamer Names Others as Gorrell Plot Witnesses," *TT*, December 14, 1934, pages 1 and 12.

"Witness Found in Born Case; Sweeney Will Ask Grand Jury to Delve into Gorrell Killing," *TDW*, December 15, 1934, pages 1 and 9.

"Sheriff Sounds Plea for Facts in Slaying Quiz," *TDW*, December 16, page 1.

"Worry Over Escapades with Phil Kennamer Led Born to Kill Himself, Police Say; Auto Wreck and Drinking Party Revealed, *TDW*, December 12, 1934, pages 1 and 8.

"Theory in Born Case Exploded," *TDW*, December 25, 1934, page 1.

"Wilcox Boy Fined $75 and Second Youth is Arrested: Judge Lectures Young Man for Shooting Out Lights at Scene of Gorrell Slaying but Two Hours Earlier," *TT*, December 12, 1934, pages 1 and 8.

"Shooting Out Lights," Editorial, *TDW*, December 14, 1934.

"Marble Machines are Object of New Move by Authorities," *TDW*, December 11, 1934, page 2.

"PTA Council Asks for Drastic Action," *TT*, December 12, 1934, pages 1 and 8.

"Pastors Open Campaign to Build Civic Righteousness," *TT*, December 13, 1934, pages 1 and 14.

"Improved Social, Recreational Opportunity for Tulsa Youth, High School P.T.A. Plan," *TT*, December 14, 1934, page 14.

"Midnight Parties," Editorial, *TDW*, December 19, 1934.

"A Season of Trouble," Editorial, *TDW*, December 21, 1934.

CHAPTER 10

"Kennamer Explains His Role in Plot Leading to Killing of Gorrell," *TDW*, December 13, 1934, pages 1 and 10.

"The Truth About Tulsa's Kennamer-Gorrell Case," Part Three, by Chief of Detectives Thomas J. Higgins as told to C.F. Waers," *The Master Detective*, August 1935.

CHAPTER 11

"Kennamer Denied Visitors at Request of His Father," *TT*, December 14, 1934, page 1.

"King Here Monday to Take Part in Kennamer Hearing," *TT*, December 15, 1934, pages 1 and 8.

"King Will Stay in Kennamer Case as Special Prosecutor; Admits Hearing Bribe Effort," *TDW*, December 16, 1934, pages 1 and 21.

"Public Duty Stressed by Attorney-General," *TDW*, December 16, 1934, page 1.

"Kennamer to Court Monday, Grand Jury Probably Later," by Harmon Phillips, *TT*, December 16, 1934, pages 1 and 16.

"Officials, Investigators, Reporters Disagree on What May Develop," *TT*, by Ruth Sheldon, December 16, 1934, pages 1 and 4.

"Phil Kennamer Preliminary Opens Today; Death of Born is Handicap to Prosecution," *TDW*, December 17, pages 1 and 3.

"Throngs to Hear Kennamer Case," *TDW*, December 17, 1934, page 1.

"48 Names on 'Who's Who' List in Kennamer-Gorrell Slaying," *TDW*, December 17, 1934, page 3.

"Kennamer into Court Today to Answer Murder Charge," *TT*, December 17, 1934, page 1.

"Kennamer Held on First Degree Murder Charge; Floyd Huff, Flier, Tells Sensational Story for State," Associated Press, *TDA*, December 17, 1935, pages 1 and 8.

"King Promises Investigation of Entire Gorrell Case as Kennamer is Held for Trial," *TDW*, December 18, 1934, pages 1, 9, and 10.

"Hundreds Turned Away from Kennamer Hearing," Photo Headline, *TDW*, December 18, 1934, page 2.

"Kennamer Back to Jail after Short, Sharp Hearing," *TT*, December 18, 1934, pages 1, 4, and 8.

"Gorrell Says He is Pleased," *TT*, December 18, 1934, page 8.

"Ready for Trial, Says Flint Moss," *TDW*, December 19, 1934, page 1.

CHAPTER 12

"Tulsa," by Carl E. Gregory, *Encyclopedia of Oklahoma History and Culture*, Oklahoma Historical Society website URL: http://www.okhistory.org/publications/enc/entry.php?entry=TU003

"Tulsa County," by Larry O'Dell, *Encyclopedia of Oklahoma History and Culture*, Oklahoma Historical Society website URL: http://www.okhistory.org/publications/enc/entry.php?entry=TU008

"Tulsa: From Creek Town to Oil Capital," by Angie Debo, University of Oklahoma Press, 1943.

"Tulsa History 1880 – 1941," *Tulsa Preservation Commission,* (Website), URL: http://www.tulsapreservationcommission.org/history/education/

"Louisiana Territory," by S. Charles Bolton, *Encyclopedia of Oklahoma History and Culture*, Oklahoma Historical Society website URL: http://www.okhistory.org/publications/enc/entry.php?entry=LO019

"Oklahoma: The Land and Its People," by Kenny Franks, University of Oklahoma Press, 1997.

"The Glenn Pool Oil Field, The discovery that made Oklahoma," by Norman Hyne, *Shale Shaker, The Journal of the Oklahoma City Geological Society*, November/December 2008, pages 93-97.

"The Burning: Massacre, Destruction, and the Tulsa Race Riot of 1921," by Tim Madigan, St. Martin's Griffin, 2003.

"Death in a Promised Land: The Tulsa Race Riot of 1921,"by Scott Ellsworth, Louisiana State University Press, 1992.

"Tulsa Race Riot," by Scott Ellsworth, *Encyclopedia of Oklahoma History and Culture*, Oklahoma Historical Society website URL: http://www.okhistory.org/publications/enc/entry.php?entry=TU013

"County Attorney Charges Sheriff with Dereliction of Duty at Tulsa," *TDA*, August 30, 1920, pages 1 and 2.

Biscup, Walter. Interview by Dana Sue Walker, November 12, 1979, Junior League of Tulsa Oral History Project, Tulsa Public Library Website, URL: http://cdm15020.contentdm.oclc.org/cdm/ref/collection/p15020coll10/id/87

Foreman, Bob. Interview by Dana Sue Walker, November 7, 1979, Junior League of Tulsa Oral History Project, Tulsa Public Library Website, URL: http://cdm15020.contentdm.oclc.org/cdm/ref/collection/p15020coll10/id/170

"1935's Call to Arms," Editorial, *TT*, January 1, 1935.

"Thrill-Seeking Tulsa Youth Blamed for Marijuana Evils," *TDW*, December 14, 1934, pages 1, 10, and 11.

"Christian Endeavor Covenant Aimed at Tulsa's Lax Morals," *TDW*, December 15, 1934, page 9.

"School Crusade Scheduled Here," *TDW*, December 16, 1934, pages 1 and 21.

"Toy Guns Blamed by National P.T.A," Associated Press, *TDW*, December 16, 1934, page 21.

"Sunset Café Beer License Delayed Another Day," *TT*, December 11, 1934, page 4.

"Bloody Swath Cut Here by 7 Violent Deaths in 3 Weeks," *TDW*, December 20, 1934, page 1.

"Tulsa Youth Fatally Shot in Juvenile Gun Play; His Four Companions Held," *TT*, December 20, 1934, page 1.

"Boy, 17, Kills Companion, 16, at Play," *TDW*, December 20, 1934, pages 1 and 10.

"Ex-Convict Confesses Beating Rich Rancher to Death Following Robbery," *TDW*, December 20, 1934, pages 1 and 10.

"A Season of Trouble," Editorial, *TDW*, December 21, 1934.

"Mysterious Death of Tulsan Brings Official Inquiry," *TDW*, December 18, 1934, page 1.

"Mystery Marks Tulsan's Death," *TT*, December 19, 1934, page 3.

"Auto Reported near Death Pit," *TT*, December 21, 1934, page 2.

"New Death Quiz Conference as Police Raid Sunset Bar," *TT*, December 9, 1934, pages 1 and 8.

"Hoop Increases Detective Force," *TDW*, December 21, 1934, page 7.

"Hoop Outlines Juvenile Crime Curb Measure," *TT*, December 21, 1934, page 1.

"Hoop Anticrime Move Hits Snag," *TDW*, January 12, 1935, page 9.

"Students Dance at Central High School after 14 Years," *TT*, December 20, 1934, page 6.

"The Rambler," Column, *TT*, December 21, 1934.

"Tulsa Church Widens Scope of Entertainment for Its Youth," *TT*, February 1, 1935, page 16.

"Denouncing Tulsa," Editorial, *TDW*, December 17, 1934.

"Tulsa Youth," Editorial, *TDW*, December 28, 1934.

"Rumors," Editorial, *TDW*, December 28, 1934.

"The Rambler," Column, *TT*, January 1, 1935.

"The Rambler," Column, *TT*, January 25, 1935.

1935

CHAPTER 13

"Kennamer Penned Notes in Secret Codes to Friend," *TDW*, January 3, 1935, pages 1 and 2.

"Kennamer Code Notes 'Innocuous,'" Associated Press, *MDNR*, January 3, 1935, page 1.

"Intrigue Between Kennamer, Friend Bared by Code Notes," *TDW*, February 10, 1935, page 1 and 12.

"The Truth About Tulsa's Kennamer-Gorrell Case," Part Three, by Chief of Detectives Thomas J. Higgins as told to C.F. Waers," *The Master Detective*, August 1935.

"Phil Kennamer in Court Today," *TDW*, January 4, 1935, page 1.

"Kennamer Goes to Court Again to Enter Plea," *TT*, January 4, 1935, page 1 and 10.

"Phil Kennamer Denies Charge," *TDW*, January 5, 1935, pages 1 and 4.

"Kennamer Now Set for Trial," *TT*, January 5, 1935, page 8.

"The Rambler," Column, *TT*, January 5, 1935.

"Kennamer's Trial Set for Jan. 28," *TDW*, January 6, 1935, page 6.

"Five Homicide Trials are Set," *TT*, January 9, 1935, page 9.

"Kennamer Flu Victim," *TT*, January 11, 1935, page 1.

"Mrs. Clara Maddux Kills Woman Friend of Husband's in Front of Nave Hotel in Childress Sunday," *Wichita Daily Times*, Wichita Falls, Texas, September 8, 1924, page 1.

"Woman Freed of Killing Another," *The Mexia Daily News*, Mexia, Texas, January 23, 1925, page 7.

"Kennamer Trial Not First of Knotty Cases for Judge Hurst," by William P. Steven, *TT*, January 15, 1935, page 4.

CHAPTER 14

"When Flaming Youth in an Oil Town Brought in a Gusher of Crime," King Features Syndicate, April 7, 1935.

"Kennamer Case Splits Tulsa," by William Voigt, Associated Press, *TDA*, January 12, 1935, pages 1 and 5.

"Kennamer Case is Given Study," by William Voigt, Associated Press, *MDNR*, January 16, 1935, page 3.

"Roadhouse Row is Closed as Deputies Deliver Warnings," by Harmon Phillips, *TT*, January 8, 1935, page 3.

"Police Nab 30 in Gambling Raids," *TDW*, January 18, 1935, page 20.

"Kennamer Defense Finds Young Set Wary of Testifying," Associated Press, *MDNR*, January 17, 1935, page 1.

"Alienists See Kennamer at County Jail," *TT*, January 14, 1935, page 1 and 10.

"Alienists, Delay, Twin Hopes for Phil Kennamer," by Harmon Phillips, *TT*, January 15, 1935, pages 1 and 10.

"Kennamer Insane, Alienists Claim," Associated Press, *TAEN*, January 15, 1935, page 1.

"Murray Grants 13 Clemencies," *TDW*, December 15, 1934, page 13.

"Murray Grants 12 Clemencies," *TDW*, December 18, 1934, page 4.

"Governor Turns Six More Loose," *TDW*, December 28, 1934, page 1.

"Witness 'Tampering' Assailed by State as Defense Claims Phil Kennamer Mentally Ill," *TDW*, January 16, 1935, pages 1 and 7.

"Experts," Editorial, *TDW*, January 16, 1935.

"Names Given in Kennamer Case Tamper Case," *TT*, January 16, 1935, page 7.

"Holly Anderson Replies to Moss," *TDW*, January 17, 1935, page 18.

"More Subpoenas in Kennamer Case, *TDW*, January 18, 1935, page 5.

"150 Called for Kennamer Jury," *TT*, January 18, 1935, page 4.

"State Ready in Kennamer Case," Associated Press, *MDNR*, January 18, 1935, page 4.

"Anderson Says Young Morton Took the Knife," *TT*, January 20, 1935, page 6B.

"Kennamer Defense to Seek Change of Venue; Letter New Case Sensation," by Harmon Phillips, *TT*, January 21, 1935, pages 1 and 7.

"Defense Prepares to Ask for Change of Venue in Kennamer Murder Case; Publicity Cited in Motion to be Made to Court," Associated Press, *MDNR*, January 21, 1935, page 6.

"Phil Kennamer's Lawyer Will Ask Change of Venue," *TDW*, January 22, 1935, pages 1 and 8.

"State in a Spirited Attack on Kennamer's Delay Move," *TT*, January 22, 1935, pages 1 and 12.

"Newspapers and Investigators Attacked in Kennamer Petition," *TT*, January 22, 1935, page 12.

"Judge Kennamer Will Aid His Son," *TDW*, January 23, 1935, pages 1 and 12.

"Kennamer Will Demand Airing of Bribe Offer," *TT*, January 23, 1935, pages 1 and 14.

"Opposing Kennamer Case Legal Batteries Promise Fiery Clash of Courtroom Tactics," by Harmon Phillips, *TT*, January 23, 1935, page 3.

"Bribe Evidence in Tulsa Case?," Associated Press, *MDNR*, January 23, 1935, pages 1 and 3.

"County Opposes Kennamer Move," *TDW*, January 24, 1935, pages 1 and 8.

"Kennamer Attorneys Fling 'Unfair' into Court," *TT*, January 24, 1935, pages 1 and 10.

"Several Witnesses Assert Belief Young Kennamer Can't Get Fair Trial in Tulsa; Defense to Quiz Tulsa Officials as to Bribe Hint," Associated Press, *MDNR*, January 24, 1935, pages 2 and 3.

"Kennamer's Attorneys Win Fight to Transfer Murder Hearing to Pawnee," *TDW*, January 25, 1935, pages 1 and 8.

"Kennamer Trial on February 11, Hurst's Decree," *TT*, January 25, 1935, pages 1 and 2.

"Kennamer Trial Set for Feb. 11," *TDW*, January 26, 1935, pages 1 and 12.

CHAPTER 15

"Pawnee Abuzz with Kennamer Trial Promising a Sensation," by William P. Steven, *TT*, January 25, 1935, pages 1 and 2.

"Kennamer Defense Bares Wilcox Extortion Note," by Harmon Phillips, *TT*, January 26, 1935, page 1.

"Text of Kennamer Case Extortion Note," *TT*, January 26, 1935, page 1.

"Kennamer Author of Kidnap 'Note' Attorney Charges," *TDW*, January 27, 1935, pages 1 and 9.

"Kennamer Tells His First Connected Version of Plot and Killing of John Gorrell," by Harmon Phillips, *TT*, January 27, 1935, pages 1 and 4.

"Note Made Public in Kennamer Case," Associated Press, *TAEN*, January 27, 1935, page 2.

"State Hoots at Extortion Note," *TT*, January 28, 1935, page 1.

"Kennamer to Get No Special Treatment in Jail at Pawnee," by William P. Steven, *TT*, January 27, 1935, page 1.

"Ordinary Cell in Model 1889 Jail Will Be Occupied by Defendant," *TDW*, January 27, 1935, page 9.

"Pawnee Citizens Resent Jibes But Prepare for Murder Trial," *TDW*, January 29, 1935, Page 8.

"Corner Stone of New Court House Laid in Due Form with Impressive Ceremonies," *The Pawnee Courier-Dispatch*, Pawnee, Oklahoma, April 28, 1932, page 1.

"Pawnee County Courthouse Construction Began in 1932," by William Howell, *The Pawnee Chief*, March 5, 1987, page 15.

"Kennamer Panel Will Be Selected," *TDW*, January 30, 1935, pages 1 and 3.

"New Kennamer Angle Sifted," Associated Press, *MDNR*, January 30, 1935, page 6.

"Witnesses, Jurors Are Called for Kennamer Trial," *TDW*, January 31, 1935, pages 1 and 6.

"100 Will Testify in Kennamer Case," *TDW*, February 1, 1935, page 1.

"No Pictures in Kennamer Case," *TT*, February 1, 1935, page 4.

"Kennamer Trial Plans Discussed," *TDW*, February 2, 1935, page 1.

"Wilcox Family May Appear in Kennamer Case," *TT*, February 3, 1935, page 1.

"Kennamer Placed Kidnap Note with Catholic Priest," *TDW*, February 6, 1935, page 1.

"State Summons Young Wilcox and His Sister," *TT*, February 6, 1935, pages 1 and 6.

"Special Rules are Drawn up Kennamer Witnesses, Spectators," *TDW*, February 7, 1935, page 9.

"State Statutes Cover 'Insanity,'" *TDW*, February 7, 1935, page 9.

"Another Name Enters Quiz in Kennamer Case," *TT*, February 8, 1935, pages 1 and 18.

"Subpoenas to 107 in Kennamer Case," *TDW*, February 9, 1935, pages 1 and 15.

"53 Persons Parade Across Kennamer Trial Stage, Gorrell Slaying Case is Reviewed," *TDW*, February 9, 1935, pages 14 and 15.

"Judge Hurst to be in Home Town During Kennamer Trial," *TDW*, February 9, 1935, page 14.

"State to Ask Death Penalty for Kennamer," *TT*, February 9, 1935, pages 1 and 20.

"State Will Ask Death Penalty," *TDW*, February 10, 1935, pages 1 and 2.

"Phil Kennamer Transferred to Pawnee Today with Trial for Gorrell Killing Monday," by Harmon Phillips, *TT*, February 10, 1935, pages 1 and 10.

"Jury Selection to be Drawn out Affair," *TT*, February 10, 1935, page 1.

"Hy-Hat Members Subpoenaed in Case," *TT*, February 10, 1935, page 1.

"Brief View of Kennamer Case," *TT*, February 10, 1935, page 10.

"Kennamer Case Routine to Few," *TT*, February 10, 1935, page 10.

"The Kennamer Case Up to Date," *TT*, February 10, 1935, page 11.

"Kennamer Trial Opens in Pawnee Today with Prosecution Expecting to Obtain Jury in Two Days, Youth Visits Mother," *TDW*, February 11, 1935, pages 1 and 7.

"Phil Kennamer Unleashes Verbal Barrage at Tulsa Photographer," *TDW*, February 11, 1935, page 1.

"Pawnee Personalities," *TDW*, February 11, 1935.

"Kennamer Likes Jail and Prisoners like Their New Associate," *TDW*, February 12, 1935, page 2.

"Krupnick Barred for Photographs," *TDW*, February 12, 1935, page 3.

Part Three

CHAPTER 16

"Young Slayer Sleeps Well in New Cell," by Ruth Sheldon, *TT*, February 12, 1935, page 1.

"'You Are Guilty' Sign Ordered Removed from Store at Pawnee,'" Baron Creager, *TDW*, February 12, 1935, pages 1 and 2.

"11 Jurors Tentatively Seated as Clash between Prosecution and Defense Marks Tedious Routine," by Walter Biscup, *TDW*, February 12, 1935, pages 1 and 2.

"Jury Striking Begins at Pawnee, Court Qualifies Box and State Uses First Challenge for Change," by Harmon Phillips, *TT*, February 12, 1935, pages 1, 8, and 10.

"Just Before Trial Began for Kennamer," *TT*, February 12, 1935, page 9.

"Pawnee Personalities," *TDW*, February 12, 1935.

"The Jury," *TT*, February 13, 1935, page 1.

"Kennamer Trial Begins Today with First Witnessed Called," by Walter Biscup, *TDW*, February 13, 1935, pages 1 and 9.

"Tulsa World Map Helps Kennamer Prosecutor," *TDW*, February 13, 1935, page 8.

"Kennamer Remains Calm during Statement to Jury," *TDW*, February 13, 1935, pages 1 and 8.

"Pawnee Personalities," *TDW*, February 13, 1935.

"Kennamer Plotter State Charges, Planned Wilcox Threat as Well as Murder," by Harmon Phillips, *TT*, February 13, 1935, pages 1 and 8.

"Kennamer and Anderson Split on New Story," *TT*, February 12, 1935, page 10.

"The Rambler," Column, *TT*, February 13, 1935.

"Kansas City Man Gives Evidence," *TDW*, February 14, 1935, pages 8 and 9.

CHAPTER 17

"Kennamer Case Witness Held for Contempt; Deny Mistrial," by Walter Biscup, *TDW*, February 14, 1935, pages 1, 7, and 10.

"Snedden Tells of Kennamer's Threats While Drunk, Phil Taken Home to End His Life," *TDW*, February 15, 1935, pages 10, 11,

"Jack Snedden on Witness Stand! Kennamer Case on Again After Near Mistrial," by Harmon Phillips, *TT*, February 14, 1935, pages 1, 2, and 6.

"Mad Love for Wilcox Girl Told to Jury," by Harmon Phillips, *TT*, February 14, 1935, pages 1 and 6.

"Kennamer Loses Temper, Calls Snedden Liar," *TDW*, February 14, 1935, page 1.

"Pawnee Personalities," *TDW*, February 14, 1935.

"Kennamer Defense Alienists Specialist in Queer People," *TT*, February 14, 1935, page 5.

CHAPTERS 18-19

"Kennamer is Described as 'Incorrigible' as Defense Opens Fight to Save Him," by Walter Biscup, *TDW*, February 15, 1935, pages 1 and 12.

"Attorney Describes Wild Career of Phil Kennamer," *TDW*, February 15, 1935, pages 1 and 12.

"Girl Who Covered Flemington Trial Likes Pawnee Comforts," *TDW*, February 15, 1935, page 11.

"Pawnee Personalities," *TDW*, February 15, 1935.

"Virginia Wilcox Will Take Stand to Clear Tragedy," *TDW*, February 15, 1935, page 1.

"Kennamer's Fate on Insanity Plea, Moss Calls Him Almost Genius," by Harmon Phillips, *TT*, February 15, 1935, pages 1, and 10.

"Wilcox Threat Note Exhibited as Slain Boy's," by Harmon Phillips, *TT*, February 15, 1935, pages 1, 7, and 9.

"Noted at the Pawnee Trial," by Ruth Sheldon, *TT*, February 15, 1935, page 9.

"Kennamer's Letter for Mrs. Wilcox," *TT*, February 15, 1935, page 9.

"The Rambler," Column, *TT*, February 15, 1935.

CHAPTER 20

"Love for Virginia Wilcox Led Kennamer to Slay Gorrell, Defense Contends, Unbalanced by Fear for Her," Associated Press, *MDNR*, February 15, 1935, page 2.

"Judge Kennamer Weeps as He Describes Phil's Abnormalities," by Walter Biscup, *TDW*, February 16, 1935, pages 1 and 12.

"Gorrell Wrote Note, Admitted," *TDW*, February 16, 1935, pages 12, 13, 14, and 15.

"Pawnee Personalities," *TDW*, February 16, 1935.

"Virginia Wilcox and Brother on Witness Stand," by Harmon Phillips, *TT*, February 16, 1935, pages 1 and 8.

"Phil Gets a Shave, Leers at His Pals," Copeland Burg, International News Service, *TT*, February 16, 1935, page 1.

"Judge Kennamer Weeps on Stand, Tells Story of Boy's Life to Crowded Room," by Harmon Phillips, *TT*, February 16, 1935, pages 1 and 20.

"The Rambler," Column, *TT*, February 16, 1935.

"Kennamer Witness Drawn into Damaging Admission under Cross Examination," by Walter Biscup, *TDW*, February 17, 1935, pages 1, 6 and 7.

"Kennamer Goes on Stand Monday to Tell Own Story of Love for Miss Wilcox," by Harmon Phillips, *TT*, February 17, 1935, pages 1 and 7.

"Many Salient Facts Already Presented in Kennamer Trial," *TT*, February 17, 1935, page 1.

CHAPTERS 21

"Two Alienists Will Testify for Kennamer," by Walter Biscup, *TDW*, February 18, 1935, pages 1 and 2.

"Moss, Gilmer Forays Witty," *TT*, February 18, 1935, page 1.

"Hysterical Mob Rushes Pawnee Courthouse to Hear Kennamer," *TDW*, February 19, 1935, page 9.

"Kansas Psychiatrist Claims Phil Kennamer Insane, Egotism Blamed for Rash Action," *TDW*, February 19, 1935, page 9, 10, and 11.

"Kennamer Was Crazy When He Killed, Is Now, Says Doctor, Adding He Should Be Confined," by Harmon Phillips, *TT*, February 19, 1935, pages 1 and 7.

"Phil Kennamer Testifies He Entered into Plot with Gorrell to Thwart It; Killing Was in Self-Defense, Witness Says," Associated Press, *MDNR*, February 18, 1935, page 6.

"Young Kennamer Repudiates Insanity Plea as He Calmly Details Version of Slaying," by Walter Biscup," *TDW*, February 19, 1935, pages 1, 12, and 13.

"Kennamer Winds up His Defense, Sticks to Story of Self-Defense, Names Others in Note Plot," by Harmon Phillips, *TT*, February 19, 1935, pages 1, 6, and 12.

"Pawnee Personalities," *TDW*, February 19, 1935.

"Doctors Testify about Defendant," *TDW*, February 20, 1935, pages 8 and 9.

"Pawnee Personalities," *TDW*, February 20, 1935.

CHAPTER 22

"Hursts Instructs Kennamer Jurors; Arguments Today," by Walter Biscup, *TDW*, February 20, 1935, pages 1, 9, and 10.

"Judge Hurst Instructs Jurors as State, Defense Rests Case," *TDW*, February 20, 1935, page 9.

"Judge Instructs Kennamer Jury, State Makes Three Thrusts," by Harmon Phillips, *TT*, February 20, 1935, pages 1, 3 and 7.

"The Rambler," Column, *TT*, February 20, 1935.

"Quirk of Law May Free Phil of Detention," by Ruth Sheldon, *TT*, February 20, 1935, page 7.

"Phil Kennamer Branded 'Reckless Killer;' Extolled as Girl's Defender; Stress Put on Life Sentence by Prosecutor," Associated Press, *MDNR*, February 20, pages 1 and 6.

"Wallace Asks Murder Vote During Plea," *TT*, February 21, 1935, page 12.

"Moss Chiefly Urges Vote of Self-Defense," *TT*, February 21, 1935, page 12.

"King Asks Jury to Forget Plea for Death Chair," *TT*, February 21, 1935, pages 1 and 13.

"Jury to Get Kennamer Case after Anderson, Stuart End Arguments at Pawnee Today," by Walter Biscup, *TDW*, February 21, 1935, pages 1, 8, 9, and 10.

"Kennamer Case to Jury Thursday, Two Arguments Left after Day of Bitter Pleas," by Harmon Phillips, *TT*, February 21, 1935, pages 1 and 8.

"Young Lawyer Last Kennamer Guilty Pleader," *TT*, February 22, 1935, page 6.

"Stuart in Last Demand to Jury for Kennamer," *TT*, February 22, 1935, page 7.

"Pawnee Personalities," *TDW*, February 21, 1935.

"Few Signs from Jurors to Indicate Their Views While These Lawyers Ask for Boy's Life," by Ruth Sheldon, *TT*, February 21, 1935, page 12.

"Phil Kennamer Murder Case Goes to Jury," Associated Press, *MDNR*, February 21, 1935, pages 1 and 3.

"Gorrells, Worn by Trial, are Seeking Quiet," *TDW*, February 22, 1935, pages 1 and 11.

"Two Grilled in Born Mystery," *TT*, February 21, 1935, page 13.

"The Rambler," Column, *TT*, February 21, 1935.

"Highly Organized Staff Brought Kennamer Case to World Readers," *TDW*, February 22, 1935, page 10.

"Kennamer Jury, Out Since Noon, Gives No Sign of Early Verdict," by Harmon Phillips, *TT*, February 22, 1935, pages 1

"The Rambler," *TT*, February 22, 1935.

"Kennamer Awaits Hour of Sentence with Usual Calm," *TDW*, February 23, 1935, pages 1 and 5.

"Kennamer Guilty of Manslaughter, Verdict of Jury Leaves Punishment of Gorrell's Slayer to Judge Hurst," by Walter Biscup, *TDW*, February 22, 1935, pages 1, 10, and 11.

"Kennamer Manslaughter Verdict on Twelfth Vote After 9 to 3 First Ballot," by Harmon Phillips, *TT*, February 23, 1935, pages 1 and 4.

"Phil Kennamer, Found Guilty of Manslaughter, Will be Sentenced Saturday," Associated Press, *MDNR*, February 22, 1935, pages 1 and 4.

"Two Guns Used in Slaying of John Gorrell," *TT*, February 23, 1935, page 1.

"The Rambler," Column, *TT*, February 23, 1935.

CHAPTER 23

"Judge Hurst Sentences Phil Kennamer to 25 years in M'Alester State Prison; His Appeal Bond is Fixed at $25,000," by Walter Biscup, *TDW*, February 24, 1935, pages 1 and 10.

"Hurst Holds to Theory that All Should Have Equal Rights," *TDW*, February 24, 1935, pages 1 and 10.

"Phil Kennamer Back to Jail with 25 Years in Prison as Penalty for Gorrell Killing," by Harmon Phillips, *TT*, February 24, 1935, pages 1 and 4.

"Gentlemen for the State No Gentlemen," *TT*, February 24, 1935, page 1.

"Phil Kennamer Gets 25 Years in Prison; Youth Unmoved as He Received Penalty," Associated Press, *MDNR*, February 24, 1935, pages 1 and 2.

"Illness Delays Kennamer Bond," *TDW*, February 25, 1935, page 1.

"Vaudeville and Justice," Editorial, *TDW*, February 25, 1935.

"Phil Kennamer Looses Bitter Flood of Words," *TT*, February 25, 1935, page 1.

"Route to Liberty Leads Through Pen," *TDW*, February 26, 1935, page 1.

"A Verdict of Justice," Editorial, *TDW*, February 26, 1935.

"Kennamer Jury May Join in a Parole Appeal," by Harmon Phillips, *TT*, February 26, 1935, page 1.

"The Rambler," Column, *TT*, February 26, 1935.

"Kennamer Appeal Filed at Pawnee," *TDW*, February 27, 1935, page 1 and 10.

"Moss Will Join in Prosecution of Mrs. Harman," *TT*, February 27, 1935, pages 1 and 12.

"Phil Kennamer Ready to Start Term in Prison," *TT*, February 27, 1935, page 12.

"US Judge Bids Good-Bye to Son," *TDW*, February 28, 1935, page 1.

"Gorrell's Bloody Coat Removed as Slayer Prepares for Prison," *TDW*, March 1, 1935, page 1.

"Leniency Denied; Phil Kennamer to Serve Long Term," Walter Biscup, *TDW*, March 3, 1935, pages 1 and 13.

"Phil Now 31-420 at State Prison," *TDW*, March 5, 1935, page 1 and 8.

"A Lawyer's Bad Break," Editorial, *TDW*, March 5, 1935.

"Prison's Doors Closed behind Phil Kennamer," by Harmon Phillips, *TT*, March 5, 1935, pages 1 and 5.

"Kennamer Working in Prison Factory," *TDW*, March 6, 1935, page 1.

Part Four

CHAPTER 24

"Mrs. Harman Trial Set for Tomorrow," *TDW*, March 10, 1935, page 1.

"Contempt Case Moves to Court," Associated Press, *MDNR*, March 11, 1935, page 6.

"Threats Figure in Harman Case," *TDW*, March 12, 1935, pages 1 and 12.

"Letter Sent by Mrs. Harman, Says Witness," *TT*, March 12, 1935, pages 1 and 8.

"'Help' Letter in Kennamer Case is Aired," *TDO*, March 12, 1935, page 10.

"Term in Jail, Fine for Mrs. Harman," *TDW*, March 13, 1935, page 1.

"Mrs. Harman to Jail in Court Contempt Case," *TT*, March 13, 1935, pages 1 and 12.

"Woman's Screams in Court Room Bring Fine, Jail Term," *TDO*, March 13, 1935, page 12.

"Mrs. Harman Plans Appeal of Sentence," *TT*, March 14, 1935, page 1.

"Mrs. Harman Makes Bond, Takes Appeal," *TDO*, March 15, 1935, page 1.

"Conviction of Woman Upheld," Associated Press, *TDA*, March 20, 1936, page 1.

"Mrs. Harman Convicted of Contempt, Loses in Higher Court," Associated Press, *TT*, March 21, 1936, page 1.

"Mrs. Harman Must Serve Jail Term," Associated Press, *MDNR*, September 18, 1936, page 6.

"Kennamer Witness to Jail Monday," *TT*, September 19, 1936, page 7.

"To Jail," *TDO*, September 19, 1936, page 5.

"Mrs. Harman Seeks Bail," Associated Press, *MDNR*, November 6, 1936, page 5.

"Stay Bond Denied Kennamer Witness," *TDO*, November 8, 1936, page 34.

"Kennamer Contempt Case in Spotlight," *TDO*, January 21, 1937, page 10.

"Parole Advocated for Mrs. Harman," Associated Press, *MDNR*, January 21, 1937, page 1.

"Mrs. Harman Goes Free Under Parole," Associated Press, *MDNR*, January 22, 1937, page 1.

"US Help Asked in Gorrell Quiz," *TDW*, March 9, 1935, pages 1 and 9.

"Gorrell Killing Quiz Reopened in Gun Request," *TT*, March 9, 1935, pages 1 and 13.

"Phil Kennamer Learns Inmates Not So Honest," *TT*, March 9, 1935, page 1.

"Four Witnessed Gorrell Slaying Sweeney is Told," *TDW*, March 10, 1935, pages 1 and 11.

"Kennamer Case Chapter to be Closed Monday," *TT*, March 10, 1935, page 1.

"Gilmer Balked in Pistol Probe," *TDW*, March 11, 1935, page 1.

"Gilmer's Gun Test Delayed," *TT*, March 12, 1935, page 4.

"Trial Delaying Pistol Inquiry," *TT*, March 13, 1935, page 3.

"Renew Inquiry in Tulsa Murder," *The Circleville (Ohio) Record,* February 19, 1935, page 5.

"Sid Born Slain, an Arrest Near, Father Declares," Associated Press, *TT*, February 16, 1935, page 1.

"Dr. Born Positive Son Murdered," *TDW*, February 16, 1935, pages 1 and 15.

"Hurst Will Call Grand Jury Quiz," *TDW*, March 14, pages 1 and 7.

"Sweeny Files Jury Petition," *TT*, March 14, 1935, pages 1 and 3.

"Witnesses Being Called for Grand Jury Tuesday," *TT*, April 9, 1935, pages 1 and 7.

"County Grand Jury at Work Behind Closed Doors," *TT*, April 10, 1935, pages 1 and 3.

"Young Kennamer May Be Witness in Jury's Probe," *TDW*, April 12, 1935, page 1.

"Hoop, Maddux, Pastor, Before Grand Jurors," *TT*, April 12, 1935, page 1.

"Wilcox Before Grand Jury in Kennamer Quiz," *TT*, April 13, 1935, pages 1 and 16.

"Jury Quiz Shifts to Born Mystery," *TDW*, April 16, 1935, page 1.

"Born Quizzed by Jury Again," *TT*, April 16, 1935, page 1.

"Grand Jury at Work," Editorial, *TDW*, April 17, 1935.

"Chief Carr is Called by Jury," *TT*, April 18, 1935, page 9.

"Grand Jury to Quiz Sweeney," *TT*, April 19, 1935, page 3.

"Criminologist H.B. Maddux Told to Quit or Get 'Fired' in Session with Hoop, Carr," *TDW*, April 20, 1935, pages 1 and 12.

"Grand Jury Near End of Its Probe," *TDW*, April 20, 1935, page 1.

"City Police Officials Will Not Eliminate Criminologist Unit," *TDW*, April 20, 1935, page 12.

"Maddux Resigns; New Fight Looms Over Police Setup," *TT*, April 20, 1935, page 1.

"Slayer of Born is Known Here, Kennamer Avers," *TDW*, April 21, 1935, page 1.

"Jurors Prompted Action by Hoop," *TDW*, April 21, 1935, pages 1 and 12.

"Personal Issue, Munroe Says in Maddux Fight," *TT*, April 21, 1935, pages 1 and 5.

"Kennamer May Discuss Born," *TT*, April 21, 1935, page 3.

"Personal Issue, Munroe Says in Maddux Fight," *TT*, April 22, 1935, page 1.

"City Will Ignore Maddux Petition," *TDW*, April 23, 1935, page 1.

"Kennamer Story Limited in Value as Help to Probe," *TDW*, April 23, 1935, pages 1 and 5.

"Moore Mentioned for Maddux Post," *TDW*, April 23, 1935, page 5.

"Case of Maddux Shifts to Court," *TDW*, April 24, 1935, pages 1 and 4.

"Jurors May Take Extended Recess," *TDW*, April 24, 1935, page 1.

"Resignation of Maddux Taken; Munroe Absent," *TT*, April 24, 1935, page 1.

"Tulsa Grand Jury Scores Policeman," Associated Press, *San Antonio Express*, April 24, 1935, page 3.

"Grand Jury Fails in 12-Day Search for Bribery Facts," *TDW*, April 25, 1935, pages 1 and 4.

"Dr. Born Purposes to Prove Murder," *TDW*, April 25, 1935, page 1.

"Grand Jury Reports Without Indicting; Maddux Scored," *TT*, April 25, 1935, page 1.

"Father Expects to Show Young Born was Slain," Associated Press, *The Hutchinson News*, Hutchinson, Kansas, April 25, 1935, page 1.

"In Abatement of Rumor," Editorial, *TDW*, April 26, 1935.

"Grand Jury Digs into City Affairs," *TDW*, May 8, 1935, page 4.

CHAPTER 25

"Phil Kennamer Out on Bond of $25,000; Dines Late in Tulsa," *TDW*, May 22, 1935, pages 1 and 7.

"Bond Approved for Kennamer; Release is Near," *TT*, May 22, 1935, page 1.

"Kennamer out of State Cell," *TDO*, May 22, 1935, page 1.

"Mystery Shrouds Phil's Activities," *TDW*, May 23, 1935, page 1.

"Kennamer out of Prison, on Chelsea Farm," *TT*, May 23, 1935, page 1.

"Loopholes for All," Editorial, *TDO*, May 25, 1935.

"19 Alleged Errors Cited," *TDA*, June 16, 1935, page 1.

"State Appellate Judges to Study Kennamer Appeal," by Walter Biscup, *TDW*, October 2, 1936, pages 1 and 4.

"Reversal for Kennamer is Plea of Moss," *TT*, October 2, 1935, pages 1 and 3.

"State Demand for Kennamer Term is Made," *TDO*, October 2, 1935, page 1.

"Ruling is Due on Kennamer," *TDO*, March 13, 1936, page 2.

"Appeals Court Upholds Conviction of Kennamer in Slaying of Gorrell," Associated Press, *MDNR*, March 13, 1936, pages 1 and 2.

"Kennamer Verdict Upheld by Court, Clemency Blocked," *TDW*, March 14, 1936, pages 1 and 5.

"Kennamer Decision Rejected, High Families Involved Here," *TDW*, March 14, 1936, page 3.

"Principals Speak Views on Kennamer Decision," *TDW*, March 14, 1936, page 3.

"Phil Kennamer Loses Appeal, Faces Return to Prison in 15 days," *TT*, March 14, 1936, page 1.

"Marland Sets Clemency Ban on Kennamer," *TDO*, March 14, 1936, page 1.

"Judge Kennamer Opens Fight to Free Son," Associated Press, *MDNR*, March 17, 1936, pages 1 and 6.

"New Kennamer Trial is Sought," *TDW*, March 18, 1936, pages 1 and 2.

"Kennamer to Demand New Death Probe," Associated Press, *TT*, March 18, 1936, page 1.

"Kennamer's Hope is Put in Claim of New Wilcox Extortion Note Evidence, Plea Will be Filed Monday, Lawyer Says," *TDO*, March 18, 1936, page 12.

"Assistant Prosecutor Scoffs at New Move to Clear Young Phil Kennamer; Plot Evidence Immaterial in Gilmer's View," Associated Press, *MDNR*, March 18, 1936, page 2.

"State Doubts Another Trial for Kennamer," *TT*, March 19, 1936, page 4.

"Extortion Plot Basis for New Kennamer Trial," *TDW*, March 20, 1936, page 1.

"Fight Mapped by Kennamer in City Parley," *TDO*, March 20, 1936, page 2.

"Kennamer Gets Time Extension," *TDW*, March 21, 1936, page 4.

"Kennamer Gets Time Extension," *TT*, March 21, 1936, pages 1 and 4.

"Kennamer to Cite Decision in City Case," *TDO*, March 21, 1936, page 2.

"Stuart Visits Farm to Talk to Kennamer," *TDO*, March 23, 1936, page 1.

"Kennamer Appeal Tactics Flayed by Prosecutors," *TDW*, April 12, 1936, pages 1 and 20.

"Prosecutors Strike Back at Kennamer's Fight for New Trial," *TT*, April 12, 1936, pages 1 and 2.

"Statement of John Gorrell's College Mate," *TT*, April 12, 1936, page 2.

"Motion Says Juror Biased, Admitted It," *TDO*, April 12, 1936, page 1.

"Kennamer Case Flares Anew Over Efforts to Keep Youth out of Prison; Slain Gorrell is Target of New Evidence," Associated Press, *MDNR*, April 12, 1936, page 2.

"Attorneys Seek New Hearing for Phil Kennamer," Associated Press, *The Ada Evening-News*, April 12, 1936, page 1.

"New Trial Sought for Phil Kennamer," United Service, *The Cedar Rapids Gazette*, April 12, 1936, page 1.

"Doubt Raised on Kennamer," *TDO*, April 13, 1936, page 2.

"Kennamer's Plea Strongly Opposed," Associated Press, *TAEN*, April 13, 1936, page 2.

"Snedden Says Phil Tried to Change Story," *TT*, April 14, 1936, page 1.

"Wire Upholds Youth's Story," Associated Press, *TDO*, April 14, 1936, page 1.

"New Actions in Kennamer Case," Associated Press, *MDNR*, April 15, 1936, page 6.

"Argument Due on Kennamer," *TDO*, April 15, 1936, page 1.

"Court Reduces Kennamer Hope," *TDW*, April 16, 1936, pages 1 and 10.

"Court Refuses Oral Arguments for Kennamer," United Press, *TT*, April 16, 1936, page 1.

"Ruling Friday Due on Plea of Kennamer," *TDO*, April 16, 1936, page 5.

"One Move Left for Kennamers," *TDW*, April 17, 1936, page 1 and 7.

"Kennamer Adds Owen to Staff; Denied a Delay," *TT*, April 17, 1936, page 1.

"Appeals Court Orders Phil Kennamer Back to Prison," Associated Press, *MDNR*, April 17, 1936, pages 1 and 2.

"Kennamer Term Must Be Served," *TDW*, April 18, 1936, pages 1 and 12.

"Appeals Court Denies New Kennamer Hearing, Enjoins Pawnee Court from Acting," *TT*, April 18, 1936, pages 1 and 4.

"Prison Twine Awaits Youth," *TDO*, April 18, 1936, page 1.

"Defense Criticized in Kennamer Ruling," Associated Press, *MDNR*, April 20, 1936, page 2.

"Phil's Pen Trip May Be Delayed," *TDW*, April 21, 1936, page 1.

"Phil Surrenders After Assailing Court Decisions," *TDW*, April 22, 1936, pages 1 and 10.

"Kennamer Back in Cell," *TDO*, April 22, 1936, page 1.

"Phil Kennamer Back in Prison," Associated Press, *MDNR*, April 22, 1936, page 8.

"Solo Trip to Prison Final Gesture by Phil Kennamer," *TT*, April 22, 1936, page 1.

"Kennamer Order Spread on Record," *TDW*, April 23, 1936, page 1.

"Prison Gates Closed Again on Kennamer," *TT*, April 23, 1936, page 1.

"Books Closed on Kennamer," *TDO*, April 23, 1936, page 1.

CHAPTER 26

1936

"Jack Snedden, Son of Oil Man and Kennamer Trial Witness, is Bridegroom," Associated Press, *TDO*, October 3, 1936, page 1.

"Clemency Plea Not Presented," Associated Press, *TAEN*, October 5, 1936, page 4.

"New Kennamer Clamor Quieted," Associated Press, *MDNR*, October 8, 1936, page 6.

"Kennamer Leaves Prison for Parley," Associated Press, *San Antonio Express*, October 13, 1936, page 2.

1937

"Marland Acts in Behalf of Kennamer," *TDO*, April 7, 1937, page 1.

"Opposition to New Kennamer Clemency Step," Associated Press, *TT*, April 7, 1937, page 1.

"Gorrell, Gilmer Before Marland," *TDW*, April 8, 1937, page 1.

"Marland Bares Kennamer Plan," *TDW*, April 9, 1937, page 1.

"Open Hearing Promise Made," *TDO*, April 9, 1937, page 5.

"Kennamer Parole Will be Opposed," *TDW*, May 29, 1937, page 1.

"Opponents of Kennamer Parole Plan Petitions," *TT*, May 29, 1937, page 1.

"Marland May Want to Talk to Kennamer," *TDO*, May 29, 1937, page 11.

"Hopes Raised on Clemency by Governor," *TDO*, May 30, 1937, page 24.

"Kennamer Parole Drawing Protest," *TDW*, June 2, 1937, page 1.

"Marland to Get Parole Protest," *TT*, June 2, 1937, page 4.

"Drive to Keep Kennamer in Prison Begins," *TDO*, June 2, 1937, page 1.

"Phil Kennamer Clemency Opposed," Associated Press, *TDA*, June 2, 1937, page 10.

"Kennamer Case in Marland's Hands," Associated Press, *TAEN*, June 6, 1937, page 16.

"Governor of Alabama Joins Kennamer Clemency Plea," *TDO*, June 11, 1937, page 11.

"Kennamer Freedom Moves Protests," *TDO*, June 13, 1937, page 33.

"Marland Receives Two More Pleas for Clemency Phil Kennamer, Former Deputy Sheriff Urges Further Probe," Associated Press, *MDNR*, June 25, 1937, page 2.

"Kennamer Parole Opposed by 5,000," *TDO*, July 4, 1937, page 18.

"Kennamer Parole Has 5,000 Protests," *TDW*, July 4, 1937, page 1.

"Kennamer Inquiry Styled Unofficial," *TDW*, July 6, 1937, page 1.

"No Kennamer Parole Probe," *TT*, July 6, 1937, page 4.

"Kennamer Punished Enough, Two Write," *TDO*, July 7, 1937, page 14.

"Anti-Kennamer Petitions Read," Associated Press, *TAEN*, July 8, 1937, page 5.

"No! No! No! Thousands Protest," *TDO*, July 20, 1937, page 18.

"Phil Kennamer Among Prisoners Given Sanity Tests by Board," *TT*, October 18, 1937, page 1.

"Young Kennamer Given Sanity Test," Associated Press, *TDO*, October 19, 1937, page 5.

1938

"Phil Planning Life in Exile if He is Freed," Associated Press, *TDW*, January 23, 1938, pages 1 and 2.

"Phil Kennamer Wants to Leave Country," Associated Press, *TDO*, January 23, 1938, pages 1 and 2.

"Kennamer, in New Bid for Freedom, Claims Principal was Perjurer," Associated Press, *TDO*, February 5, 1938, page 14A.

"Kennamer Asks Perjury Charges Against Witness," United Press, *TT*, February 6, 1938, page 1.

"Jailer to Answer Kennamer Claim," Associated Press, *TDW*, February 7, 1938, page 1.

"Pawnee Jailer Mum on Kennamer Case," Associated Press, *TDO*, February 7, 1938, page 30.

"Kennamer's Perjury Plea Strikes Snag," Associated Press, *TDO*, February 8, 1938, page 1.

"Kennamer Loses Retrial Battle," Associated Press, *TDW*, February 12, 1938, page 10.

"Kennamer Appeal for Freedom Lost," Associated Press, *TDO*, February 12, 1938, page 1.

"Gorrell Hits Parole Hint," Associated Press, *TDO*, August 14, 1938, page 4.

"Tulsa Girl Injured When Car Skids on Wet Road Near Grants," *Albuquerque Journal*, September 2, 1938, page 1.

"Marland Dashes Kennamer Hopes of Leaving Pen," *TDW*, September 13, 1938, page 1.

"Marland Against Kennamer Parole," *TDO*, September 13, 1938, page 1.

"Kennamer Case Again Agitated," *TDW*, October 4, 1938, page 1.

"Open Hearing on Kennamer Parole Hinted," *TDO*, October 4, 1938, page 1.

"Governor Orders Kennamer Parole Hearing Oct. 31," *TT*, October 21, 1938, page 1.

"Kennamer Parole Rapped by Pastor," Associated Press, *TDO*, October 24, 1938, page 1.

"State Clemency Machinery Geared to Higher Speed," *TDO*, October 26, 1938, page 1.

"Kennamer Appeals to State for Fair Play in Son's Parole Plea," *TT*, October 30, 1938, pages 1 and 5b.

"Board Adviser Fights Parole for Kennamer," *TDO*, October 30, 1938, page 17.

"Protests to Parole for Kennamer Begun at Many Enter Plea for Clemency," *TT*, by Joseph E. Howell," *TT*, October 31, 1938, pages 1 and 3.

"Two Days Likely to be Needed for Hearing on Parole for Kennamer," *TDO*, October 31, 1938, page 5.

"Sanity Hearing at Pen today May Free Kennamer after Quick Action by Marland Clemency Board, Despite Warning that Phil is a 'Dangerous Man,'" by Edward D. Burks, *TDW*, November 1, 1938, pages 1 and 3.

"Parole Hearing Arguments Heard," World Capital Bureau, *TDW*, November 1, 1938, page 3.

"Marland Awaits Report on Kennamer Sanity to Guide Six Month Parole," by Joseph E. Howell, *TT*, November 1, 1938, pages 1 and 3.

"Marland to Accept Board's Decision to Free Kennamer," *TDO*, November 1, 1938, page 1.

"Kennamer Held to Prison Schedule," *TDO*, November 1, 1938, page 2.

"Kennamer Tested, Certified as Sane, Leaves Pen Today," by Edward D. Burks, November 2, 1938, page 1.

"Kennamer Sentences Kidnap Pair as Son Wins Release," *TT*, November 2, 1938, page 1.

"Kennamer to be Out Today," *TDO*, November 2, 1938, page 1.

"Not for These," Editorial, *TDO*, November 2, 1938.

"Jaunty Kennamer Quits Pen; Will Meet Mother in Texas, Then Work on Arizona Ranch," Associated Press, *TDW*, November 3, 1938, page 1.

"Kennamer to Mother's Side," *TT*, November 3, 1938, page 1.

"Kennamer Goes to Work for Phoenix Firm," Associated Press, *TT*, November 29, 1938, page 3.

"Kennamer is Given Job by Oil Firm," *TDO*, November 29, 1938, page 1.

"Marland Sets Parole Record," *MDNR*, December 11, 1938, pages 1 and 2.

1939

"Mrs. Kennamer Taken by Death; Ill Many Years," *TDW*, March 13, 1939, pages 1 and 2.

"Mrs. Kennamer Rites Tuesday," *TT*, March 13, 1939, page 1.

"Son Arrives for Funeral," *TDO*, March 14, 1938, page 14.

"Mrs. Kennamer Laid to Rest," *TT*, March 15, 1939, page 2.

"Kennamer's Leave to Expire May 2," *TDO*, April 23, 1939, page 22.

"Phillips to Study Kennamer Case," Associated Press, *TDW*, April 26, 1939, page 1.

"Phillips to Ask for Kennamer File," *TDO*, April 26, 1939, page 11.

"Phillips Extends Slayers Leave," *TDW*, April 27, 1939, pages 1 and 2.

"Kennamer to Get 2 Weeks More Liberty," *TDO*, April 27, 1939, page 1.

"Kennamer to be Given Two Weeks," Associated Press, *TT*, April 27, 1939, page 9.

"Phil Kennamer's Leave Cancelled by Gov. Phillips," *TDW*, May 30, 1939, page 1 and 2.

"Kennamer Goes Back to Prison," *TT*, May 30, 1939, page 1.

"Kennamer Leave is Ended, Tulsa Slayer Ordered Back to M'Alester," *TDO*, May 30, 1939, page 1.

"Kennamer in Tulsa as Leave Ends Friday," *TDW*, May 31, 1939, page 1 and 3.

"Gorrell Against Kennamer Plea," Associated Press, *TAEN*, December 10, 1939, page 1.

1940

"Kennamer Action Remains Far Off," *TDW*, February 14, 1940, page 1.

"Phillips Sees No Clemency for Kennamer," *TDO*, February 14, 1940, page 1.

"Kennamer Asks to be Retired; Savage in Line to Succeed Him," *TT*, May 15, 1940, page 1.

"Kennamer Asks to be Retired from Federal Bench," Associated Press, *MDNR*, May 15, 1940, pages 1 and 2.

"Edith Gorrell Illness Victim," *TT*, September 12, 1940, page 1.

1941

"Phillips Airs Scandal Hint in Kennamer Parole Drive," *TDO* January 16, 1941, pages 1 and 2.

"Crutcher Faces Fire in Senate; Kennamer Clemency is Issue," *TDO*, January 17, 1941, pages 1 and 2.

"Kennamer Not to Get Hearing," Associated Press, *TDA*, January 16, 1941, pages 1 and 12.

"Phillips Spurns Kennamer Move," Associated Press, *MDNR*, January 16, 1941, pages 1 and 2.

"New Kennamer Release Move," Associated Press, *MDNR*, February 12, 1941, page 8.

"F.E. Kenanmer's Wedding Bared," *TDO*, April 13, 1941, page 17.

"Divorce Granted to Kennamer," Associated Press, *TDO*, July 16, 1941, page 1.

"F.E. Kennamer Gets Divorce," Associated Press, *TDA*, July 16, 1941, page 2.

1942

"Kennamer Would Enlist if Free; Governor Told," United Press, *TT*, February 3, 1942, pages 1 and 5.

"New Phil Kennamer Clemency Plea, Reported Based on Offer to Join the Army, Placed Before Gov. Phillips," Associated Press, *MDNR*, February 3, 1942, pages 1 and 2.

"Phillips Growls at Latest Plea for Kennamer," *TDO*, February 4, 1942, page 13.

1943

"Kerr Reveals He Will Ask Parole Board to Consider Clemency for P. Kennamer," Associated Press, *MDNR*, March 2, 1943, pages 1 and 10.

"Kerr to Check Kennamer Plea to New Board," *TT*, March 2, 1943, pages 1 and 7.

"Pardon, Parole Board to Hold Session Today," DO, March 3, 1943, page 20.

"Board to Delay Kennamer Action," United Press, *TT*, March 4, 1943, page 1.

"Kennamer Plea Hearing Looms," *TDO*, March 4, 1943, page 11.

"Full Day Hearing Promised on Clemency Plea," *TDO*, March 5, 1943, page 17.

"Day to be Devoted to Kennamer Case," Associated Press, *TAEN*, March 5, page 1.

"Armed Service Kennamer Plea," United Press, *TT*, March 10, 1943, pages 1 and 2.

"Letters Plead for Kennamer," *TT*, March 11, 1943, pages 1 and 2.

"Kennamer Will Attend Hearing," Associated Press, *TT*, March 18, 1943, page 1.

"Phil Kennamer Parole Hearing Set for April," Associated Press, *MDNR*, March 18, 1943, page 1.

"Phillips Says Kerr First to Ask Pardon for Phil Kennamer," Associated Press, *TAEN*, March 29, 1943, pages 1 and 2.

"Warden Takes Neutral Stand in Phil's Case," by Joseph E. Howell, *TT*, April 13, 1943, pages 1 and 10.

"With Odds Heavily in His Favor, Young Phil Kennamer Will Make Parole Bid April 20," Associated Press, *MDNR*, April 15, 1943, page 10.

"Kennamer Out for O.C. Trip," Associated Press, *TT*, April 19, 1943, page 1.

"Kennamer to Bid for Own Freedom," by Walter Biscup, *TDW*, April 20, 1943, pages 1 and 4.

"Gilmer Denies He Agreed to Ask Kennamer Freedom," by Joseph E. Howell, *TT*, April 20, 1943, pages 1 and 13.

"Attorneys Clash Verbally As Hearing Opens Today at Capital for Phil Kennamer," by John Owen, Associated Press, *MDNR*, April 20, 1943, pages 1 and 2.

"Kennamers Wait in Seclusion; Phil Calm with Fate at Issue," Associated Press, *TT*, April 20, 1943, page 13.

"Kennamer Gains Freedom, Phil Will Seek Army Induction as Paratrooper," by Walter Biscup, *TDW*, April 21, 1943, pages 1 and 14.

"Kennamer Freed After Hot Parole Hearing," by Ray Parr, *TDO*, April 21, 1943, pages 1 and 2.

"Kennamer Finis," Editorial, *TDW*, April 21, 1943.

CHAPTER 27

"Kennamer Freed, Will Proceed to Army Enlistment," *TT*, April 21, 1943, pages 1 and 4.

"Phil Kennamer Asks Induction," Associated Press, *TDA*, April 21, 1943, page 3.

"Phi Kennamer Inducted into Army," Associated Press, *TDA*, May 25, 1943, page 3.

"Phil Kennamer to be Paratrooper," Associated Press, *TAEN*, May 29, 1943, page 2.

1944

"Phil Kennamer Killed in Action in France," by Edward D. Burks, *TDW*, September 27, 1944, pages 1 and 3.

"Death on French Battlefield of Phil Kennamer Closes Case," *TT*, September 27, 1944, pages 1 and 8.

"Parole Justified," State Capital Bureau of the Tribune, *TT*, September 27, 1944, page 1.

"Phil Kennamer Dies in France," Associated Press, *MDNR*, September 27, 1944, page 1 and 3.

"Phil Kennamer is Killed in France While Fighting with US Paratroops," *TDO*, September 27, 1944, page 1.

"For Country's Sake," Editorial, *TDO*, September 28, 1944, page 10.

"Atonement," Editorial, *Denton Record-Chronicle*, Denton, Texas, September 30, 1944, page 6.

"Phil Kennamer's Sacrifice," Editorial, *TDA*, October 1, 1944, page 10.

"Debt Paid in Full," Letter to the Editor, *TDO*, October 8, 1944, page 50.

"Army Reveals Kennamer Killed in Attack on Nazi Gun Nest," *TDO*, November 15, 1944, page 1.

"The Parachute F.A. BN Record of Events, 'D day,'" by Captain Louis Vogel, 517th Parachute Regimental Combat Team After Action Report.

Jean Loup-Gassend, discussions with author by email March, 2015. (Author: Operation Dragoon: Autopsy of a Battle: The Allied Liberation of the French Riviera August-September 1944.)

Merle McMorrow, discussions with author by email, March, 2015. (Battery C, 460th Parachute Field Artillery Battalion, Served with Phil Kennamer from 1943-1944, and author of *From Breckenridge to Bastogne: The Accounts of a World War II Paratrooper*.)

SSGT Milton D. Rogers, "How I Saw It," October 2007. Website: *517th Parachute Regimental Combat Team 1943-1945*. URL: http://www.517prct.org/bios/milton_d_rogers.htm

460th Parachute Field Artillery Battalion Unit History, Website: *www.ww2-airborne.us*, URL: http://www.ww2-airborne.us/units/460/460.html

"Operation Dragoon," *Wikipedia*, URL: http://en.wikipedia.org/wiki/Operation_Dragoon

"Phil Kennamer Dies After Heroic Battle," *TT*, January 12, 1945, page 14.

Epilogue

Holly Anderson

1. "House Debates Gin Marriages," Associated Press, *MDNR*, January 26, 1939, page 1.

2. "Tulsa Legislative Nominee Drops Out," Associated Press, *TAEN*, August 12, 1942, page 3.

3. "Holly L Anderson," Ancestry.com, URL: http://records.ancestry.com/holly_l_anderson_records.ashx?pid=3009196

William "Dixie" Gilmer

"Gilmer, William Franklin," by Carolyn G. Hanneman, *The Encyclopedia of Oklahoma Culture and History*, Oklahoma Historical Society website, URL: http://www.okhistory.org/publications/enc/entry.php?entry=GI008

J. Berry King

"Notable Notes on Business and Finance," Column, by J. Willis Baker, Financial Editor, *TDO*, October 28, 1962, page 78.

"Former State Attorney Dies, Rites Tuesday," *TDO*, November 26, 1962, page 4.

Henry B. Maddux

"Hudspeth's Albuquerque City Directory," 1950, page 425.

"New Risk Manager," *Albuquerque Journal*, September 3, 1952, page 10.

"Henry Bailess Maddux," Ancestry.com URL: http://records.ancestry.com/henry_bailess_maddux_records.ashx?pid=179204357

"Henry B. Maddux, 52, Insurance Man Dies," *Albuquerque Journal*, January 5, 1953, page 4.

"Funeral Held for Former Resident Henry B. Maddux," *Roswell Daily Record*, Roswell, New Mexico, January 7, 1953, page 16.

Austin Flint Moss

"Noted Oklahoma Criminal Lawyer Plans Retirement," *TDO*, March 9, 1943, page 5.

"Flint Moss Dies in Long Beach," Associated Press, *TDO*, December 18, 1943, page 2.

"Deaths: Austin F. Moss," *The Long Beach Independent*, December 19, 1943, page 34.

Charles Stuart

"Services for C.B. Stuart Set Monday in Harding Hall," *TDO*, October 31, 1936, page 18.

"Resolutions of Respect for and in Appreciation of Honorable Charles B. Stuart," Chronicles of Oklahoma, June 1937, pages 228-137.

Judge Franklin Kennamer

"Kennamer Funeral Will Be Thursday," Associated Press, *TDO*, May 3, 1961, page 12.

"Franklin E. Kennamer, 1879-1960," *FindAGrave.com*, URL: http://www.findagrave.com/cgi-bin/fg.cgi?page=gr&GRid=100130973

"Pauline Fox Kennamer, 1908-1955," *FindAGrave.com*, URL: http://www.findagrave.com/cgi-bin/fg.cgi?page=gr&GRid=67818590

"Opal Kennamer, 1904-1989," FindAGrave.com, URL: http://www.findagrave.com/cgi-bin/fg.cgi?page=gr&GRid=100131008

Edna M. Harman

"California Death Records," *Ancestry.com*, URL: http://vitals.rootsweb.ancestry.com/ca/death/search.cgi

"Edna Harman 1930 Census Record," Year: *1930*; Census Place: *Tulsa, Tulsa, Oklahoma*; Roll: *1934*; Page: *4B*; Enumeration District: *0058*; Image: *447.0*; FHL microfilm: *2341668*

Sydney Born

"The Truth About Tulsa's Kennamer-Gorrell Case," Part Three, by Chief of Detectives Thomas J. Higgins as told to C.F. Waers," *The Master Detective*, August 1935.

Virginia Wilcox

"Virginia Francis Wilcox Hagar," *FindAGrave.com, URL:* http://www.findagrave.com/cgi-bin/fg.cgi?page=gr&GRid=121177999

"Jack Robin Snedden," *FindAGrave.com, UR:* http://www.findagrave.com/cgi-bin/fg.cgi?page=gr&GRid=13662914

Philip Kennamer

"Trans-en-Provence," First Airborne Task Force website, URL: http://1stabtf.com/monument/trans-en-provence-monument.htm

"Sister of Kennamer Plans to Publish 'Inside Story,'" *TDW*, August 26, 1947, page 3.

"Phil Kennamer Services Friday," *TT*, May 5, 1948, page 31.

"Philip Milholland Kennamer, 1915-1944," *FindAGrave.com*, URL: http://www.findagrave.com/cgi-bin/fg.cgi?page=gr&GRid=53200131

Alice and Dr. John Gorrell Sr.

"John Franklin Gorrell Sr. 1881-1961," *FindAGrave.com,* URL: http://www.findagrave.com/cgi-bin/fg.cgi?page=gr&GRid=11374441

"Alice Bair Gorrell, 1885-1959," *FindAGrave.com*, URL: http://www.findagrave.com/cgi-bin/fg.cgi?page=gr&GRid=11374458

"Benjamin Franklin Gorrell, 1919-2000," *FindAGrave.com*, URL: http://www.findagrave.com/cgi-bin/fg.cgi?page=gr&GRid=63368898

John Robert Gorrell, private discussions with author in August 2014, and April 2015.

Author

Jason Lucky Morrow is a Gulf War veteran and award winning newspaper reporter who now researches and writes vintage true crime stories for his blog, HistoricalCrimeDetective.com. His focus is on obscure but significant criminal cases that are nearly forgotten and have not been adequately explored in decades. Mr. Morrow has lived and worked in Nebraska, Texas, Alabama, Romania, and Oklahoma where he currently resides in the Tulsa area with his wife, Alina.

Visit **HistoricalCrimeDetective.com** for more vintage true crime stories and follow along for new story updates on our Facebook page.

43196541R00232

Made in the USA
Charleston, SC
16 June 2015